BEYOND THE BREACH

VOLUME
1

LOSING CALIFORNIA

ED BRISSON

DAMIAN COUCEIRO

PATRICIO DELPECHE

HASSAN OTSMANE-ELHAOU

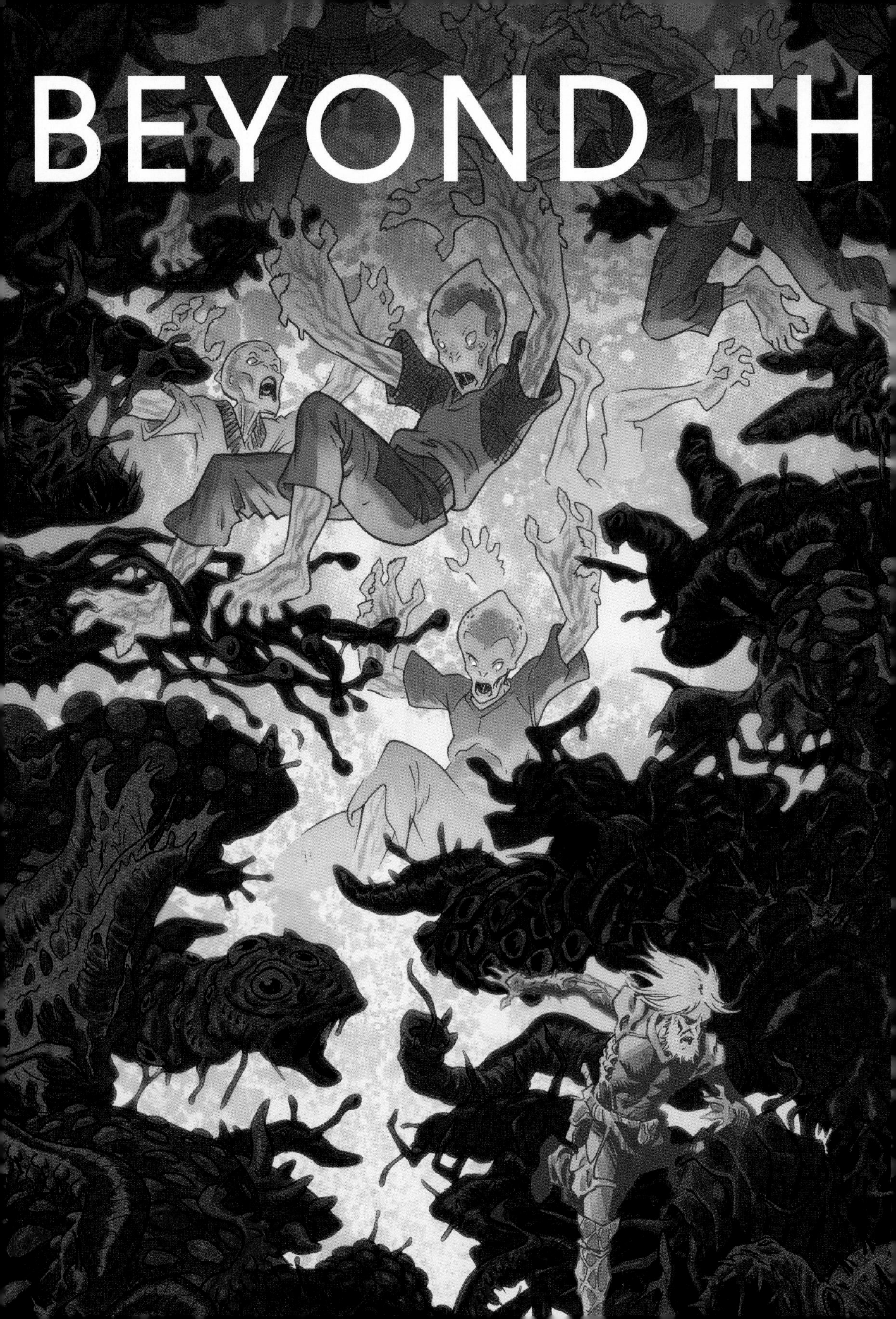
BEYOND TH

E BREACH

VOLUME 1: LOSING CALIFORNIA

ED BRISSON writer

DAMIAN COUCEIRO artist

PATRICIO DELPECHE colorist

HASSAN OTSMANE-ELHAOU letterer

DAMIAN COUCEIRO w/ **PATRICIO DELPECHE** front & original covers

DECLAN SHALVEY incentive cover

PHIL HESTER AfterShock ambassador cover

RUDY AO, NINO CAMMARATA, PEEJY CATACUTAN, GÖRKEM DEMIR, ADAM FIELDS, PHIL HESTER w/ **MARK ENGLERT, BOB TKACIK & FRANCK UZAN** variant covers

TOM MUELLER logo designer

CHARLES PRITCHETT issue #1 backmatter designer

COREY BREEN book designer

CHIRSTINA HARRINGTON editor

created by **ED BRISSON** & **DAMIAN COUCEIRO**

special thanks to **MARIA AGUSTINA VALLEJO**

AFTERSHOCK™

MIKE MARTS - Editor-in-Chief • JOE PRUETT - Publisher/CCO • LEE KRAMER - President • JON KRAMER - Chief Executive Officer
STEVE ROTTERDAM - SVP, Sales & Marketing • DAN SHIRES - VP, Film & Television UK • CHRISTINA HARRINGTON - Managing Editor
MARC HAMMOND - Sr. Retail Sales Development Manager • RUTHANN THOMPSON - Sr. Retailer Relations Manager
KATHERINE JAMISON - Marketing Manager • KELLY DIODATI - Ambassador Outreach Manager • BLAKE STOCKER - VP, Finance
AARON MARION - Publicist • LISA MOODY - Finance • RYAN CARROLL - Director, Comics/Film/TV Liaison • JAWAD QURESHI - Technology Advisor/Strategist
RACHEL PINNELAS - Social Community Manager • CHARLES PRITCHETT - Design & Production Manager • COREY BREEN - Collections Production
TEODORO LEO - Associate Editor • SARAH PRUETT - Publishing Assistant

AfterShock Logo Design by COMICRAFT
Publicity: contact AARON MARION (aaron@publichausagency.com) & RYAN CROY (ryan@publichausagency.com) at PUBLICHAUS
Special thanks to: ATOM! FREEMAN, IRA KURGAN, MARINE KSADZHIKYAN, KEITH MANZELLA, ANTHONY MILITANO, ANTONIA LIANOS, STEPHAN NILSON & ED ZAREMBA

AFTERSHOCKCOMICS.COM

I N T R O D U C T I O N

I love road trips.

I've traveled across Canada about a dozen times, from the Pacific to the Atlantic and back. As a kid, it was to spend summers with my dad. It was cheaper for him to haul my brother, sister and me across the country and back than it was for him to fly the three of us. And, so, every summer, he'd pick us up in his car — which never had air conditioning — and we'd spend four days driving across the country listening to Linda Ronstadt's *Greatest Hits* on repeat. At the end of the summer, it would be another four days back, with that same album on repeat. I prayed to the gods that my dad's tape deck would eat the cassette, but they never listened.

After graduating high school, I did the trip solo; then, later, with a girlfriend (we broke up halfway through the trip and had to spend five days trapped in the car together — *not recommended*); then a couple of years later with my brother; once by bus; and most recently when moving from the West Coast to the East. I've been lost, *intentionally* sometimes. Broken down. Nearly killed by a reckless driver in the middle of Butt-f*ck Nowhere, Ontario. Ran out of money. Ticketed for *excessive* speeding. Stranded. And once accidentally set my car engine on fire (be sure to always replace your oil cap!). I've slept in the seediest of motels, camped along the Trans-Canada Highway, snoozed in parking lots and once got eaten alive by mosquitos while attempting to sleep on a park bench because it was too hot to sleep in the car.

But, for every harrowing moment, there's one that's equally breathtaking. I've experienced the Badlands of Drumheller, the awe-inspiring Rocky Mountains, all five Great Lakes, sea lions and whales off the shores of the Pacific and the red sands of P.E.I.. From the safety of my car, I've seen grizzly bears, black bears, moose, antelope, mountain goats, mountain lions and prairie dogs.

In 2020, my wife, daughter and I were planning another cross-Canada trip, but COVID hit and disrupted the world. I don't need to tell you how chaotic it was, you were there, it screwed with your life in both minor and major ways, too. The trip, which we'd all been looking forward to, had to be put off until 2021 (and was again put off until 2022, fingers crossed).

When the pandemic hit, projects got canceled, and Damian and I found ourselves with an opening in our schedules and started discussing new projects. We wanted to build from the ground up, rather than diving into an archive of ideas that we had waiting in our back pocket. Damian and I have worked together about a dozen times over the last 15 years, both on creator-owned and on Big Two projects, he's one of my favorite artists to collaborate with and generally the first person I turn to when I have something cooking. Damian wanted to do something horror, something where he could draw monsters and unspeakable terrors. That sounded **great** to me. Because I was not willing to let go of the road trip, I decided that if I can't go on one, then at least I can experience it vicariously through our protagonist Vanessa.

We built a world not too dissimilar to what the world *was* at the time. The ground seemed to be constantly shifting and no one had any idea when we might wake up from the nightmare of COVID. The idea behind the book, much like a road trip, was that each new town or stretch of highway could bring a new adventure. The landscape, post-Breach, would be changed forever. Your maps were obsolete. We thrust Vanessa, Dougie, Kai, Samuel and Turtle into a world that seemed to change with every passing day, where no one understood the threats that lay before them. Each answer they received only opened up a myriad of new questions.

And so, here we are. The book that you hold in your hands is our thinly veiled pandemic anxiety tale. A road trip into the unknown, where answers are not easy to come by and a solution is not necessarily in the cards. It's about facing a changing world and having to adapt to it because there is no other option.

I'd be remiss if I signed off without recognizing the contributions of Patrico Delpeche, whose otherworldly colors helped breathe life into this book, and Hassan Otsmane-Elhaou, letterer extraordinaire, who gave voice to our motley crew. And of course, thanks to Christina Harrington and Mike Marts for taking a chance on this book and for their guidance on this journey.

ED BRISSON
November 2021
Halifax, Nova Scotia

1

THE DAY WE HIT THE COAST

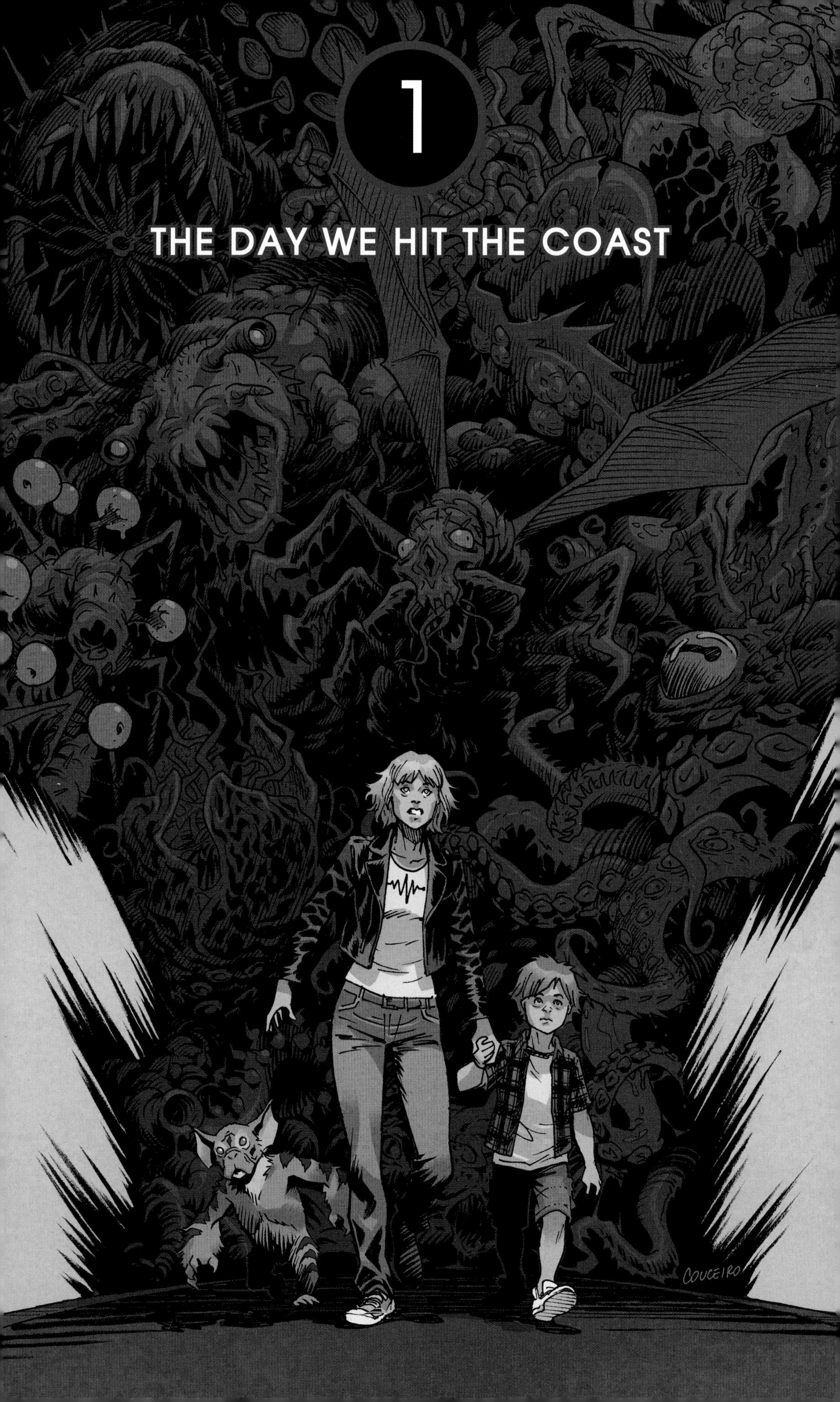
COUCEIRO

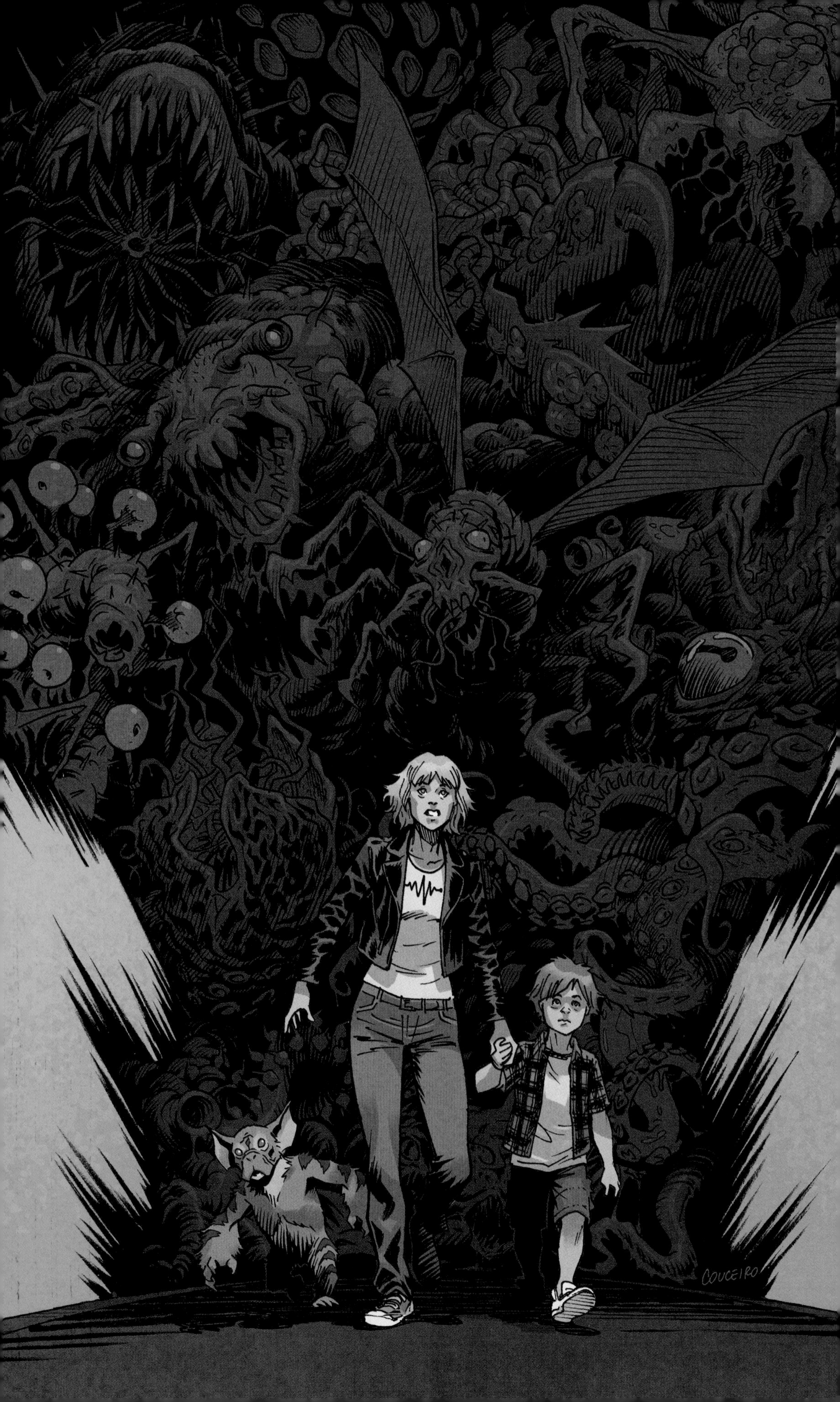
COUCEIRO

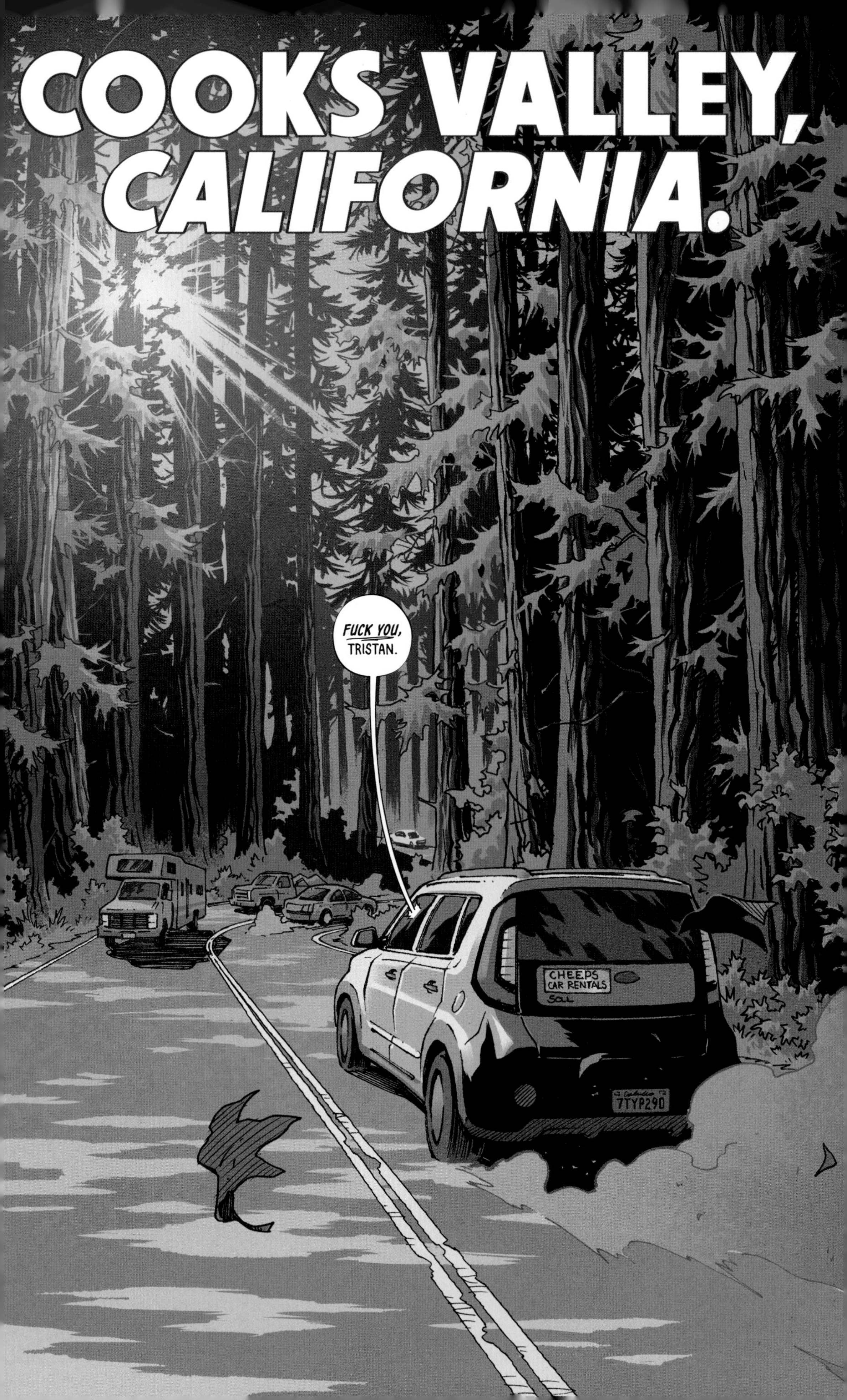
COOKS VALLEY, CALIFORNIA.
FUCK YOU, TRISTAN.
CHEEPS CAR RENTALS
7TYP290

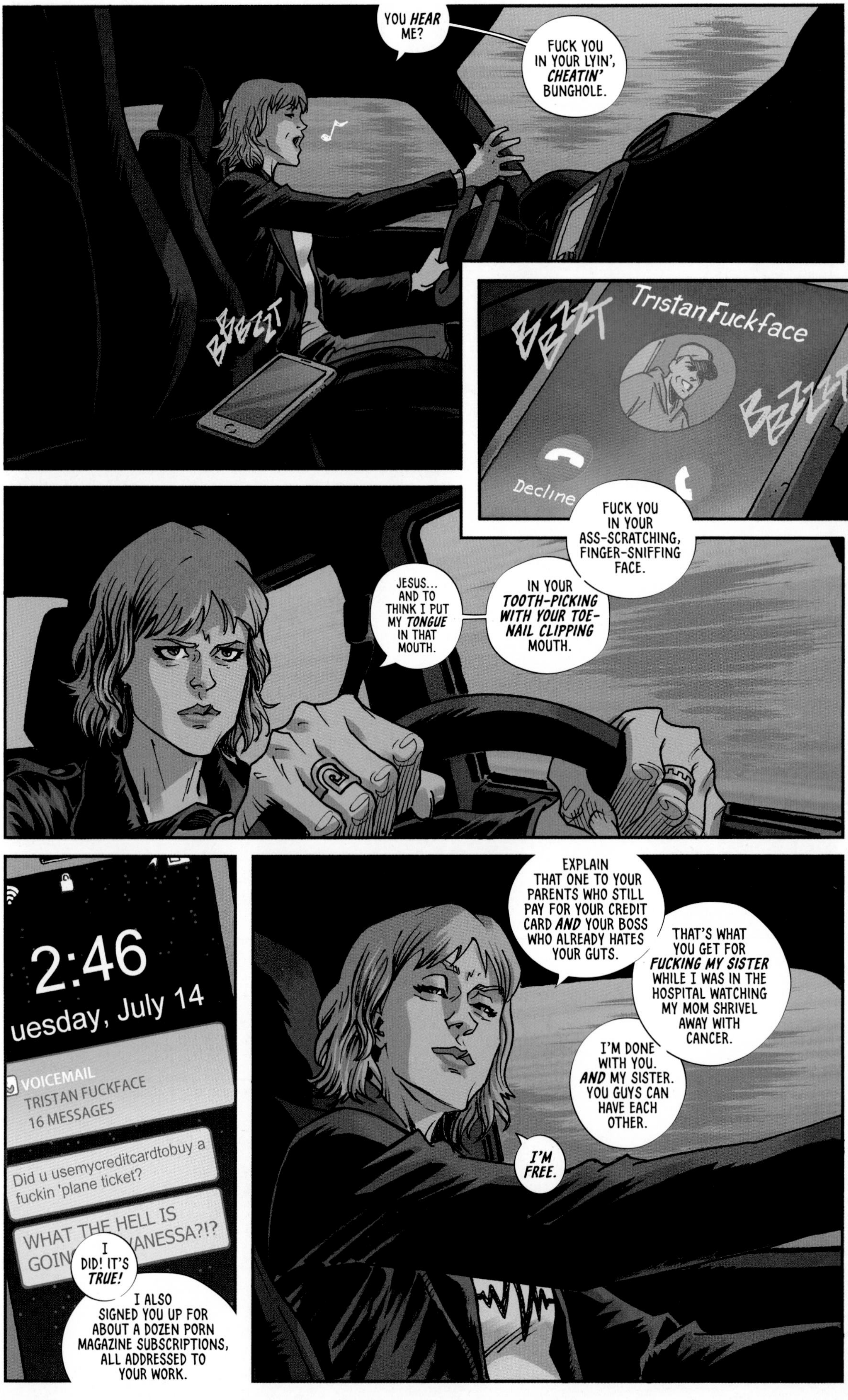
YOU HEAR ME?
FUCK YOU IN YOUR LYIN', CHEATIN' BUNGHOLE.
BZZZT
Tristan Fuckface
BZZZT
BZZZT
Decline
FUCK YOU IN YOUR ASS-SCRATCHING, FINGER-SNIFFING FACE.
IN YOUR TOOTH-PICKING WITH YOUR TOE-NAIL CLIPPING MOUTH.
JESUS... AND TO THINK I PUT MY TONGUE IN THAT MOUTH.
2:46
uesday, July 14
VOICEMAIL
TRISTAN FUCKFACE
16 MESSAGES
Did u usemycreditcardtobuy a fuckin 'plane ticket?
WHAT THE HELL IS GOIN VANESSA?!?
I DID! IT'S TRUE!
I ALSO SIGNED YOU UP FOR ABOUT A DOZEN PORN MAGAZINE SUBSCRIPTIONS, ALL ADDRESSED TO YOUR WORK.
EXPLAIN THAT ONE TO YOUR PARENTS WHO STILL PAY FOR YOUR CREDIT CARD AND YOUR BOSS WHO ALREADY HATES YOUR GUTS.
THAT'S WHAT YOU GET FOR FUCKING MY SISTER WHILE I WAS IN THE HOSPITAL WATCHING MY MOM SHRIVEL AWAY WITH CANCER.
I'M DONE WITH YOU. AND MY SISTER. YOU GUYS CAN HAVE EACH OTHER.
I'M FREE.

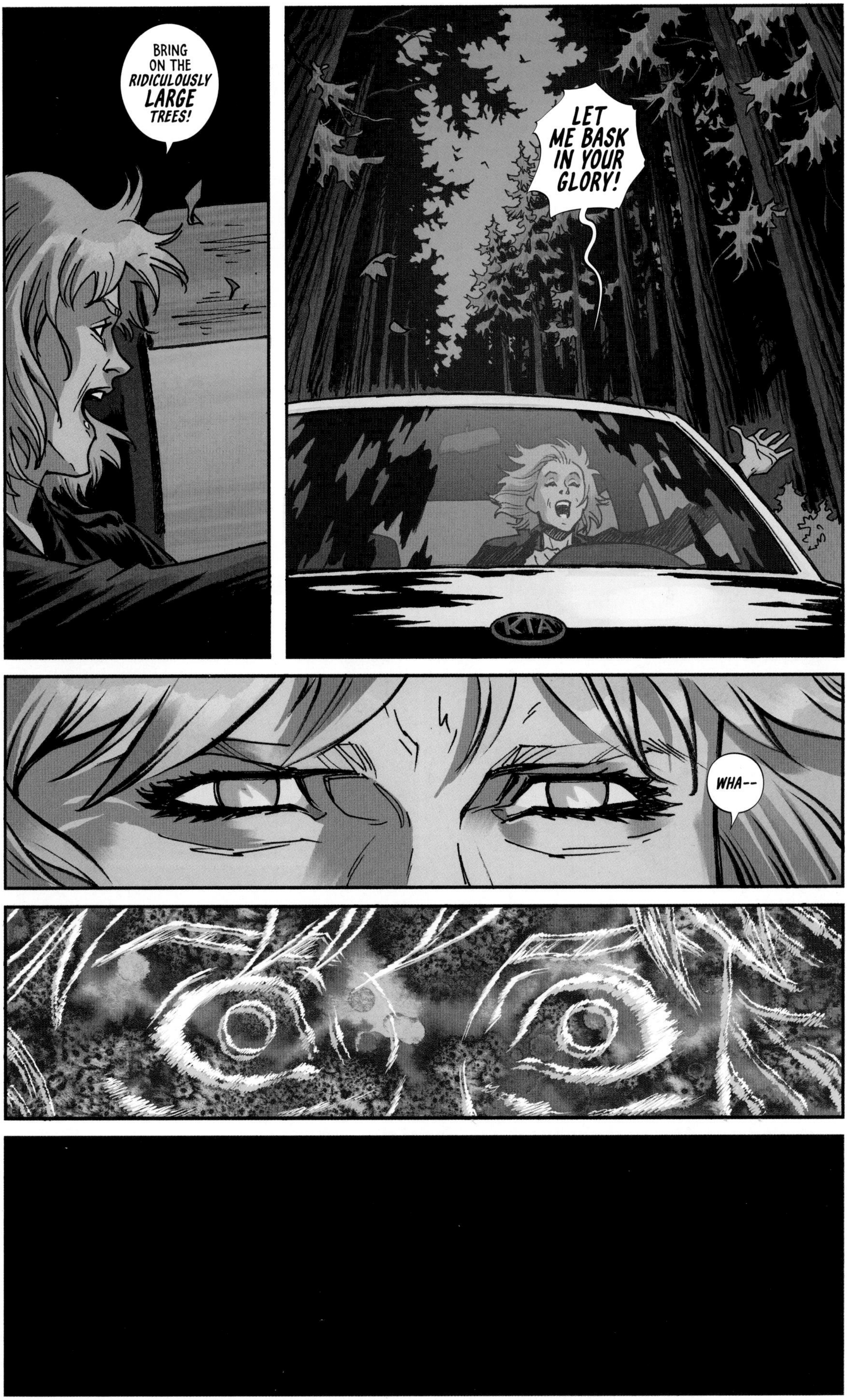
BRING ON THE RIDICULOUSLY LARGE TREES!
LET ME BASK IN YOUR GLORY!
KIA
WHA--

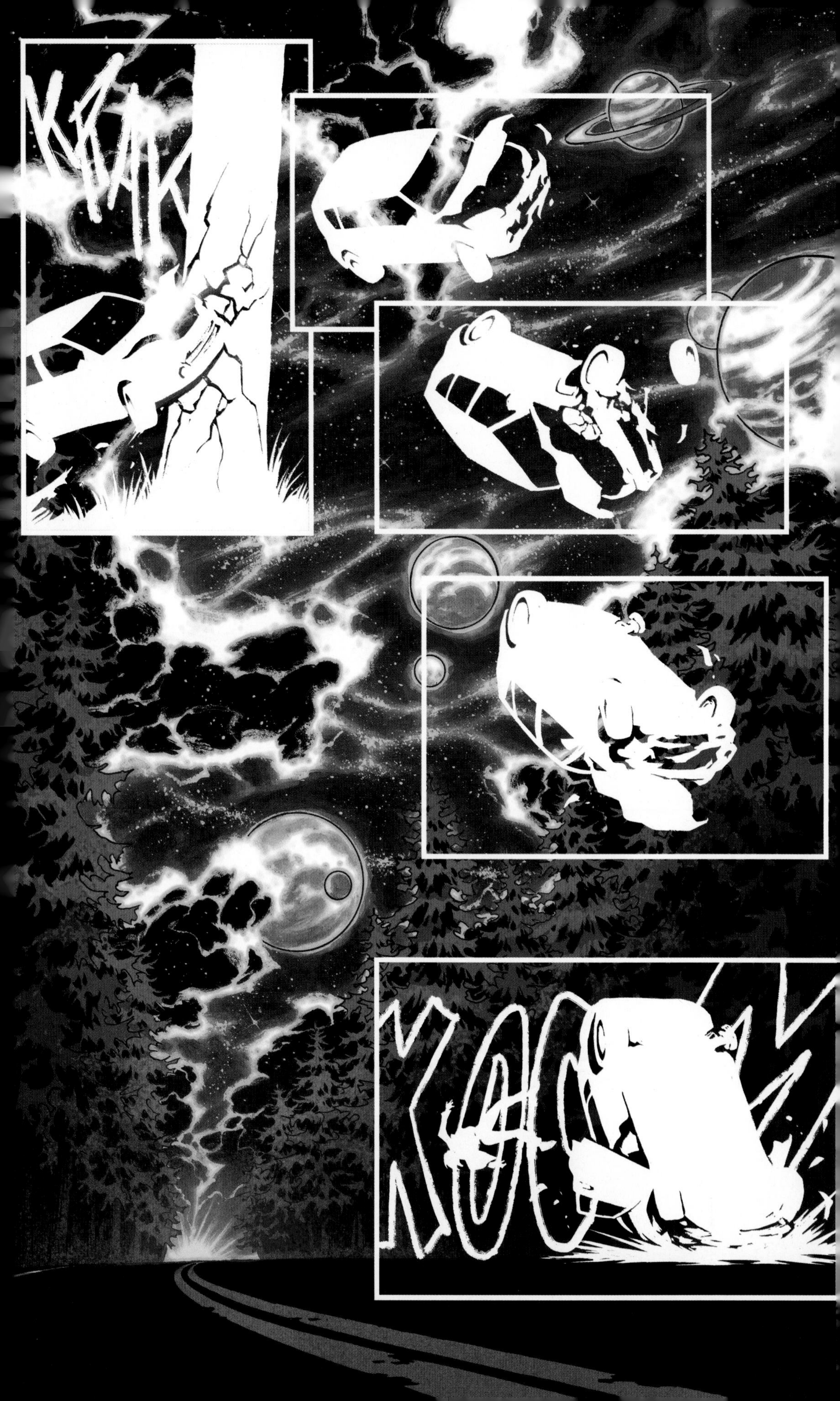
KRAK

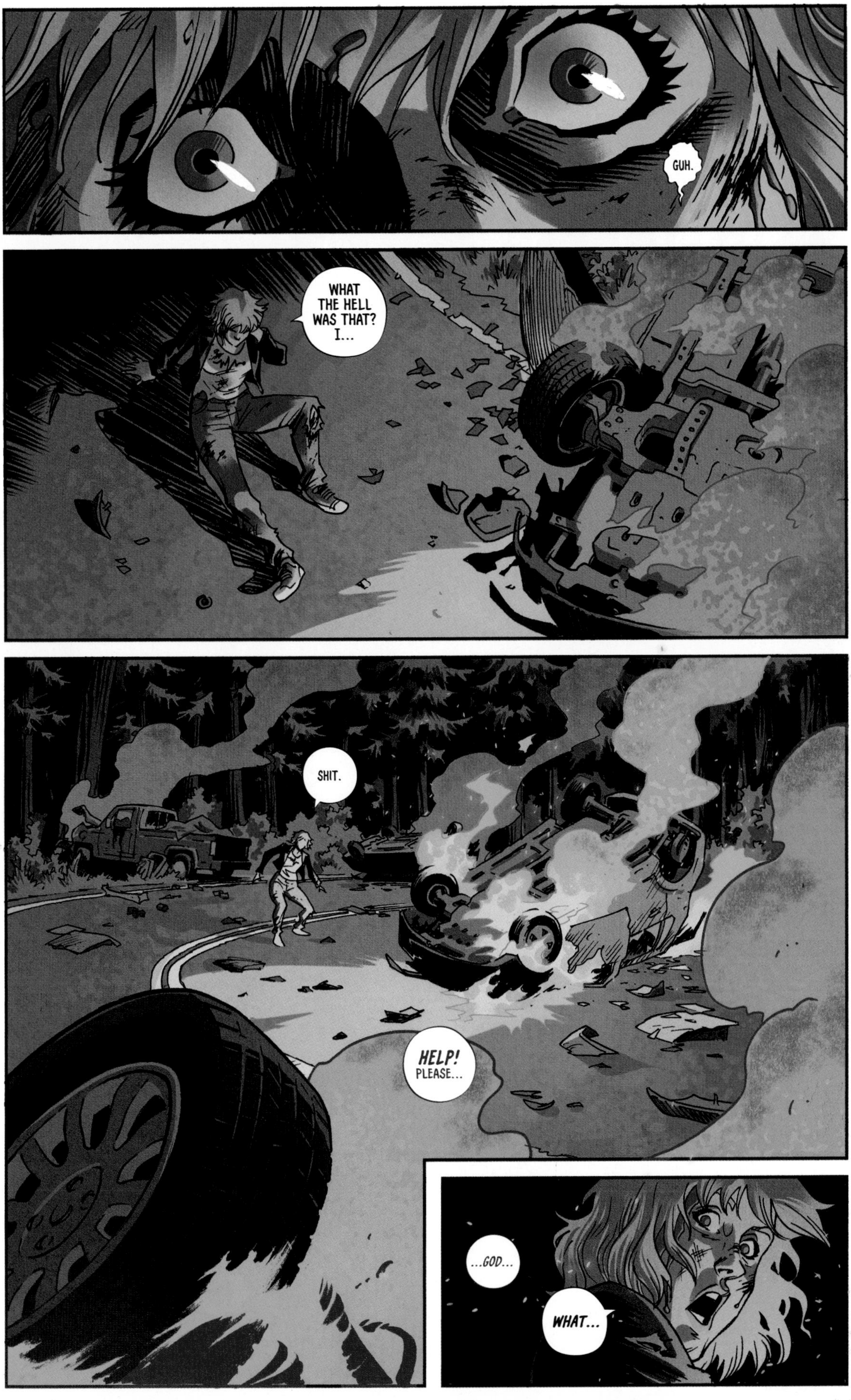
GUH.
WHAT THE HELL WAS THAT? I...
SHIT.
HELP! PLEASE...
...GOD...
WHAT...

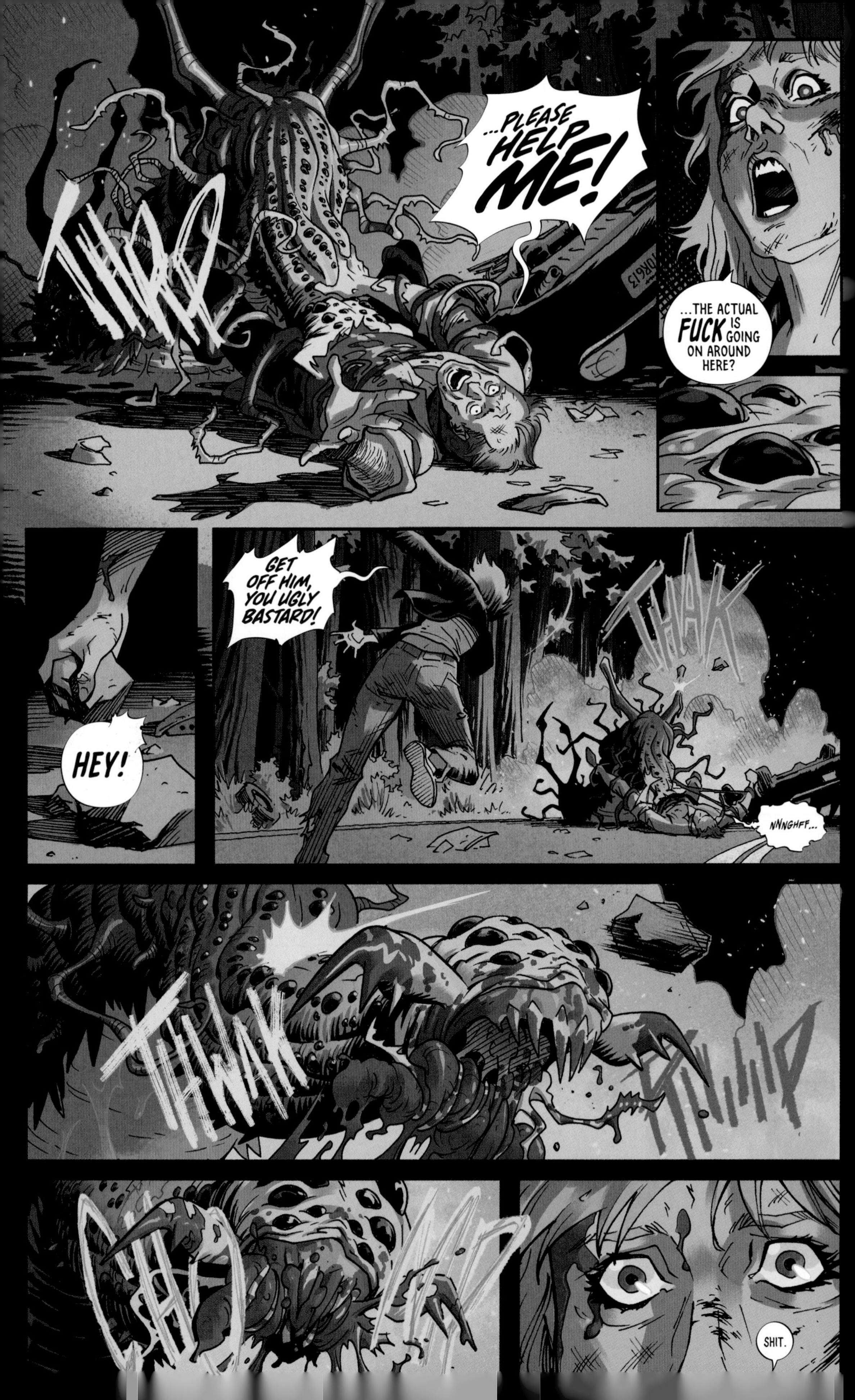
THWAP
...PLEASE HELP ME!
...THE ACTUAL FUCK IS GOING ON AROUND HERE?
HEY!
GET OFF HIM, YOU UGLY BASTARD!
THAK
NNNGHFF...
THWAK
SHIT.

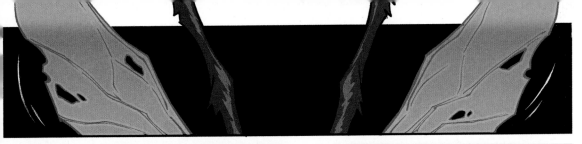

OH NO.
NO. NO.
NO.

HSSSS

UNGH!

ARE YOU...
CHRIST, WHAT
WAS THAT THING?
I...ARE YOU
OKAY?

HELLO?

I'M
SORRY
ABOUT
YOUR--

HHRRKK

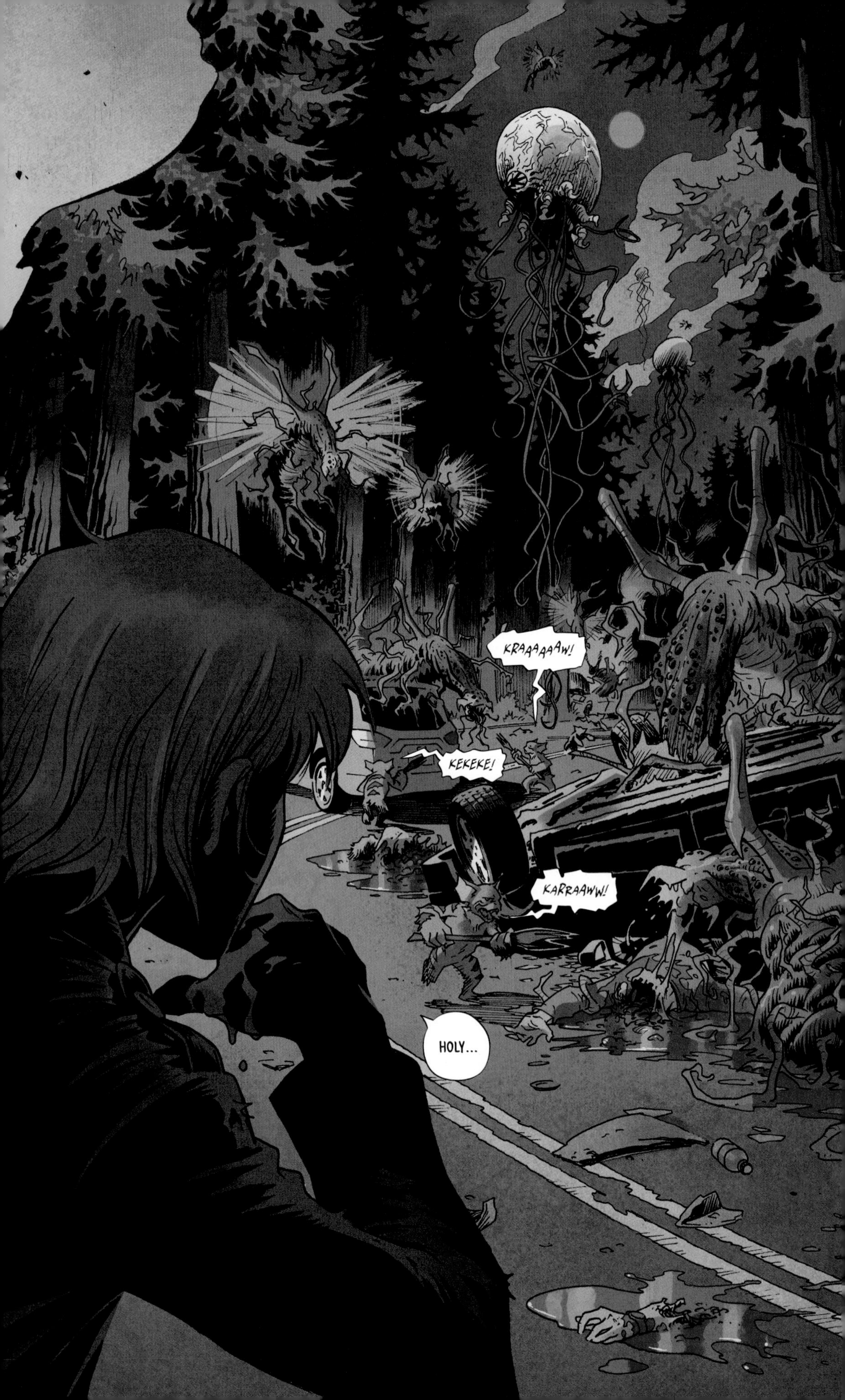
KRAAAAAAW!
KEKEKE!
KARRAAWW!
HOLY...

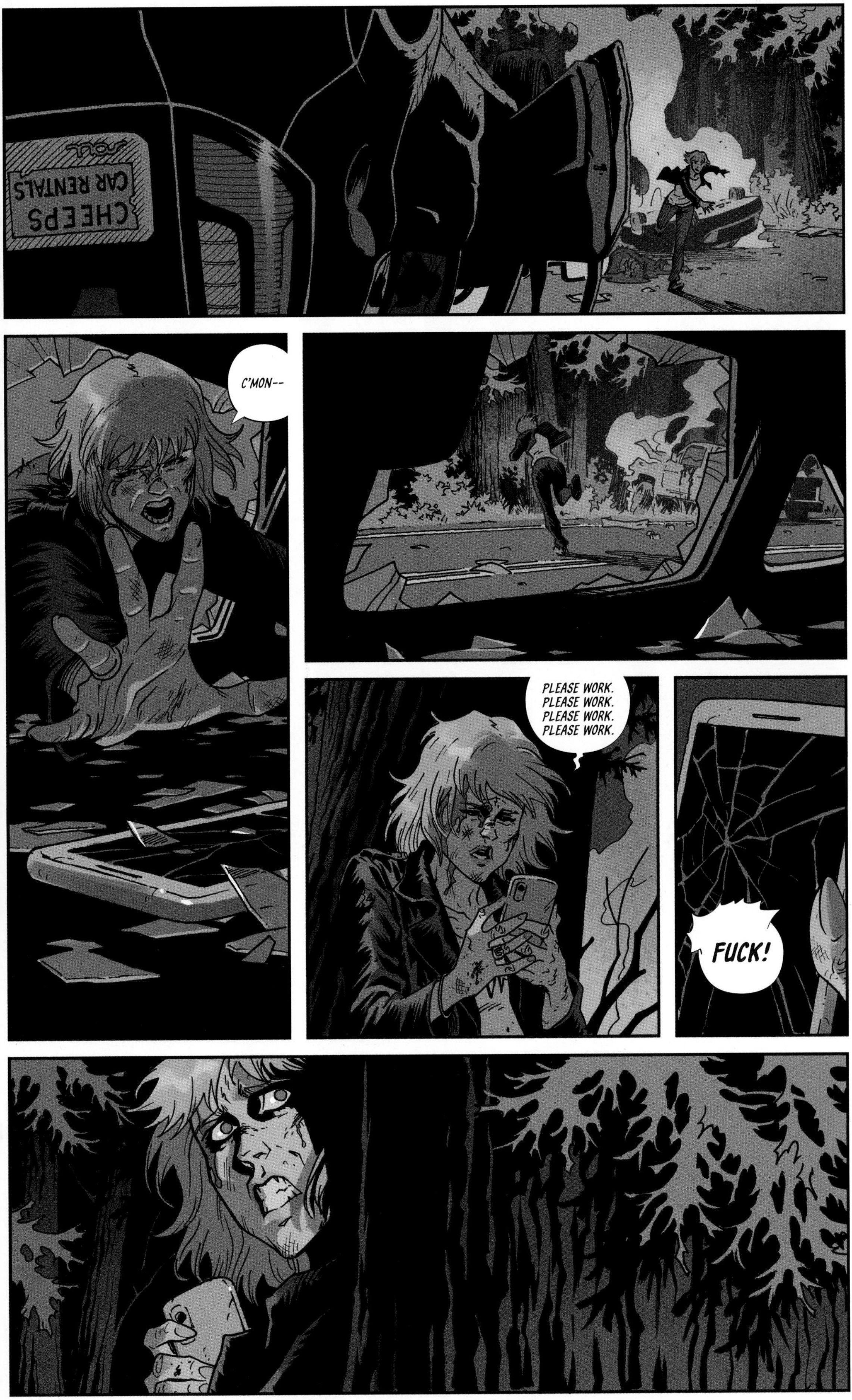
CHEEPS
CAR RENTALS
C'MON--
PLEASE WORK.
PLEASE WORK.
PLEASE WORK.
PLEASE WORK.
FUCK!

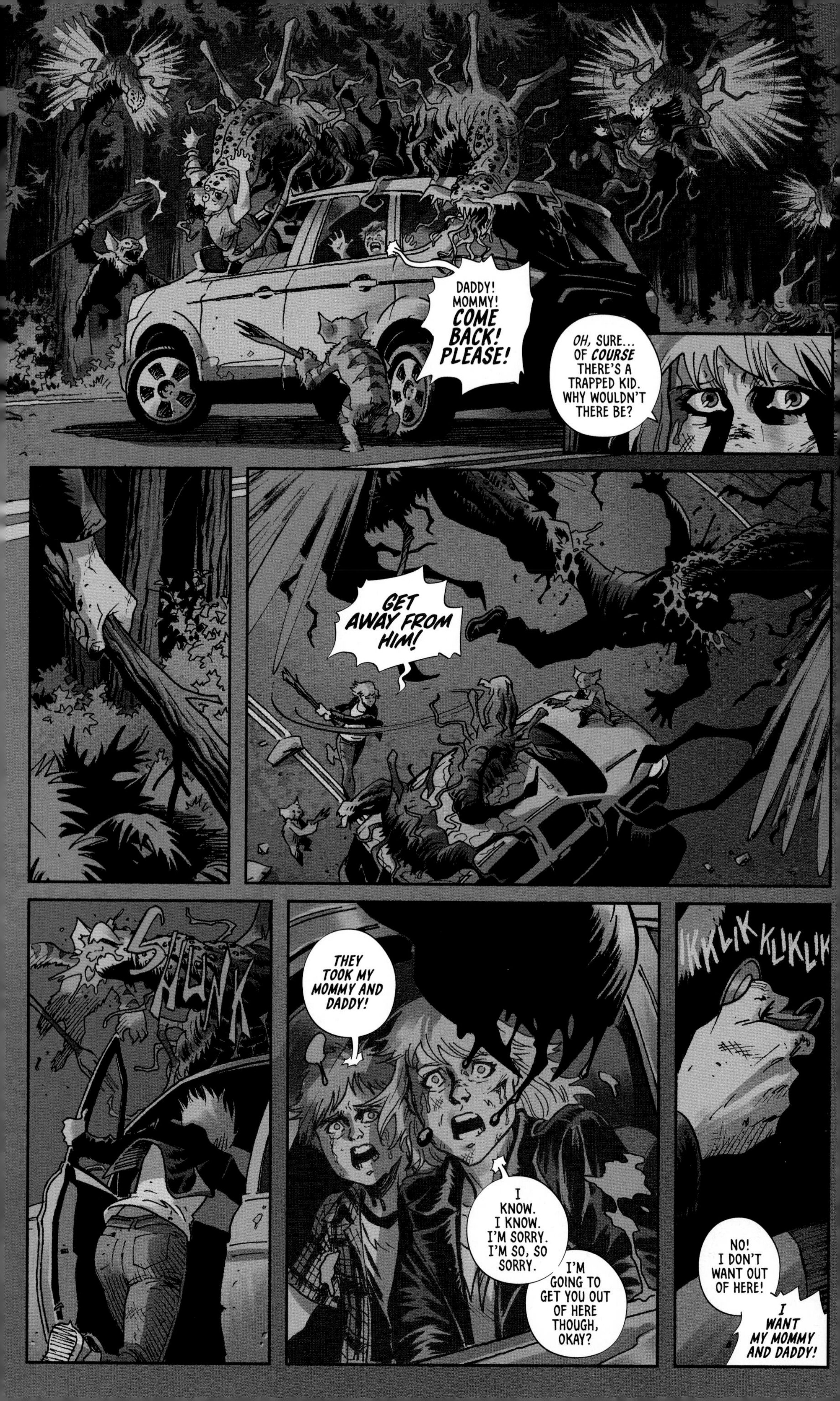
DADDY! MOMMY! COME BACK! PLEASE!
OH, SURE... OF COURSE THERE'S A TRAPPED KID. WHY WOULDN'T THERE BE?
GET AWAY FROM HIM!
SHUNK
THEY TOOK MY MOMMY AND DADDY!
I KNOW. I KNOW. I'M SORRY. I'M SO, SO SORRY.
I'M GOING TO GET YOU OUT OF HERE THOUGH, OKAY?
IKKLIK KLIKLIK
NO! I DON'T WANT OUT OF HERE!
I WANT MY MOMMY AND DADDY!

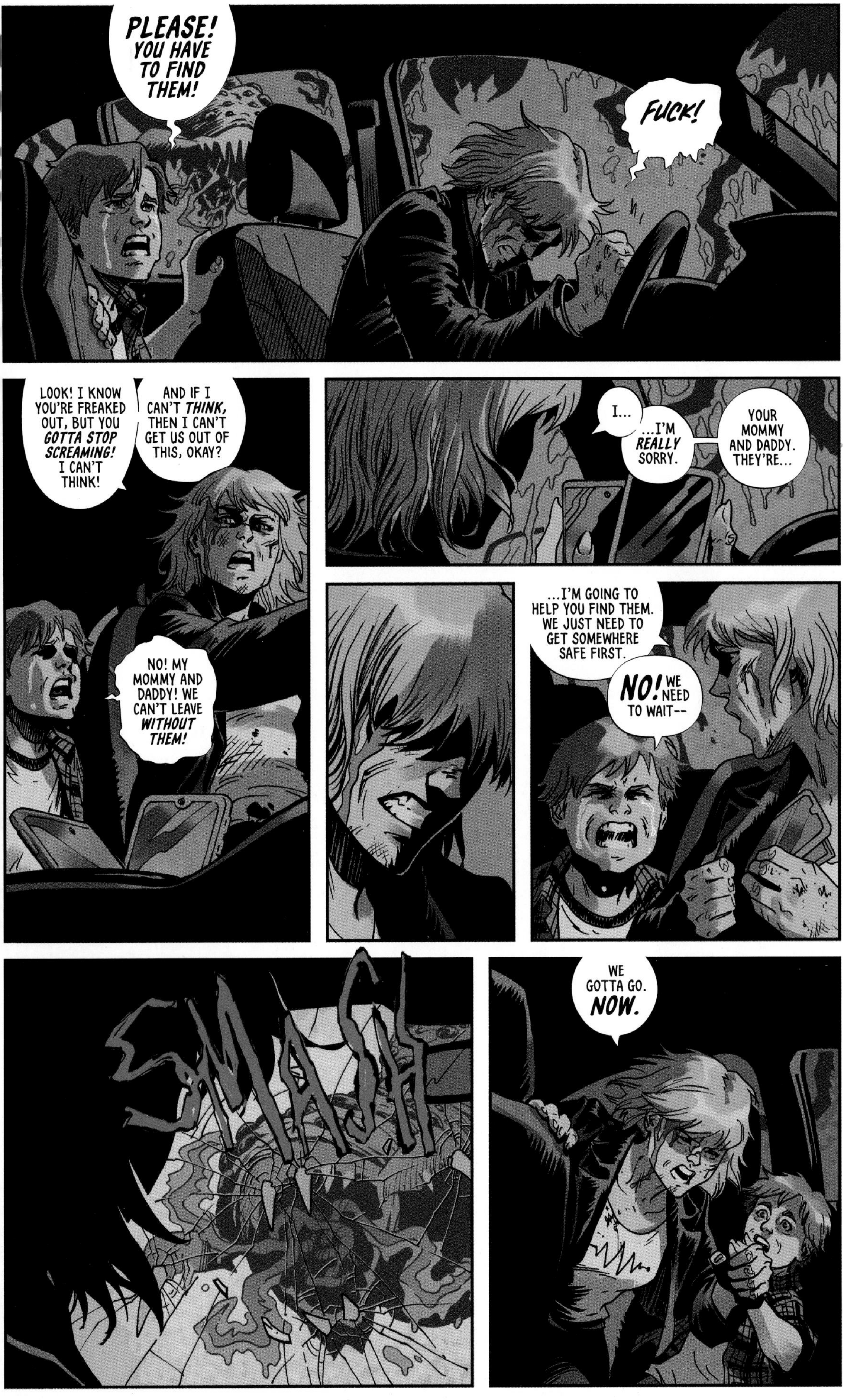
PLEASE! YOU HAVE TO FIND THEM!
FUCK!
LOOK! I KNOW YOU'RE FREAKED OUT, BUT YOU *GOTTA STOP SCREAMING!* I CAN'T THINK!
AND IF I CAN'T *THINK,* THEN I CAN'T GET US OUT OF THIS, OKAY?
NO! MY MOMMY AND DADDY! WE CAN'T LEAVE *WITHOUT THEM!*
I...
...I'M *REALLY* SORRY.
YOUR MOMMY AND DADDY. THEY'RE...
...I'M GOING TO HELP YOU FIND THEM. WE JUST NEED TO GET SOMEWHERE SAFE FIRST.
NO! WE NEED TO WAIT--
SMASH
WE GOTTA GO. NOW.

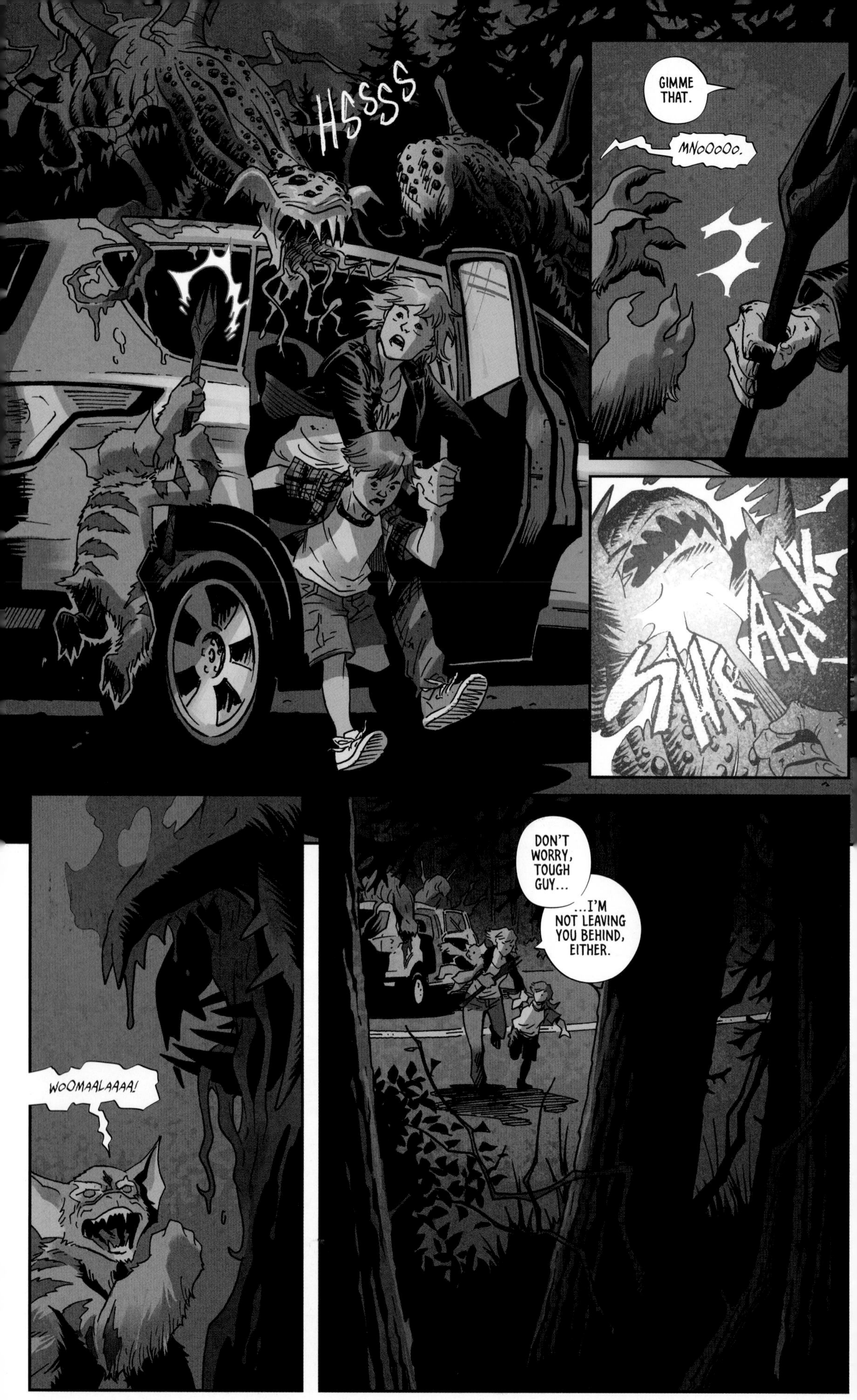
HSSSS
GIMME THAT.
MNOOOOO.
SHKRAAK
WOOMAALAAAA!
DON'T WORRY, TOUGH GUY...
...I'M NOT LEAVING YOU BEHIND, EITHER.

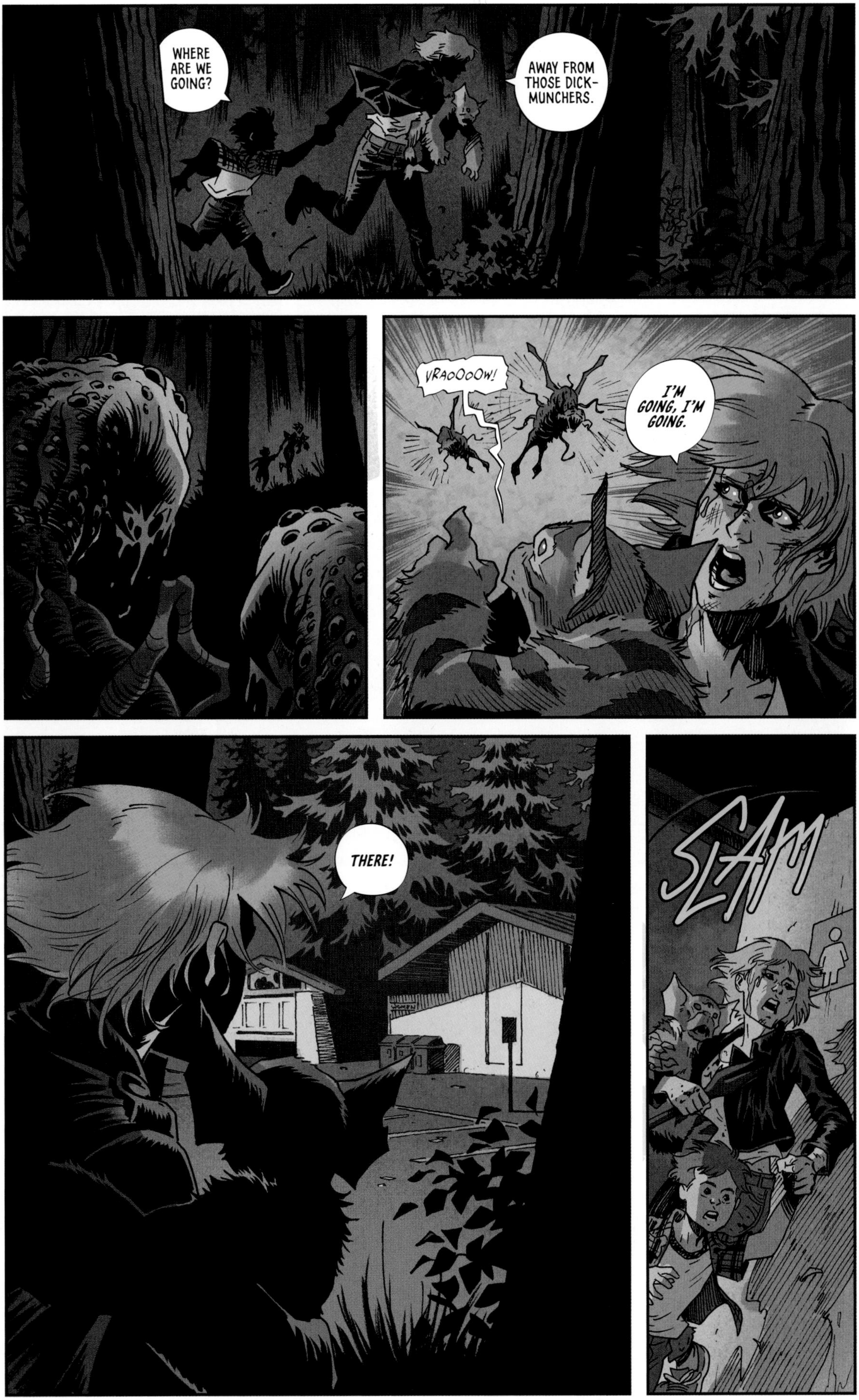
WHERE ARE WE GOING?
AWAY FROM THOSE DICK-MUNCHERS.
VRAOOOOW!
I'M GOING, I'M GOING.
THERE!
SLAM

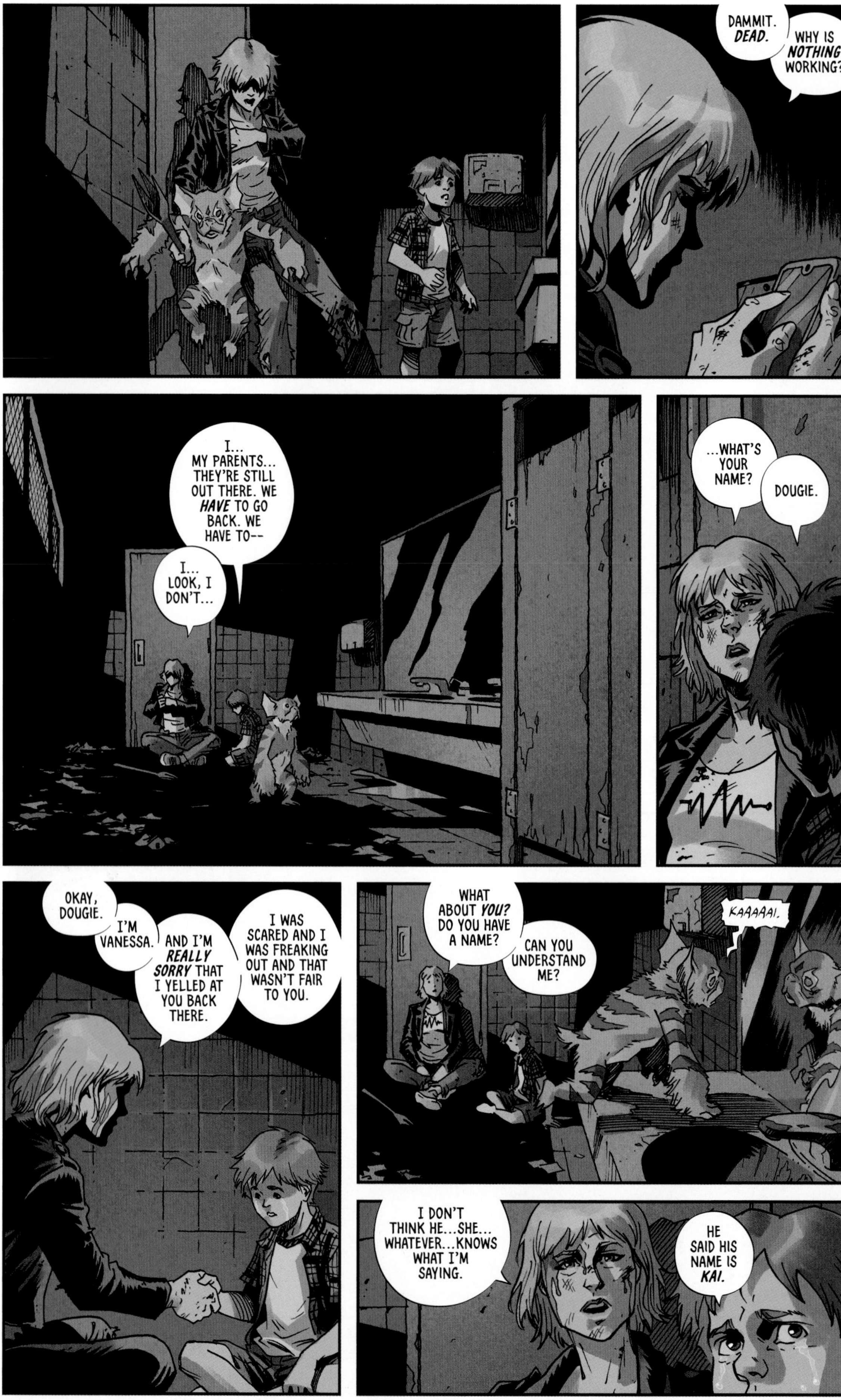
DAMMIT. *DEAD.*
WHY IS *NOTHING* WORKING?
I... MY PARENTS... THEY'RE STILL OUT THERE. WE *HAVE* TO GO BACK. WE HAVE TO--
I... LOOK, I DON'T...
...WHAT'S YOUR NAME?
DOUGIE.
OKAY, DOUGIE.
I'M VANESSA.
AND I'M *REALLY SORRY* THAT I YELLED AT YOU BACK THERE.
I WAS SCARED AND I WAS FREAKING OUT AND THAT WASN'T FAIR TO YOU.
WHAT ABOUT *YOU?* DO YOU HAVE A NAME?
CAN YOU UNDERSTAND ME?
KAAAAAI.
I DON'T THINK HE...SHE... WHATEVER...KNOWS WHAT I'M SAYING.
HE SAID HIS NAME IS *KAI.*

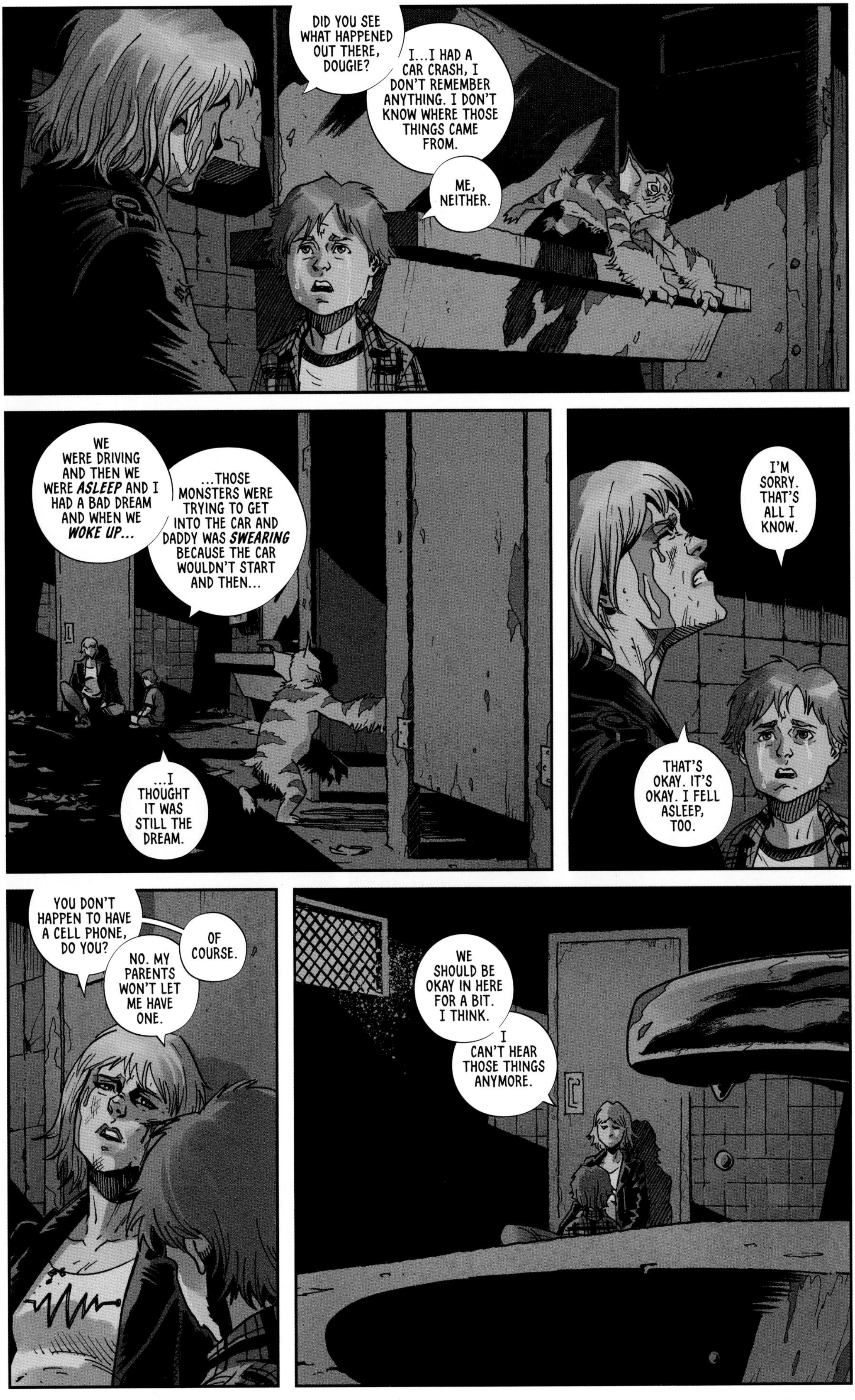
DID YOU SEE WHAT HAPPENED OUT THERE, DOUGIE?
I...I HAD A CAR CRASH, I DON'T REMEMBER ANYTHING. I DON'T KNOW WHERE THOSE THINGS CAME FROM.
ME, NEITHER.
WE WERE DRIVING AND THEN WE WERE *ASLEEP* AND I HAD A BAD DREAM AND WHEN WE *WOKE UP...*
...THOSE MONSTERS WERE TRYING TO GET INTO THE CAR AND DADDY WAS *SWEARING* BECAUSE THE CAR WOULDN'T START AND THEN...
...I THOUGHT IT WAS STILL THE DREAM.
I'M SORRY. THAT'S ALL I KNOW.
THAT'S OKAY. IT'S OKAY. I FELL ASLEEP, TOO.
YOU DON'T HAPPEN TO HAVE A CELL PHONE, DO YOU?
OF COURSE.
NO. MY PARENTS WON'T LET ME HAVE ONE.
WE SHOULD BE OKAY IN HERE FOR A BIT. I THINK.
I CAN'T HEAR THOSE THINGS ANYMORE.

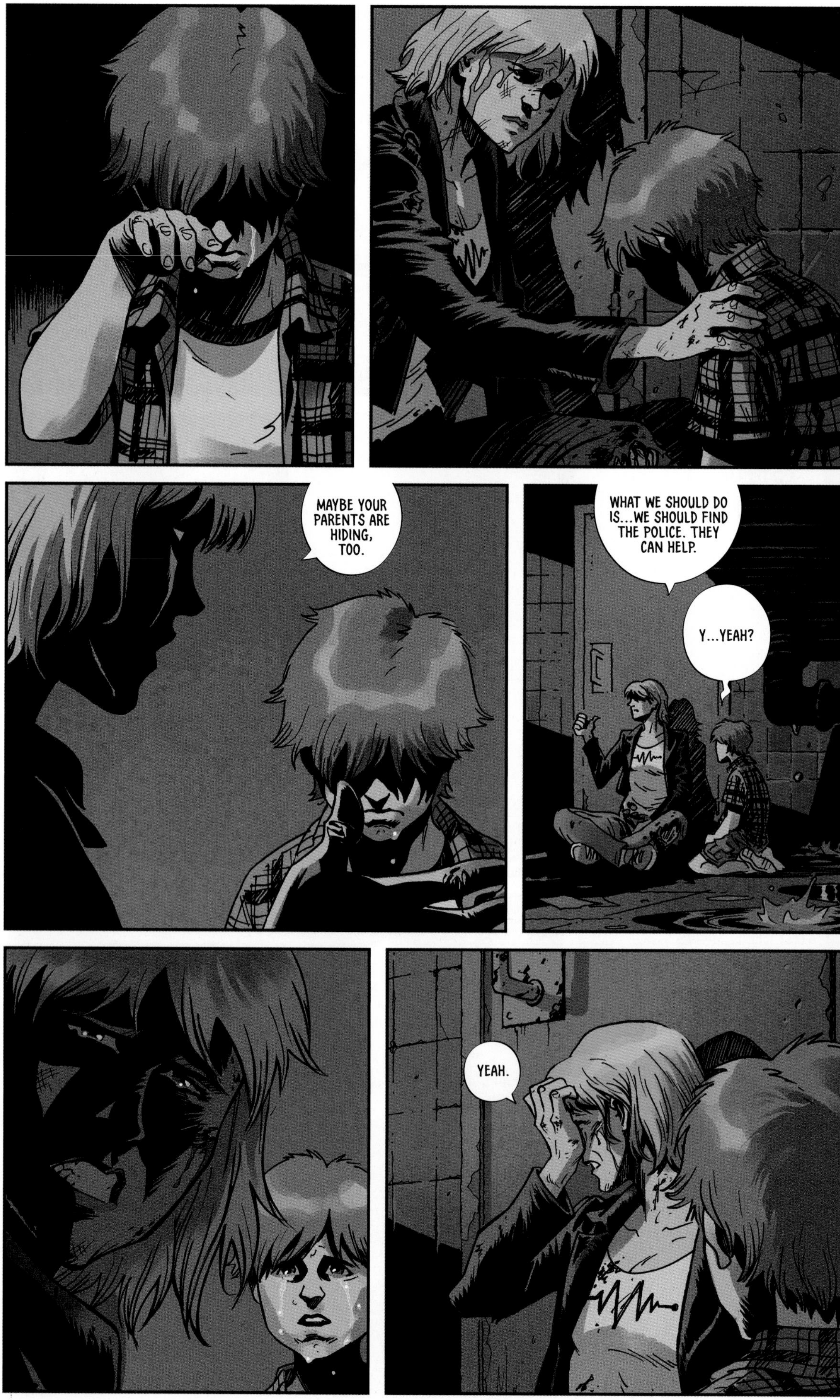
MAYBE YOUR PARENTS ARE HIDING, TOO.
WHAT WE SHOULD DO IS...WE SHOULD FIND THE POLICE. THEY CAN HELP.
Y...YEAH?
YEAH.

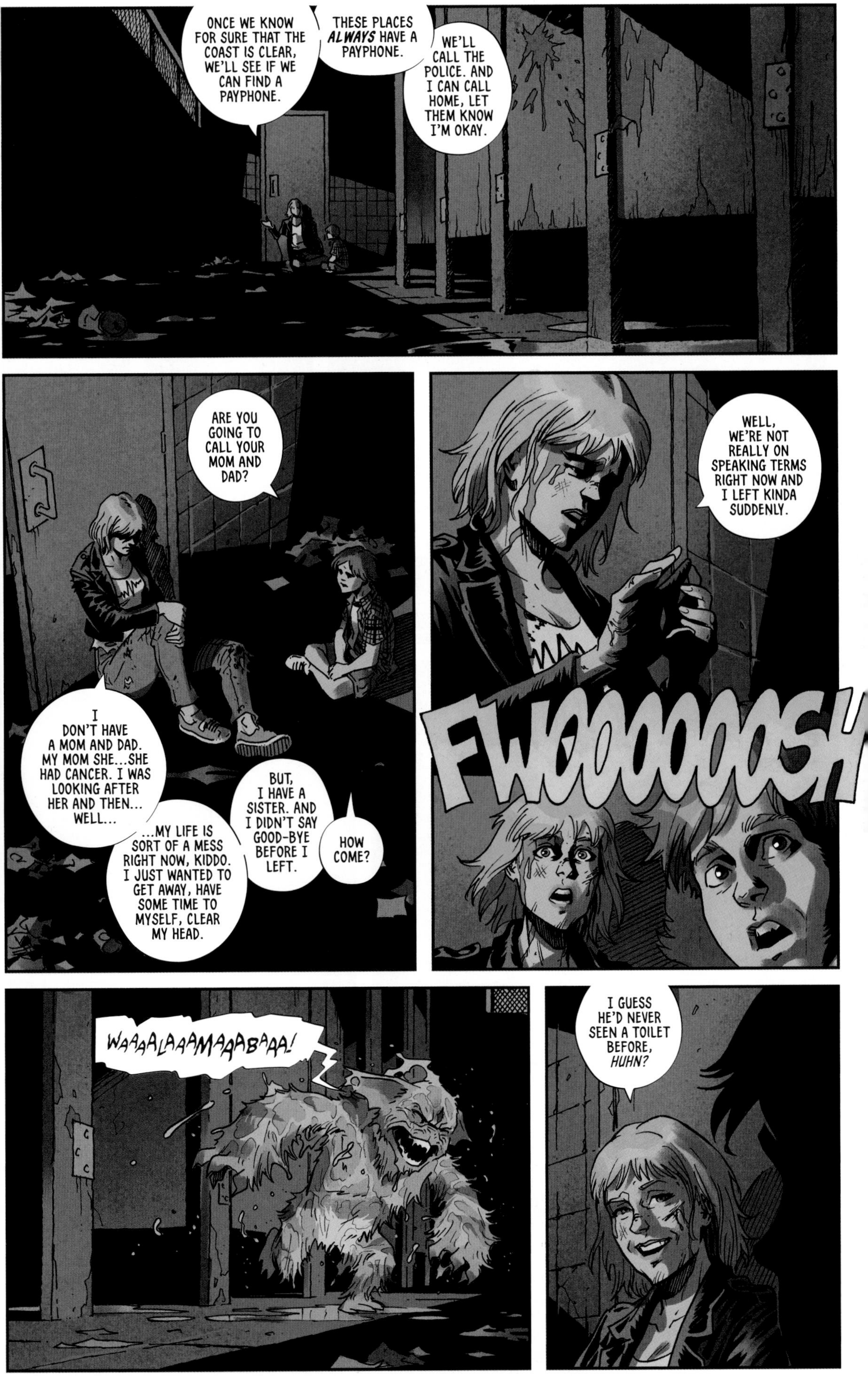
ONCE WE KNOW FOR SURE THAT THE COAST IS CLEAR, WE'LL SEE IF WE CAN FIND A PAYPHONE.
THESE PLACES *ALWAYS* HAVE A PAYPHONE.
WE'LL CALL THE POLICE. AND I CAN CALL HOME, LET THEM KNOW I'M OKAY.
ARE YOU GOING TO CALL YOUR MOM AND DAD?
I DON'T HAVE A MOM AND DAD. MY MOM SHE...SHE HAD CANCER. I WAS LOOKING AFTER HER AND THEN... WELL...
...MY LIFE IS SORT OF A MESS RIGHT NOW, KIDDO. I JUST WANTED TO GET AWAY, HAVE SOME TIME TO MYSELF, CLEAR MY HEAD.
BUT, I HAVE A SISTER. AND I DIDN'T SAY GOOD-BYE BEFORE I LEFT.
HOW COME?
WELL, WE'RE NOT REALLY ON SPEAKING TERMS RIGHT NOW AND I LEFT KINDA SUDDENLY.
FWOOOOOOSH
WAAAALAAAMAAABAAA!
I GUESS HE'D NEVER SEEN A TOILET BEFORE, *HUHN?*

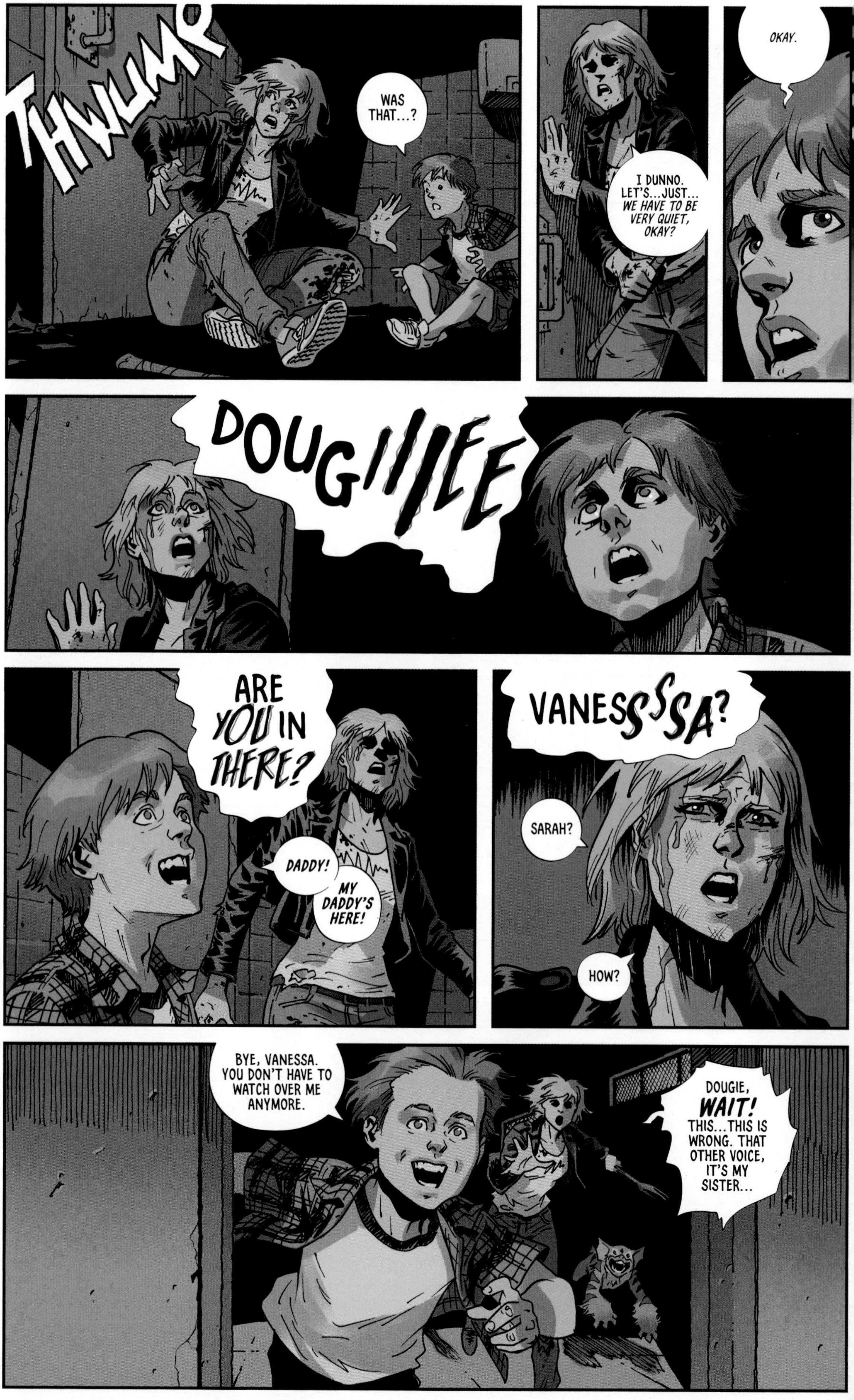
THWUMP
WAS THAT...?
I DUNNO. LET'S...JUST... WE HAVE TO BE VERY QUIET, OKAY?
OKAY.
DOUGIIIEE
ARE YOU IN THERE?
DADDY!
MY DADDY'S HERE!
VANESSSSA?
SARAH?
HOW?
BYE, VANESSA. YOU DON'T HAVE TO WATCH OVER ME ANYMORE.
DOUGIE, WAIT! THIS...THIS IS WRONG. THAT OTHER VOICE, IT'S MY SISTER...

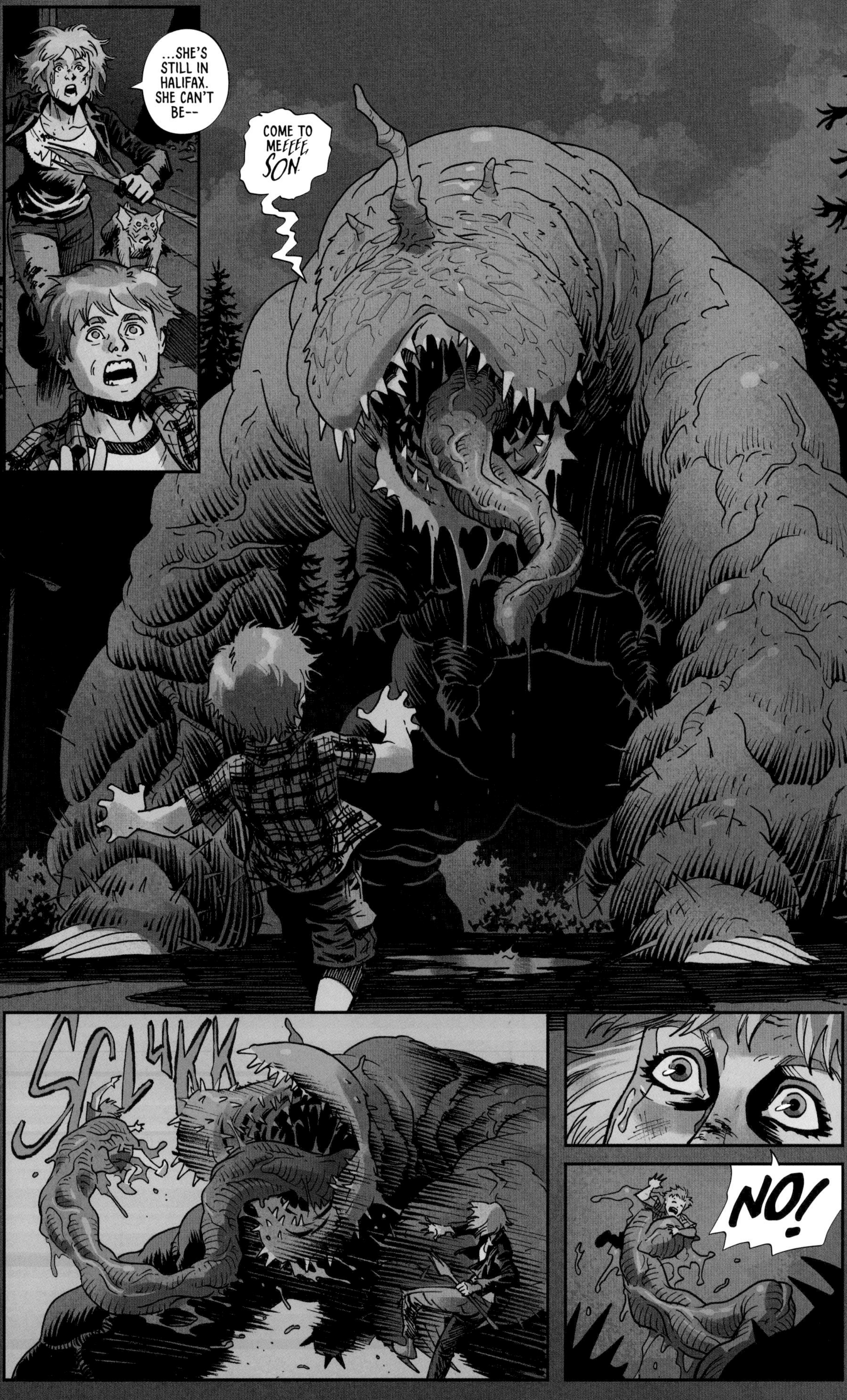
...SHE'S STILL IN HALIFAX. SHE CAN'T BE--
COME TO MEEEEE, SON.
SCLUKK
NO!

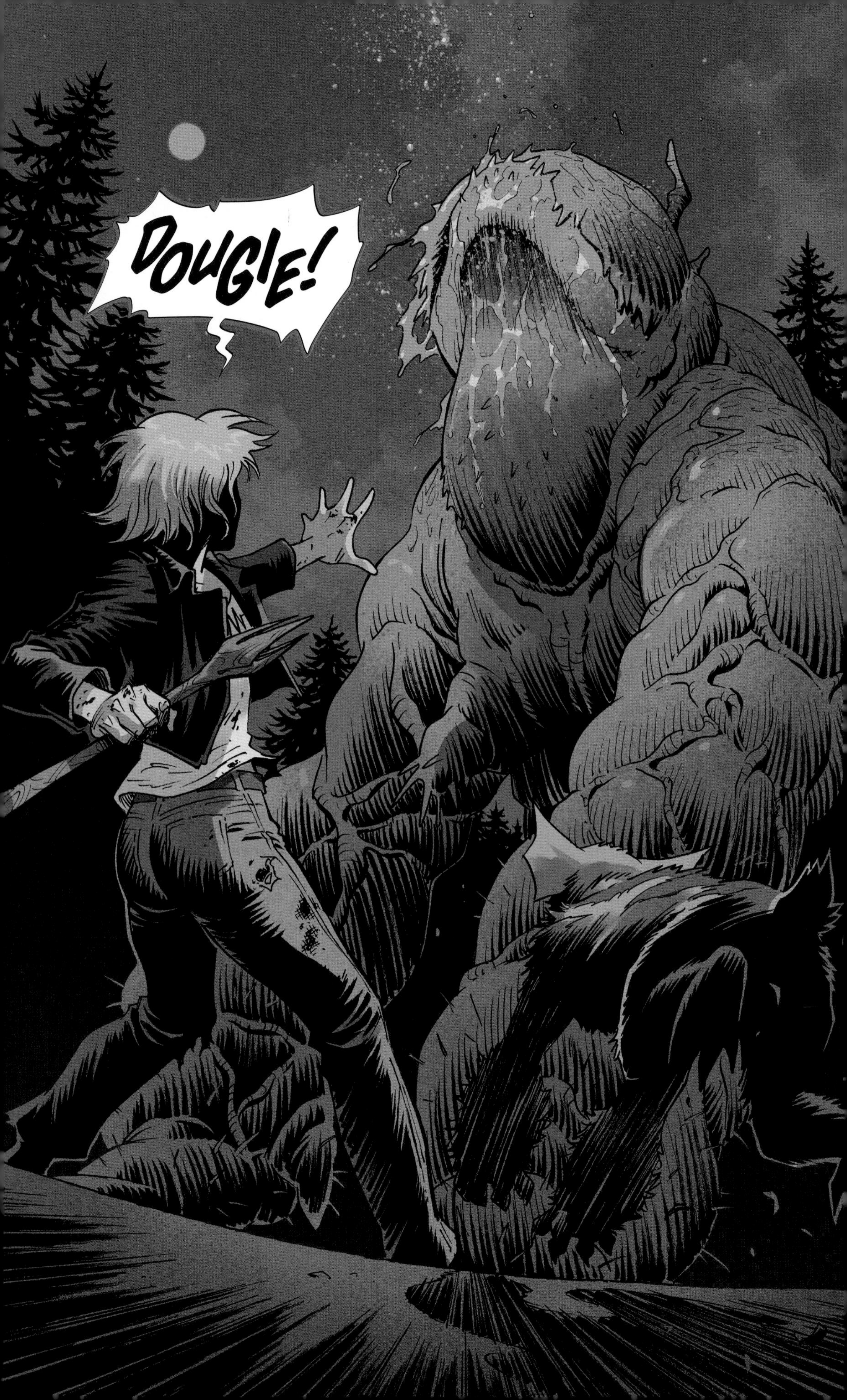
DOUGIE!

2

EVERYTHING YOU'VE DONE WRONG

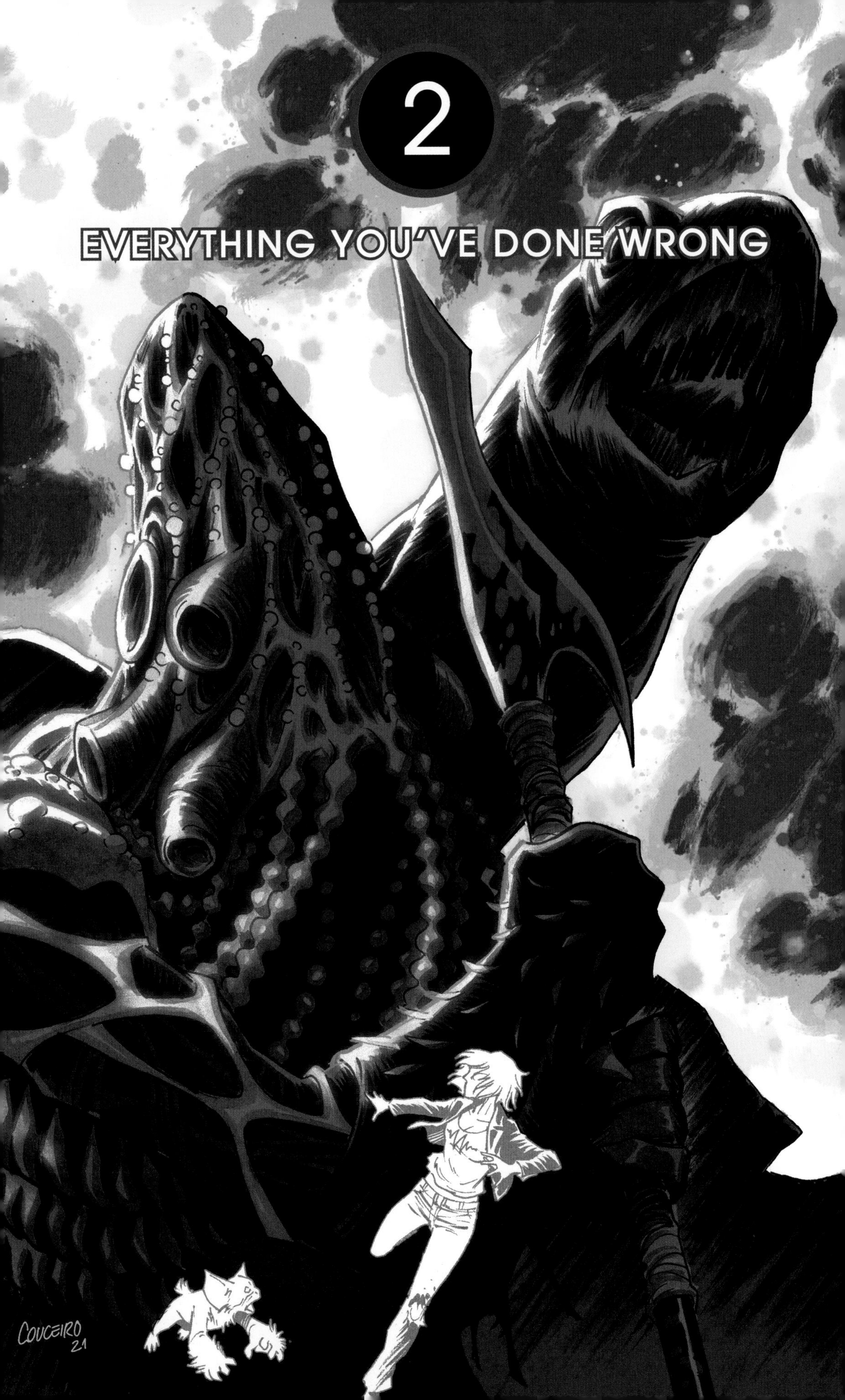
COUCEIRO 21

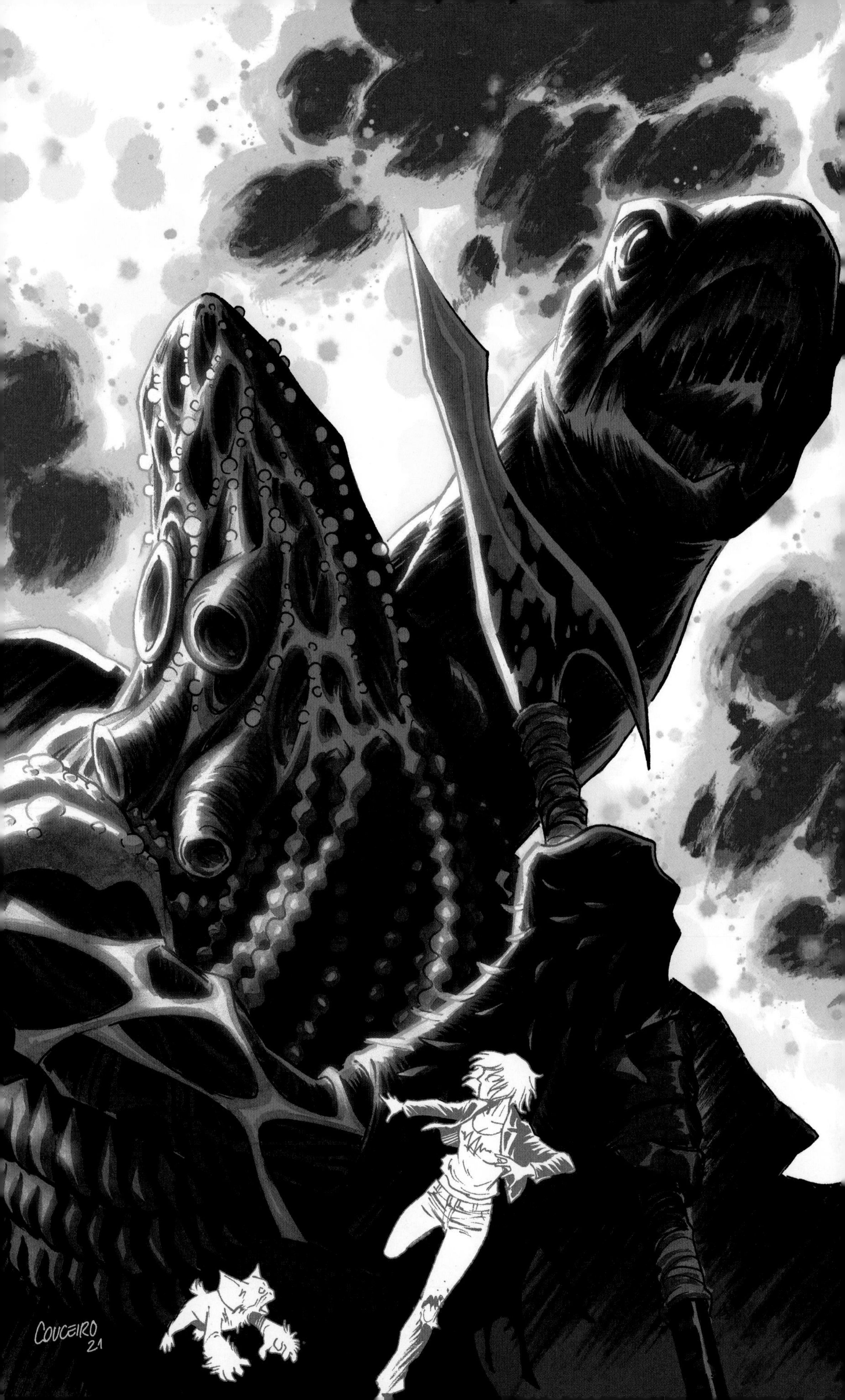
COUCEIRO
21

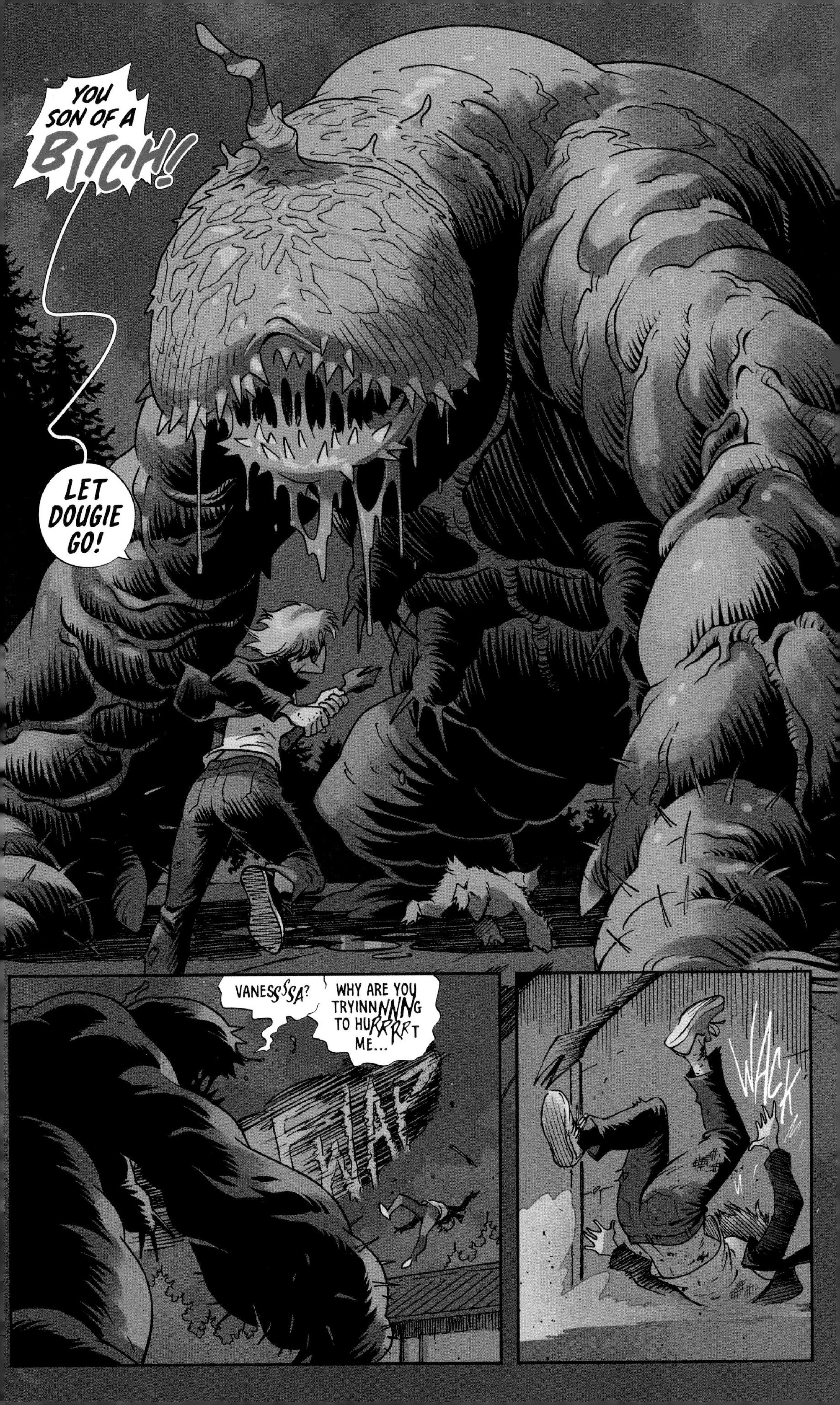
YOU SON OF A BITCH!!
LET DOUGIE GO!
VANESSSSA?
WHY ARE YOU TRYINNNNNG TO HURRRRRT ME...
WACK

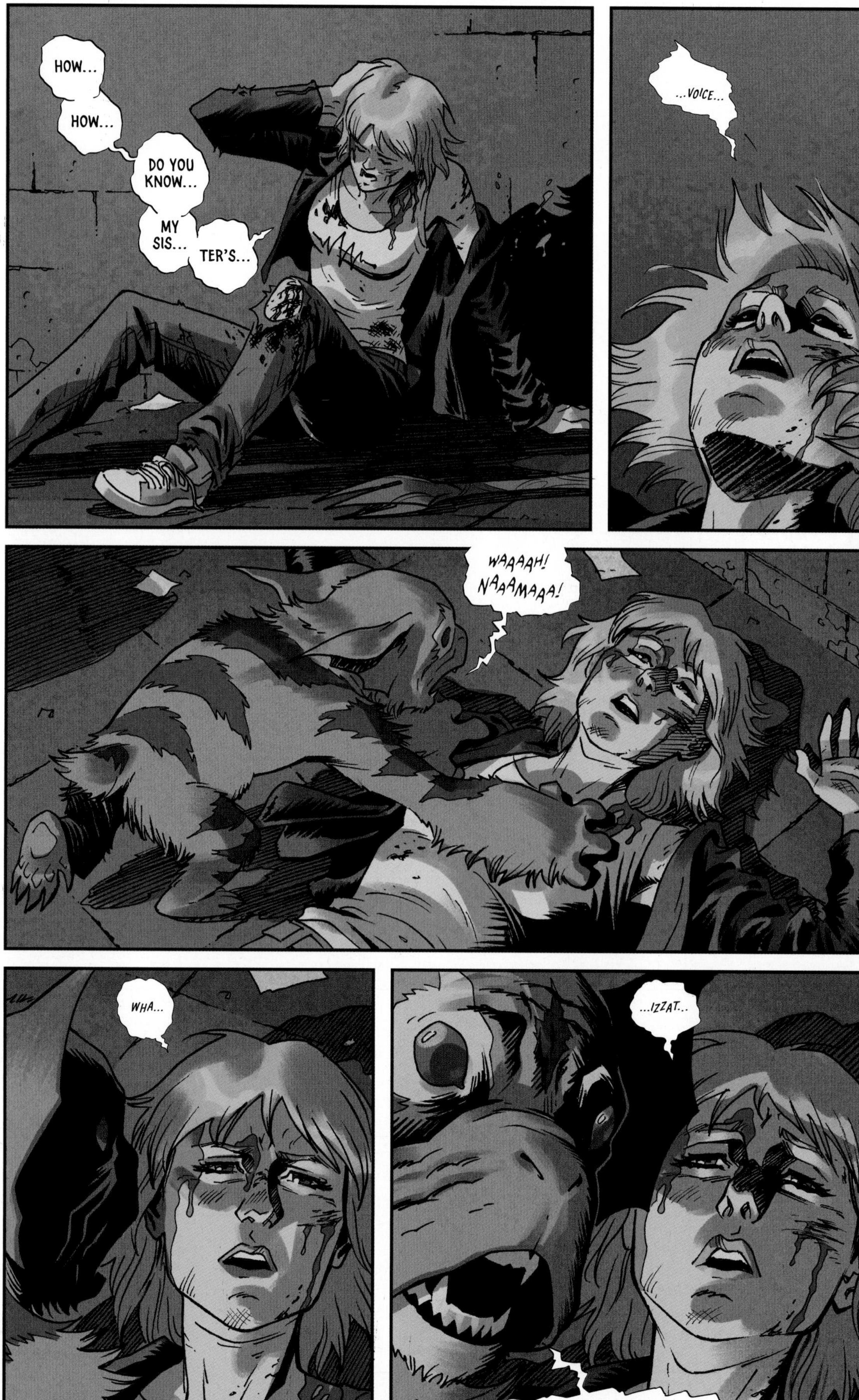
HOW...
HOW...
DO YOU KNOW...
MY SIS...
TER'S...
...VOICE...
WAAAAH! NAAAMAAA!
WHA...
...IZZAT...
WOOOOOOOMOOOOO!

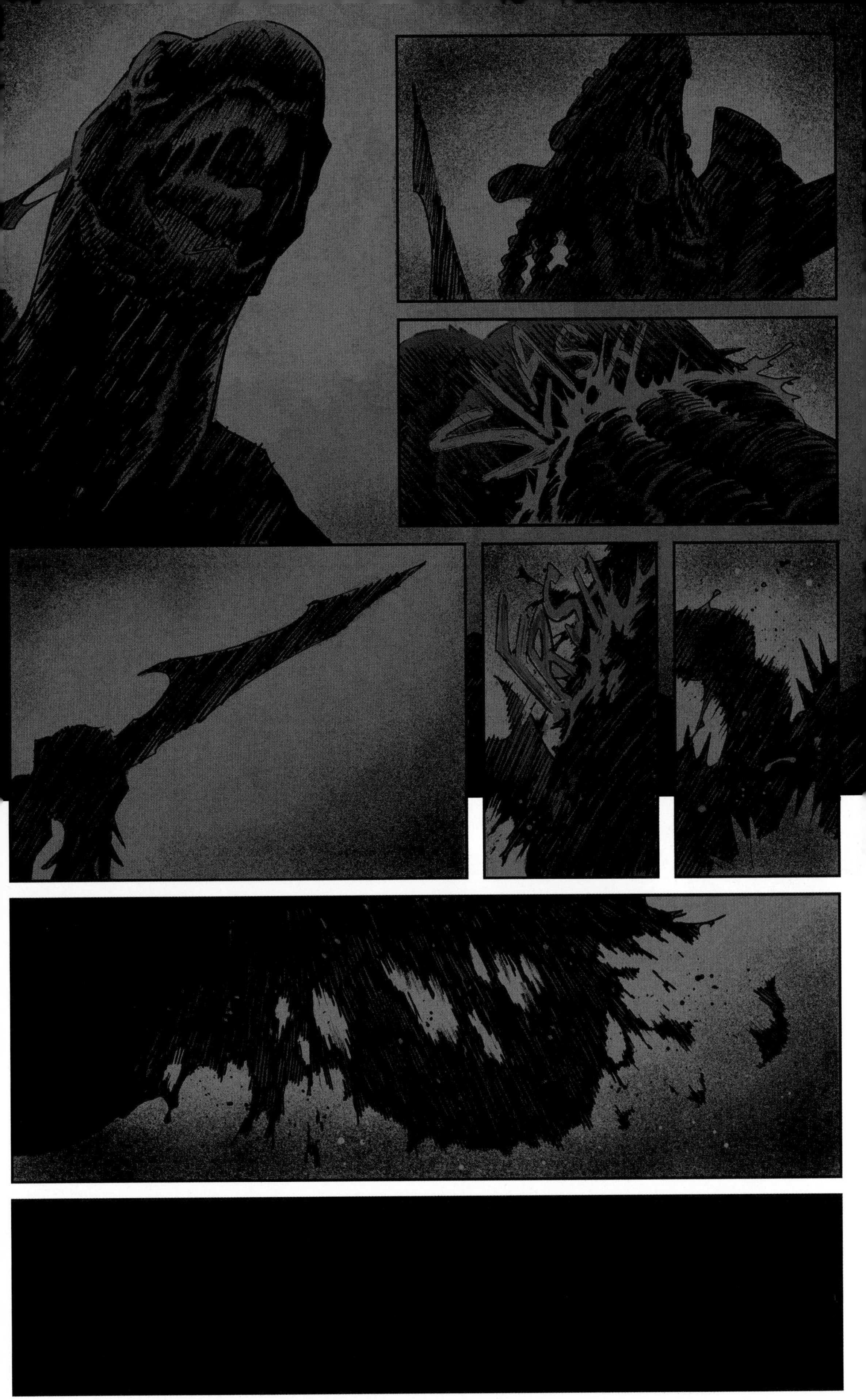

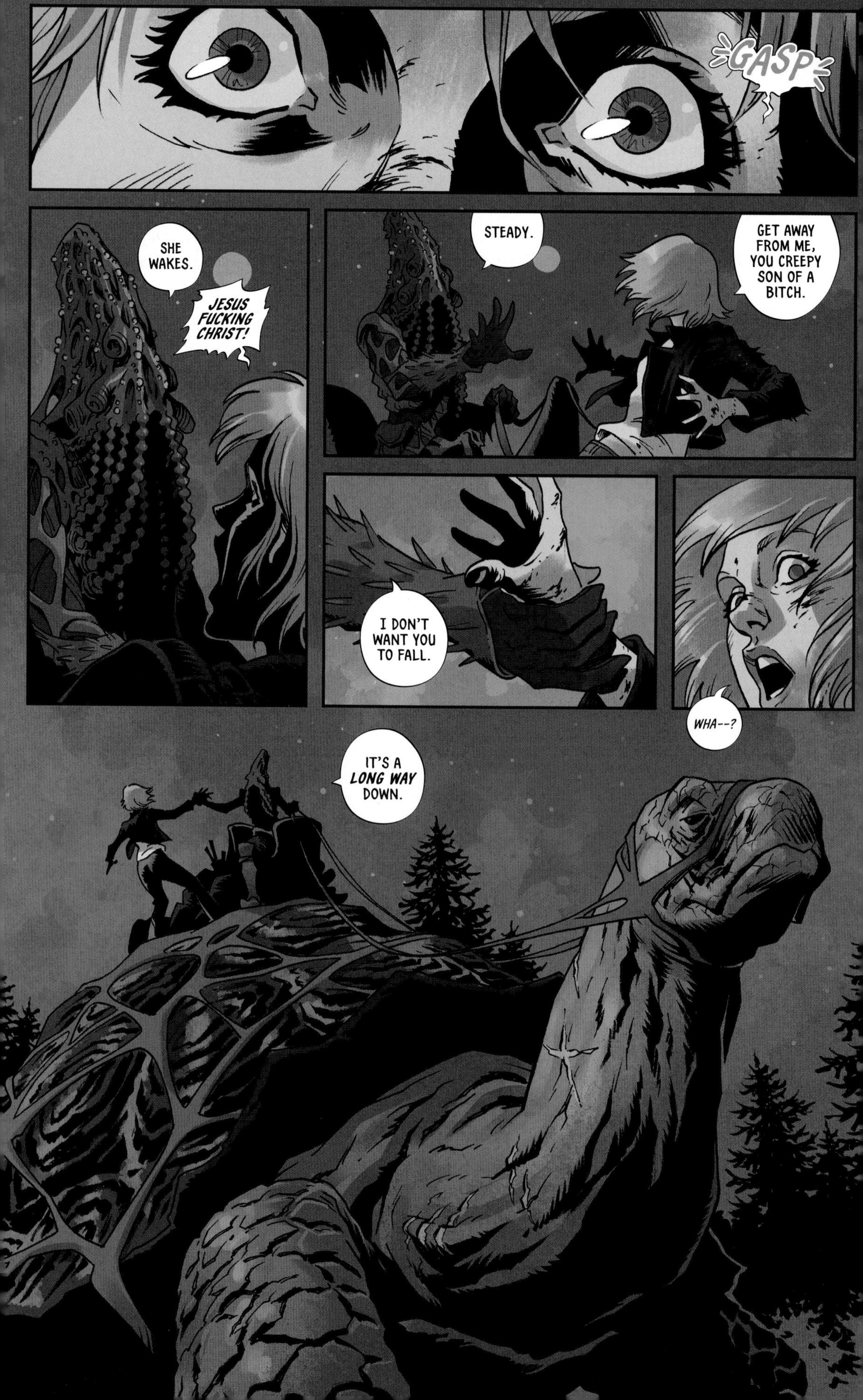
GASP
SHE WAKES.
JESUS FUCKING CHRIST!
STEADY.
GET AWAY FROM ME, YOU CREEPY SON OF A BITCH.
I DON'T WANT YOU TO FALL.
WHA--?
IT'S A LONG WAY DOWN.

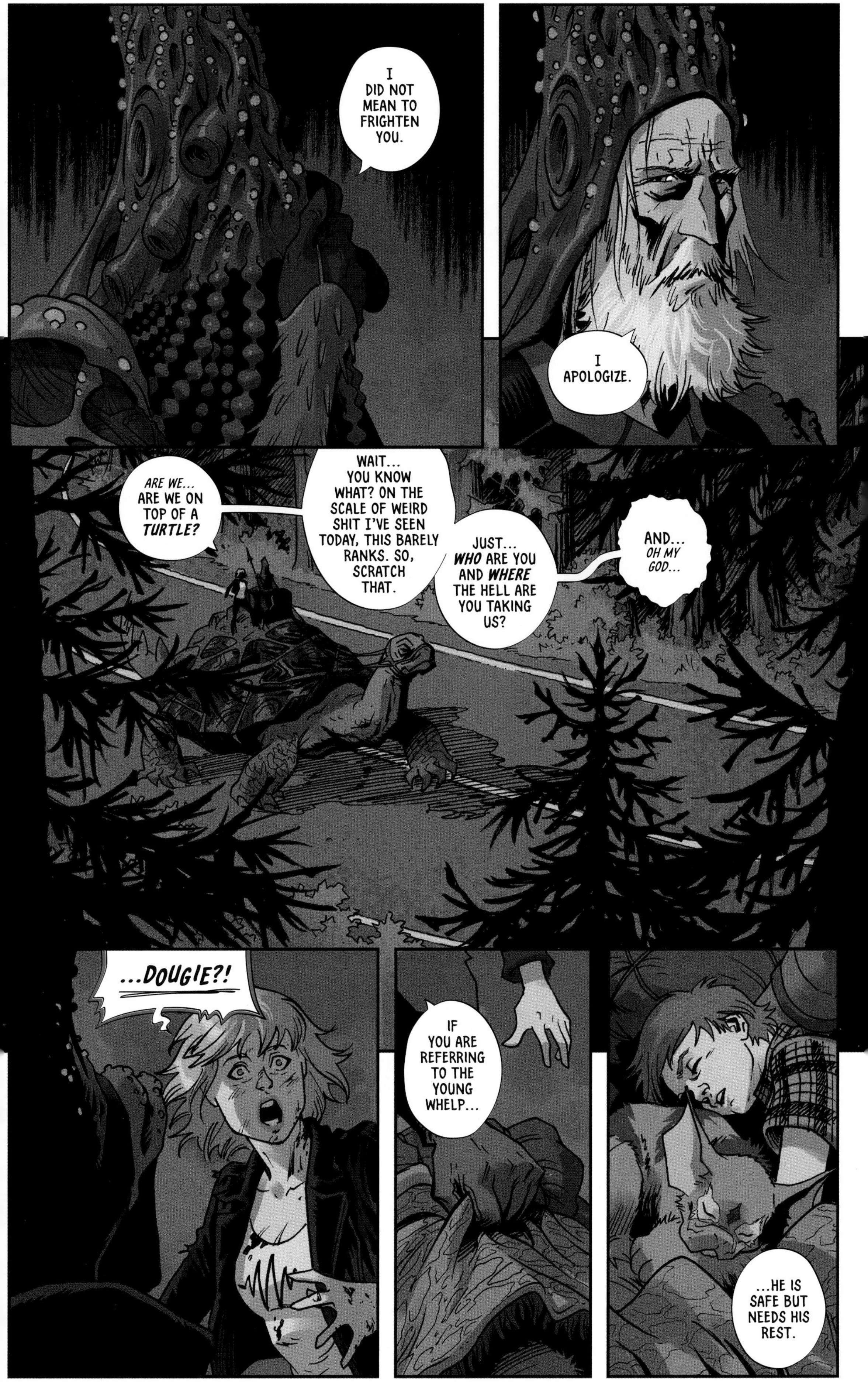

I DID NOT MEAN TO FRIGHTEN YOU.
I APOLOGIZE.
ARE WE... ARE WE ON TOP OF A *TURTLE?*
WAIT... YOU KNOW WHAT? ON THE SCALE OF WEIRD SHIT I'VE SEEN TODAY, THIS BARELY RANKS. SO, SCRATCH THAT.
JUST... ***WHO*** ARE YOU AND ***WHERE*** THE HELL ARE YOU TAKING US?
AND... *OH MY GOD...*
...DOUGIE?!
IF YOU ARE REFERRING TO THE YOUNG WHELP...
...HE IS SAFE BUT NEEDS HIS REST.

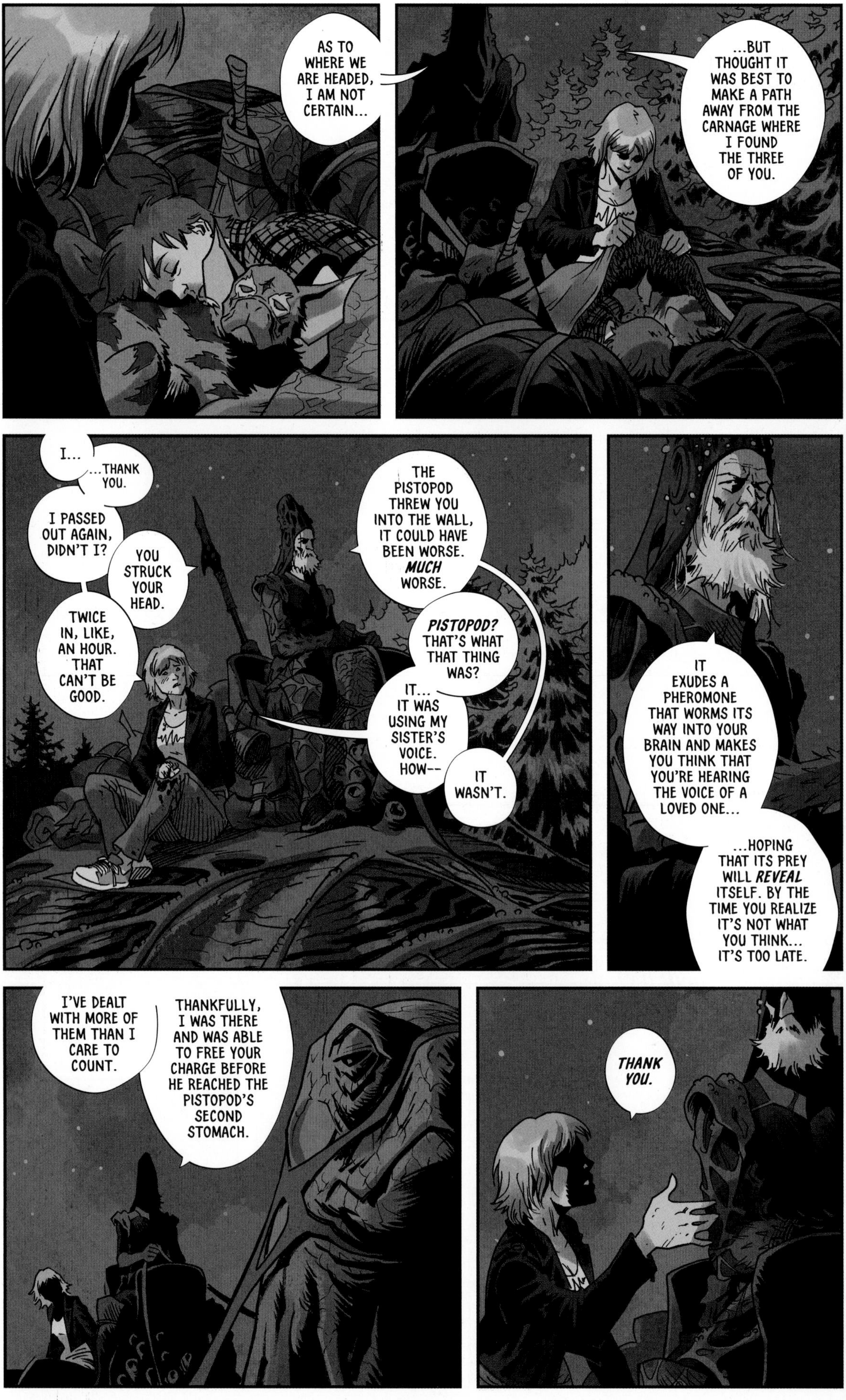
AS TO WHERE WE ARE HEADED, I AM NOT CERTAIN...
...BUT THOUGHT IT WAS BEST TO MAKE A PATH AWAY FROM THE CARNAGE WHERE I FOUND THE THREE OF YOU.
I...
...THANK YOU.
I PASSED OUT AGAIN, DIDN'T I?
YOU STRUCK YOUR HEAD.
TWICE IN, LIKE, AN HOUR. THAT CAN'T BE GOOD.
THE PISTOPOD THREW YOU INTO THE WALL, IT COULD HAVE BEEN WORSE. *MUCH* WORSE.
PISTOPOD? THAT'S WHAT THAT THING WAS?
IT... IT WAS USING MY SISTER'S VOICE. HOW--
IT WASN'T.
IT EXUDES A PHEROMONE THAT WORMS ITS WAY INTO YOUR BRAIN AND MAKES YOU THINK THAT YOU'RE HEARING THE VOICE OF A LOVED ONE...
...HOPING THAT ITS PREY WILL *REVEAL* ITSELF. BY THE TIME YOU REALIZE IT'S NOT WHAT YOU THINK... IT'S TOO LATE.
I'VE DEALT WITH MORE OF THEM THAN I CARE TO COUNT.
THANKFULLY, I WAS THERE AND WAS ABLE TO FREE YOUR CHARGE BEFORE HE REACHED THE PISTOPOD'S SECOND STOMACH.
THANK YOU.

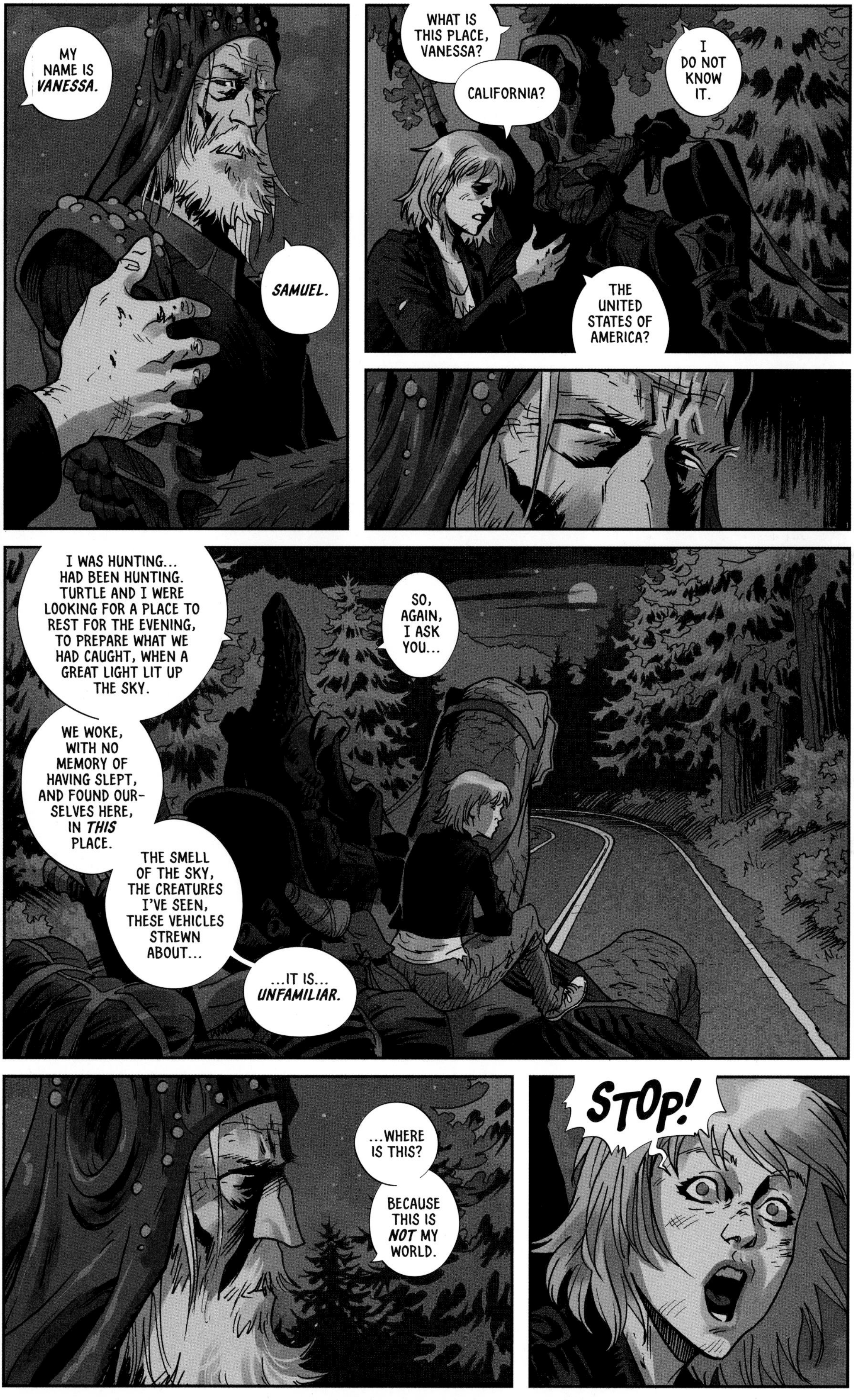
MY NAME IS *VANESSA.*
SAMUEL.
WHAT IS THIS PLACE, VANESSA?
CALIFORNIA?
I DO NOT KNOW IT.
THE UNITED STATES OF AMERICA?
I WAS HUNTING... HAD BEEN HUNTING. TURTLE AND I WERE LOOKING FOR A PLACE TO REST FOR THE EVENING, TO PREPARE WHAT WE HAD CAUGHT, WHEN A GREAT LIGHT LIT UP THE SKY.
WE WOKE, WITH NO MEMORY OF HAVING SLEPT, AND FOUND OURSELVES HERE, IN *THIS* PLACE.
THE SMELL OF THE SKY, THE CREATURES I'VE SEEN, THESE VEHICLES STREWN ABOUT...
...IT IS... *UNFAMILIAR.*
SO, AGAIN, I ASK YOU...
...WHERE IS THIS?
BECAUSE THIS IS *NOT* MY WORLD.
STOP!

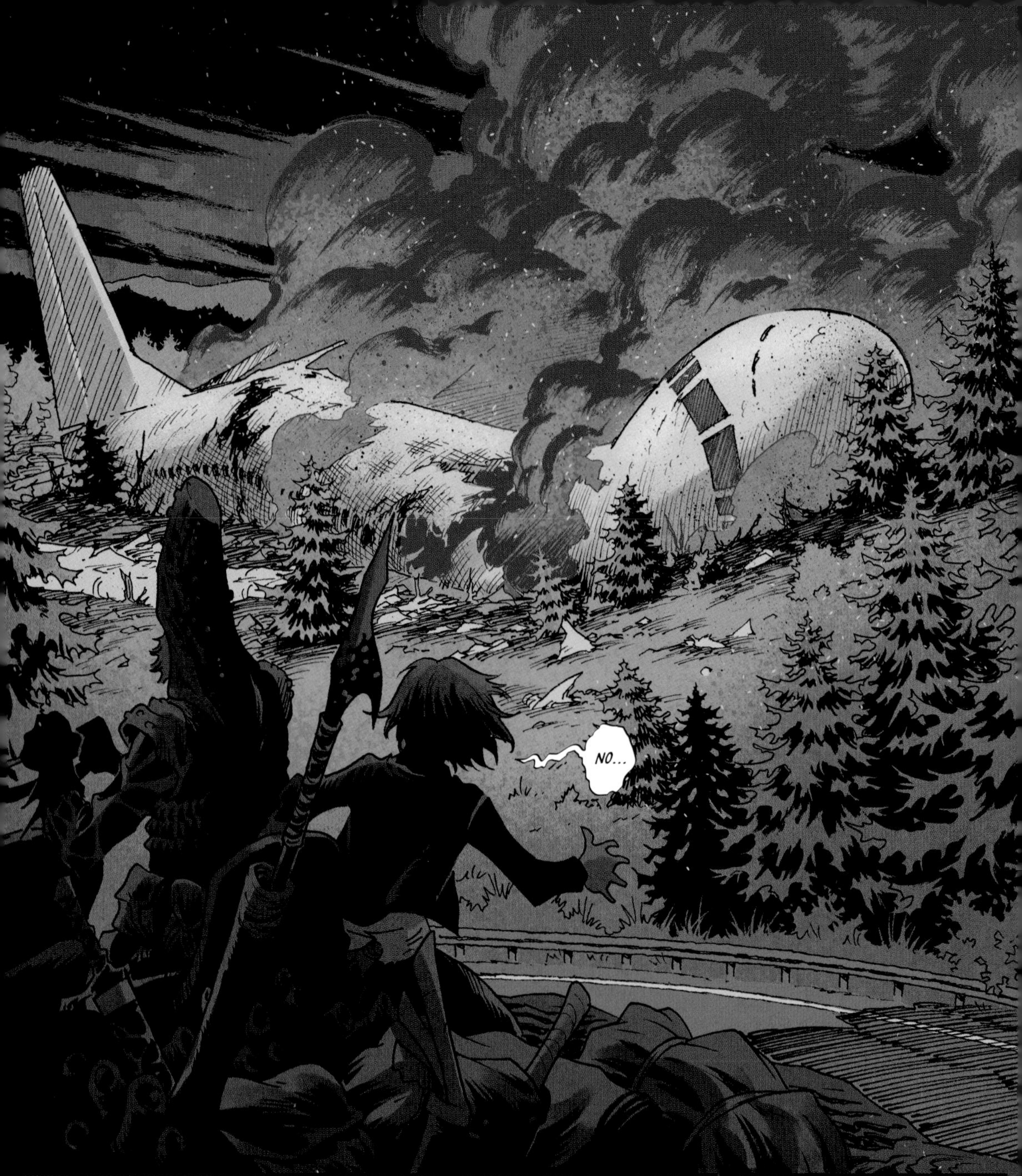
NO...
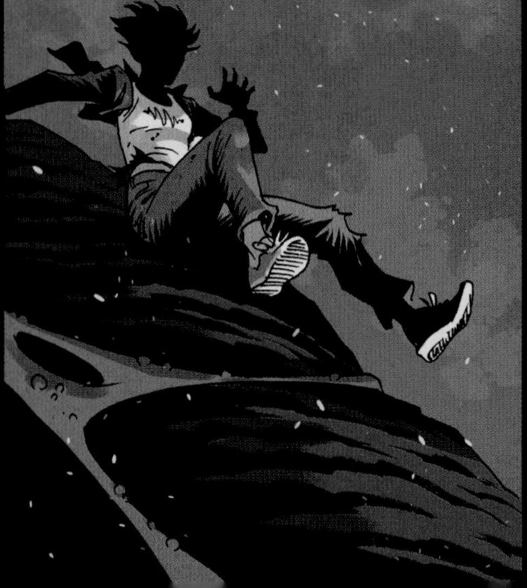
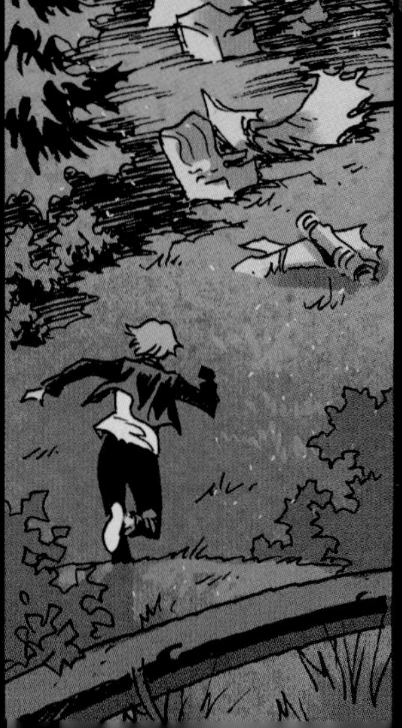
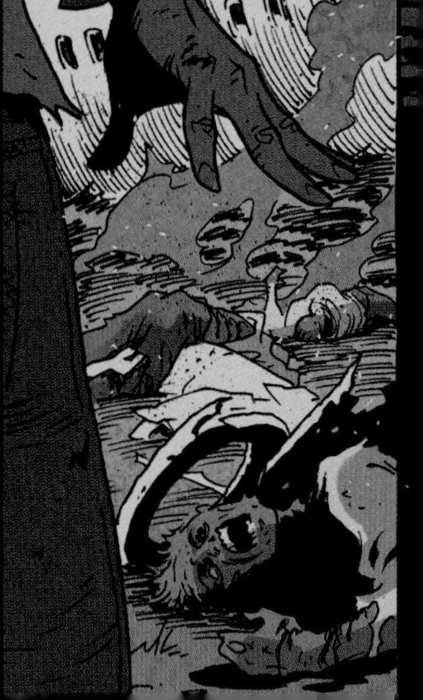

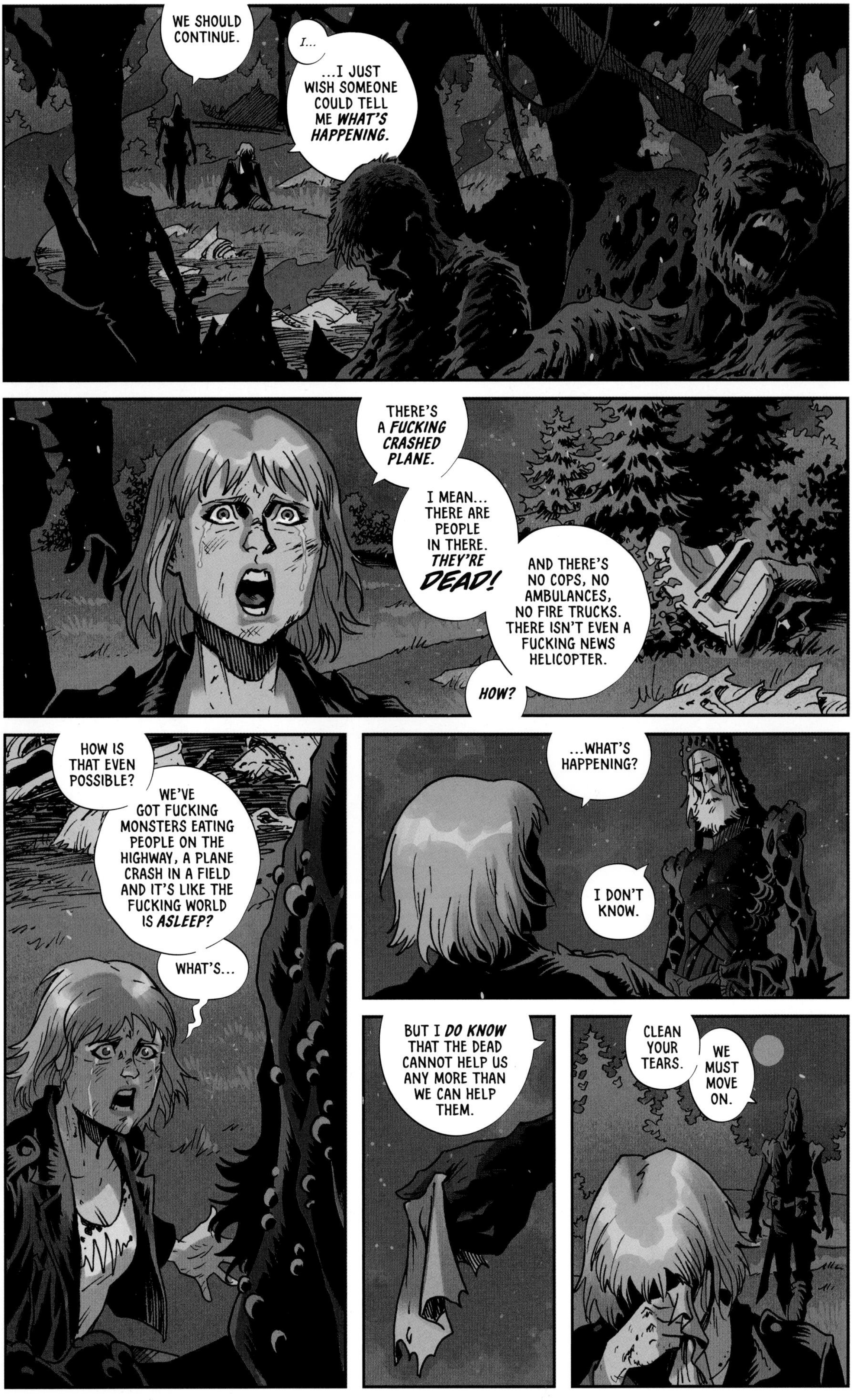
WE SHOULD CONTINUE.
I...
...I JUST WISH SOMEONE COULD TELL ME *WHAT'S HAPPENING.*
THERE'S A *FUCKING CRASHED PLANE.*
I MEAN... THERE ARE PEOPLE IN THERE. *THEY'RE* ***DEAD!***
AND THERE'S NO COPS, NO AMBULANCES, NO FIRE TRUCKS. THERE ISN'T EVEN A FUCKING NEWS HELICOPTER.
HOW?
HOW IS THAT EVEN POSSIBLE?
WE'VE GOT FUCKING MONSTERS EATING PEOPLE ON THE HIGHWAY, A PLANE CRASH IN A FIELD AND IT'S LIKE THE FUCKING WORLD IS *ASLEEP?*
WHAT'S...
...WHAT'S HAPPENING?
I DON'T KNOW.
BUT I *DO KNOW* THAT THE DEAD CANNOT HELP US ANY MORE THAN WE CAN HELP THEM.
CLEAN YOUR TEARS.
WE MUST MOVE ON.

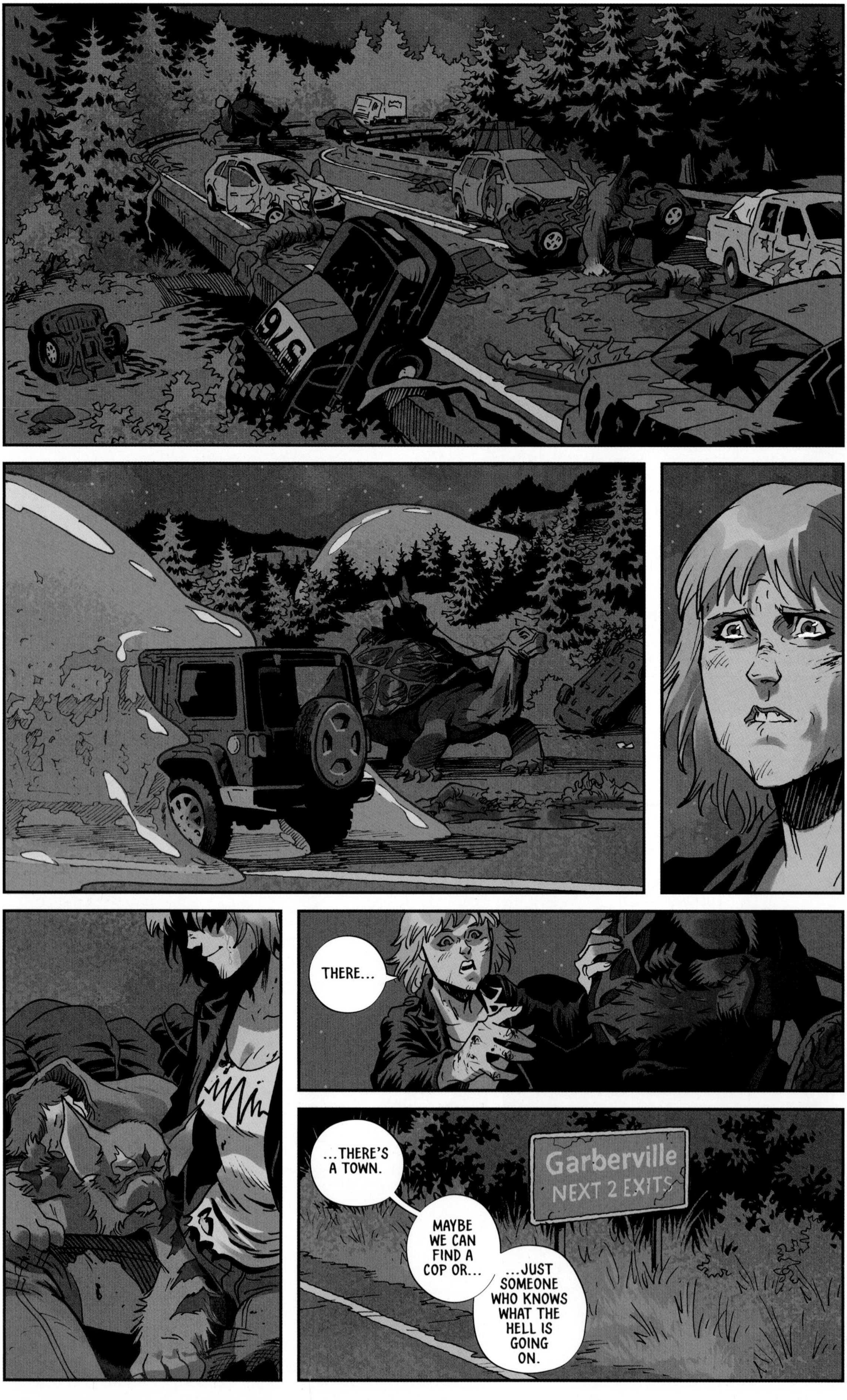
976
THERE...
...THERE'S A TOWN.
Garberville
NEXT 2 EXITS
MAYBE WE CAN FIND A COP OR...
...JUST SOMEONE WHO KNOWS WHAT THE HELL IS GOING ON.

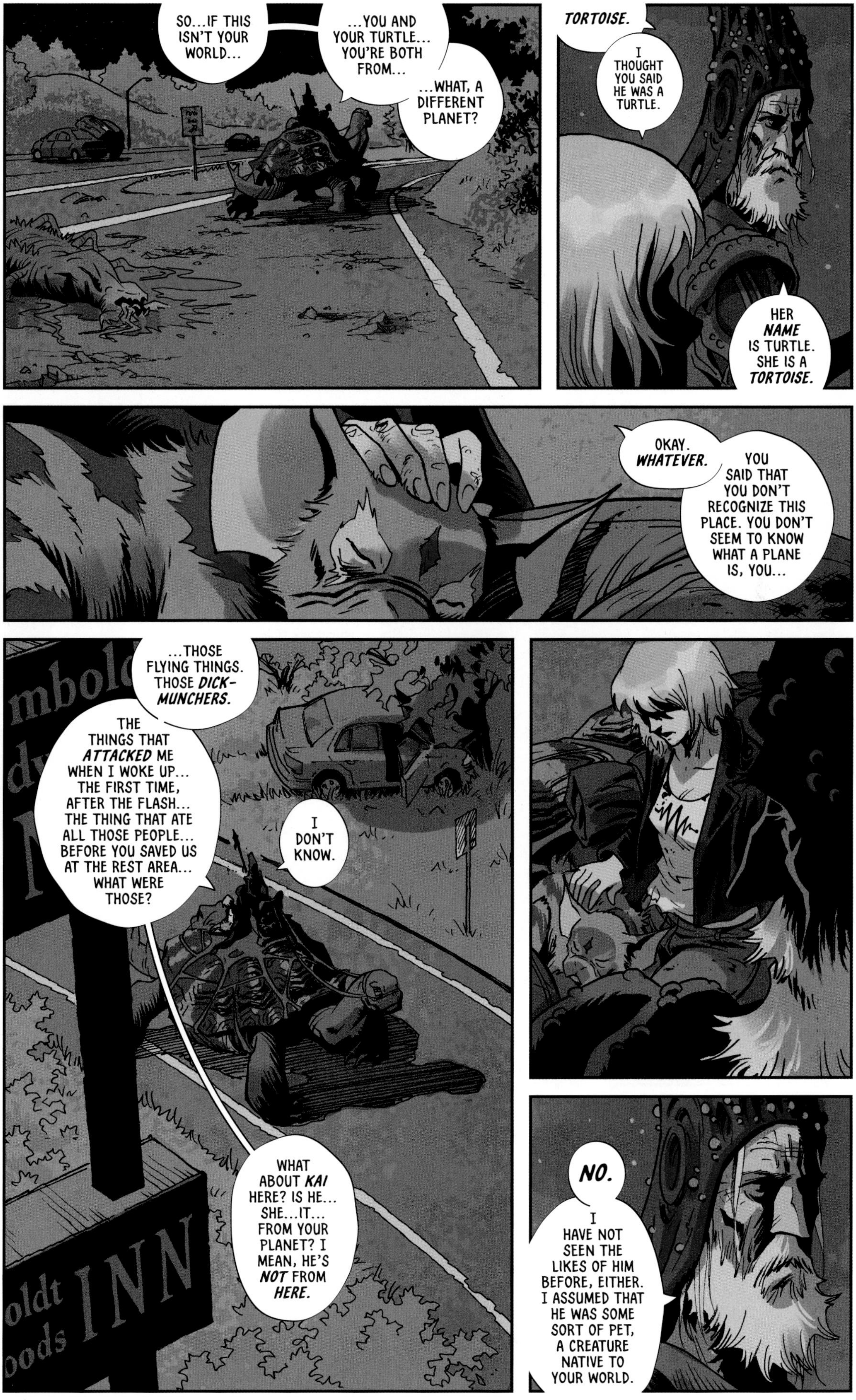
SO...IF THIS ISN'T YOUR WORLD...
...YOU AND YOUR TURTLE... YOU'RE BOTH FROM...
...WHAT, A DIFFERENT PLANET?
TORTOISE.
I THOUGHT YOU SAID HE WAS A TURTLE.
HER NAME IS TURTLE. SHE IS A TORTOISE.
OKAY. WHATEVER.
YOU SAID THAT YOU DON'T RECOGNIZE THIS PLACE. YOU DON'T SEEM TO KNOW WHAT A PLANE IS, YOU...
...THOSE FLYING THINGS. THOSE DICK-MUNCHERS.
THE THINGS THAT ATTACKED ME WHEN I WOKE UP... THE FIRST TIME, AFTER THE FLASH... THE THING THAT ATE ALL THOSE PEOPLE... BEFORE YOU SAVED US AT THE REST AREA... WHAT WERE THOSE?
I DON'T KNOW.
WHAT ABOUT KAI HERE? IS HE... SHE...IT... FROM YOUR PLANET? I MEAN, HE'S NOT FROM HERE.
NO.
I HAVE NOT SEEN THE LIKES OF HIM BEFORE, EITHER. I ASSUMED THAT HE WAS SOME SORT OF PET, A CREATURE NATIVE TO YOUR WORLD.

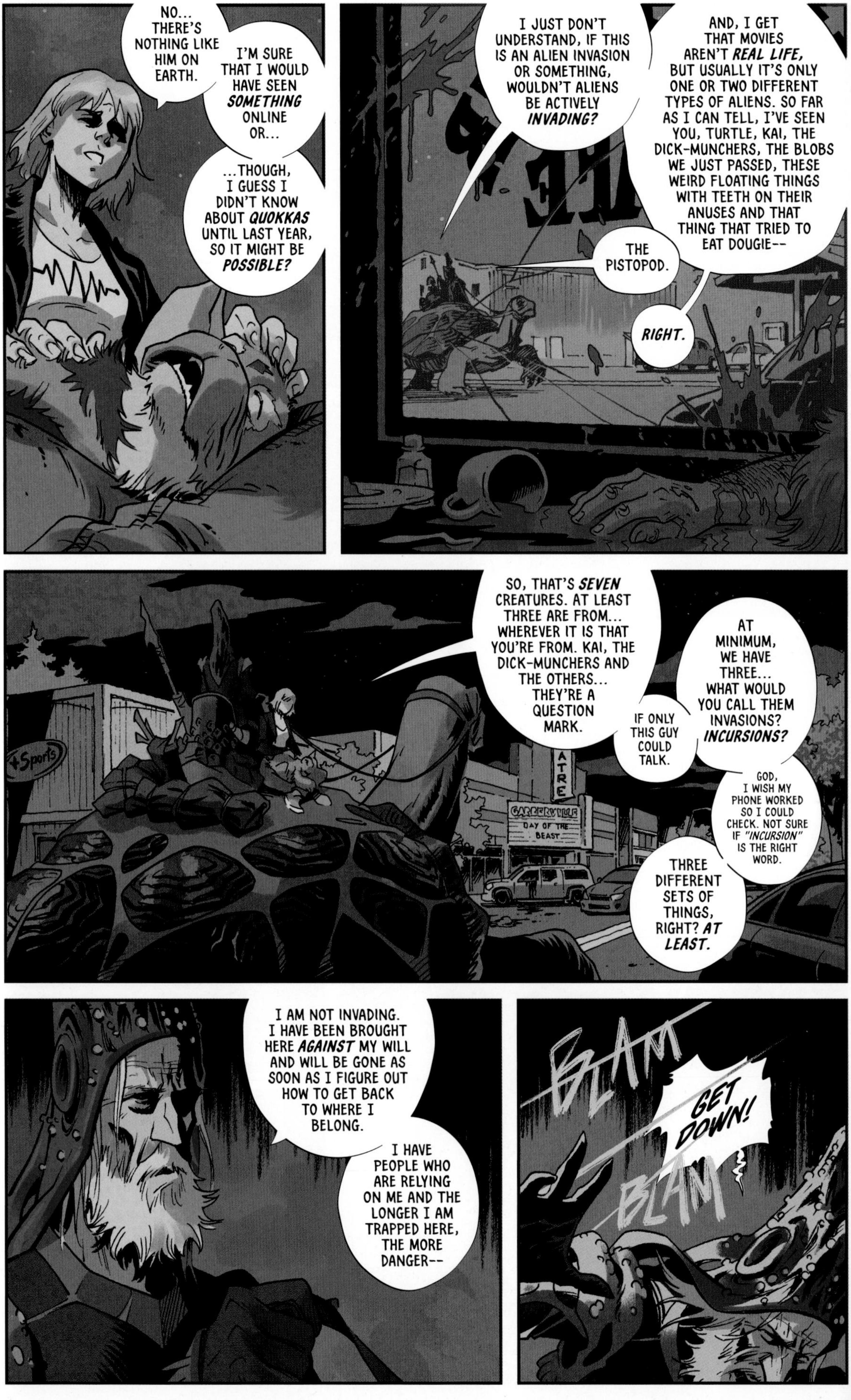
NO... THERE'S NOTHING LIKE HIM ON EARTH.
I'M SURE THAT I WOULD HAVE SEEN SOMETHING ONLINE OR...
...THOUGH, I GUESS I DIDN'T KNOW ABOUT QUOKKAS UNTIL LAST YEAR, SO IT MIGHT BE POSSIBLE?
I JUST DON'T UNDERSTAND, IF THIS IS AN ALIEN INVASION OR SOMETHING, WOULDN'T ALIENS BE ACTIVELY INVADING?
AND, I GET THAT MOVIES AREN'T REAL LIFE, BUT USUALLY IT'S ONLY ONE OR TWO DIFFERENT TYPES OF ALIENS. SO FAR AS I CAN TELL, I'VE SEEN YOU, TURTLE, KAI, THE DICK-MUNCHERS, THE BLOBS WE JUST PASSED, THESE WEIRD FLOATING THINGS WITH TEETH ON THEIR ANUSES AND THAT THING THAT TRIED TO EAT DOUGIE--
THE PISTOPOD.
RIGHT.
SO, THAT'S SEVEN CREATURES. AT LEAST THREE ARE FROM... WHEREVER IT IS THAT YOU'RE FROM. KAI, THE DICK-MUNCHERS AND THE OTHERS... THEY'RE A QUESTION MARK.
IF ONLY THIS GUY COULD TALK.
AT MINIMUM, WE HAVE THREE... WHAT WOULD YOU CALL THEM INVASIONS? INCURSIONS?
GOD, I WISH MY PHONE WORKED SO I COULD CHECK. NOT SURE IF "INCURSION" IS THE RIGHT WORD.
THREE DIFFERENT SETS OF THINGS, RIGHT? AT LEAST.
+Sports
ATRE
GARBERVILLE
DAY OF THE BEAST
I AM NOT INVADING. I HAVE BEEN BROUGHT HERE AGAINST MY WILL AND WILL BE GONE AS SOON AS I FIGURE OUT HOW TO GET BACK TO WHERE I BELONG.
I HAVE PEOPLE WHO ARE RELYING ON ME AND THE LONGER I AM TRAPPED HERE, THE MORE DANGER--
BLAM
GET DOWN!
BLAM

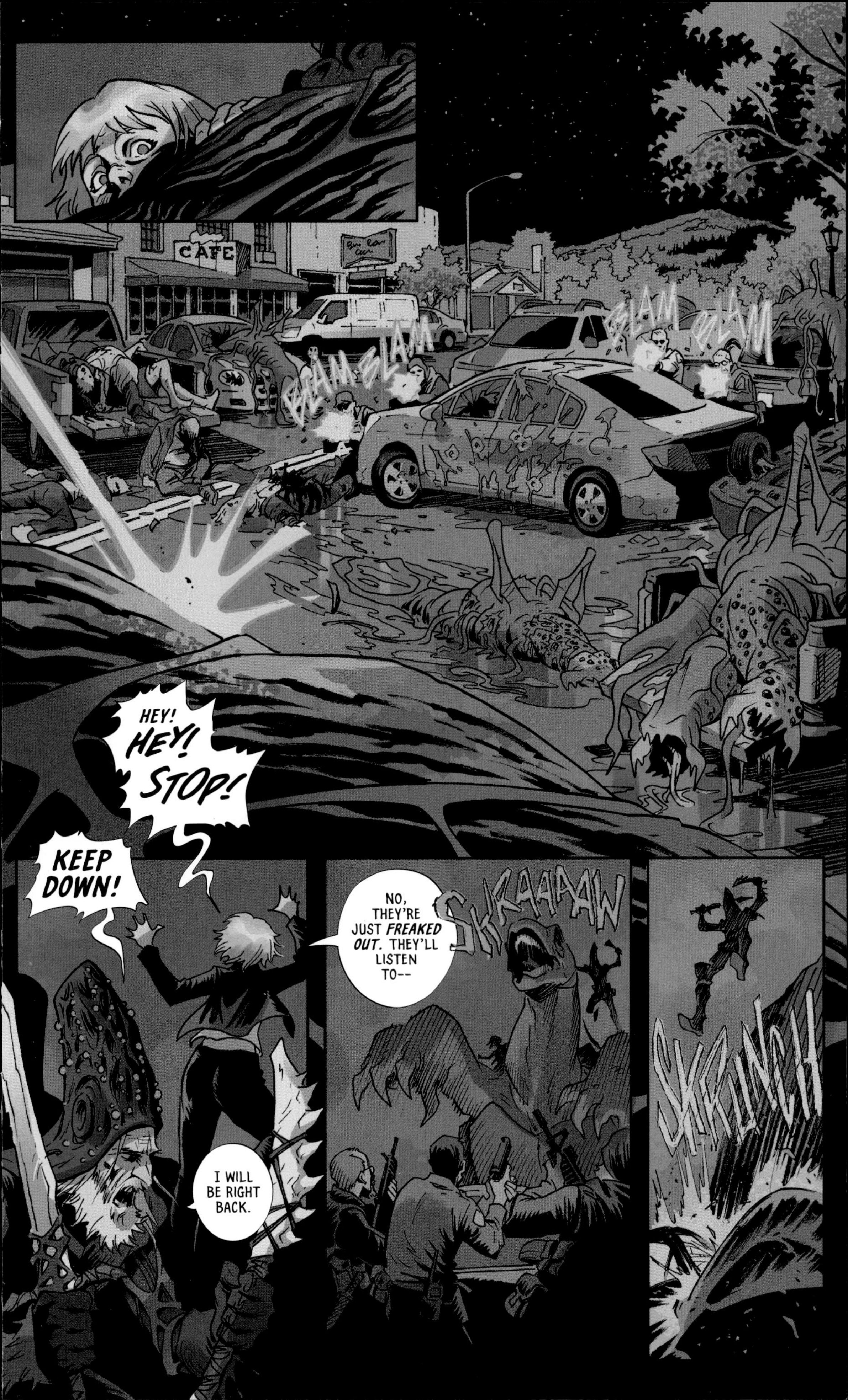
CAFE
BLAM BLAM
BLAM BLAM
HEY! HEY! STOP!
KEEP DOWN!
NO, THEY'RE JUST *FREAKED OUT.* THEY'LL LISTEN TO--
I WILL BE RIGHT BACK.
SKRAAAAW
SKRUNCH

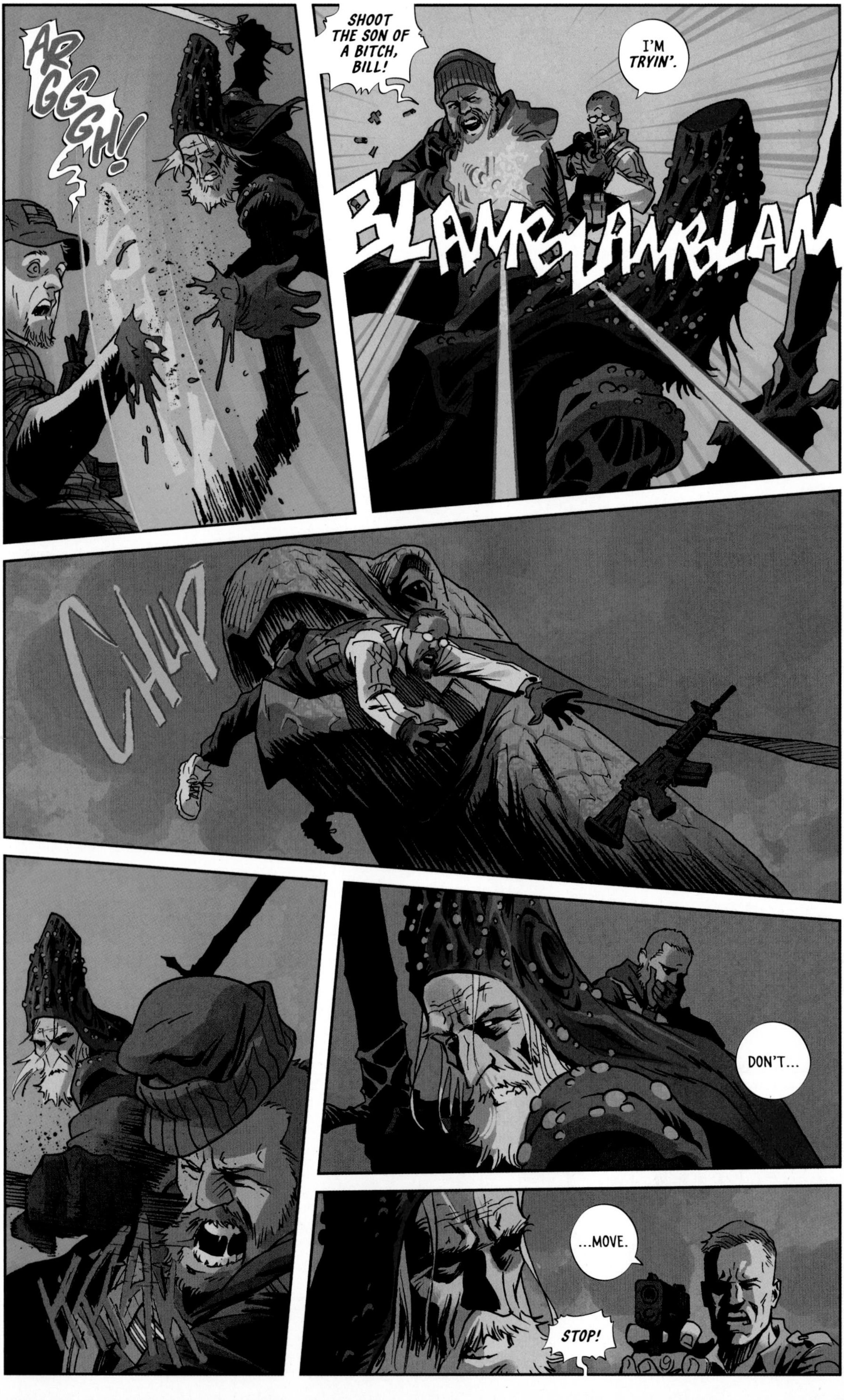
ARGGGH!
SHOOT THE SON OF A BITCH, BILL!
I'M TRYIN'.
BLAMBLAMBLAM
CHUP
DON'T...
...MOVE.
STOP!

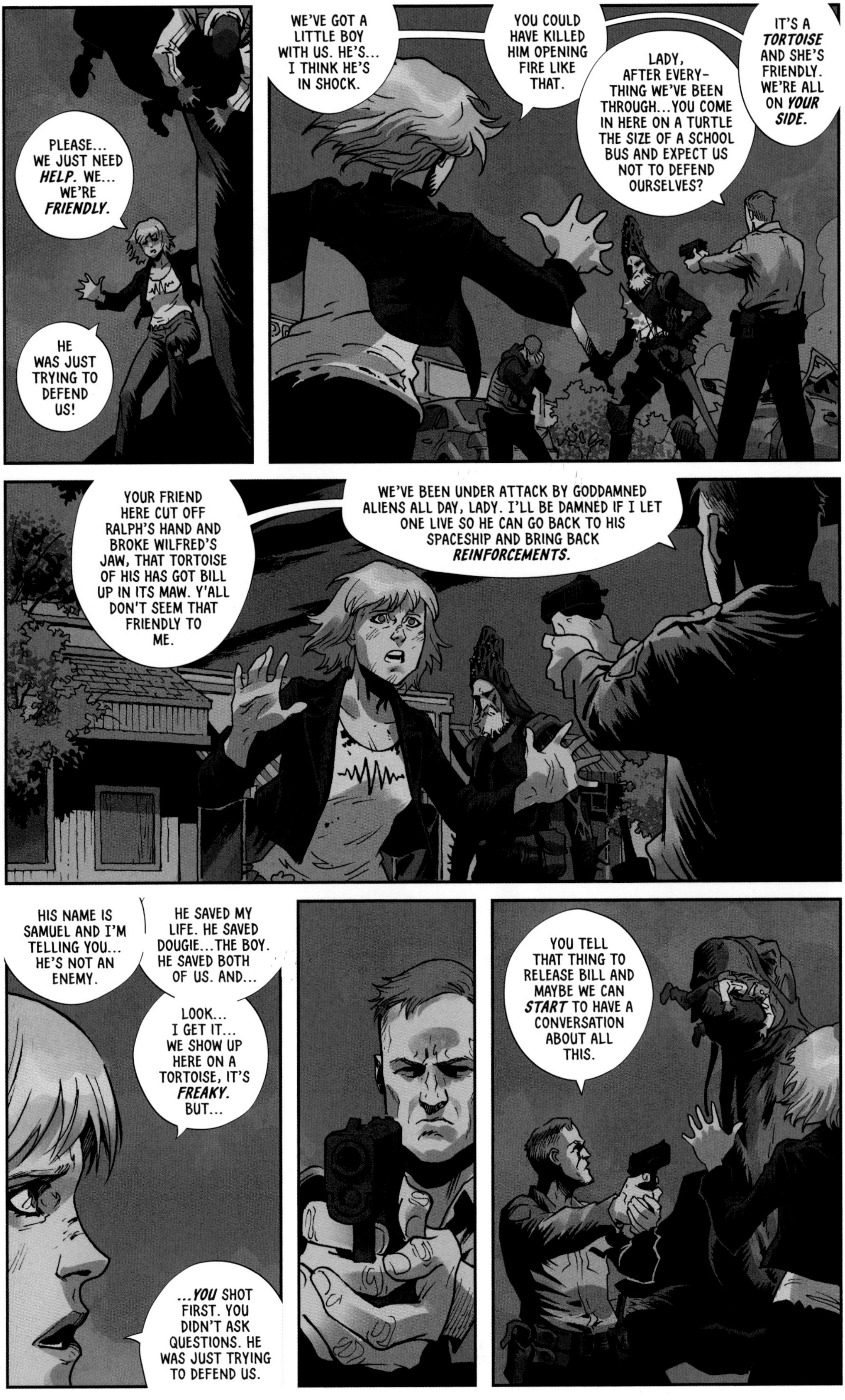
PLEASE... WE JUST NEED HELP. WE... WE'RE FRIENDLY.
HE WAS JUST TRYING TO DEFEND US!
WE'VE GOT A LITTLE BOY WITH US. HE'S... I THINK HE'S IN SHOCK.
YOU COULD HAVE KILLED HIM OPENING FIRE LIKE THAT.
LADY, AFTER EVERY-THING WE'VE BEEN THROUGH...YOU COME IN HERE ON A TURTLE THE SIZE OF A SCHOOL BUS AND EXPECT US NOT TO DEFEND OURSELVES?
IT'S A TORTOISE AND SHE'S FRIENDLY. WE'RE ALL ON YOUR SIDE.
YOUR FRIEND HERE CUT OFF RALPH'S HAND AND BROKE WILFRED'S JAW, THAT TORTOISE OF HIS HAS GOT BILL UP IN ITS MAW. Y'ALL DON'T SEEM THAT FRIENDLY TO ME.
WE'VE BEEN UNDER ATTACK BY GODDAMNED ALIENS ALL DAY, LADY. I'LL BE DAMNED IF I LET ONE LIVE SO HE CAN GO BACK TO HIS SPACESHIP AND BRING BACK REINFORCEMENTS.
HIS NAME IS SAMUEL AND I'M TELLING YOU... HE'S NOT AN ENEMY.
HE SAVED MY LIFE. HE SAVED DOUGIE...THE BOY. HE SAVED BOTH OF US. AND...
LOOK... I GET IT... WE SHOW UP HERE ON A TORTOISE, IT'S FREAKY. BUT...
...YOU SHOT FIRST. YOU DIDN'T ASK QUESTIONS. HE WAS JUST TRYING TO DEFEND US.
YOU TELL THAT THING TO RELEASE BILL AND MAYBE WE CAN START TO HAVE A CONVERSATION ABOUT ALL THIS.

GODDAMMIT!

MY FUCKING **HAND,** MAN!

DON'T IMAGINE IT TICKLES.

WHERE DO WE--?

JUST PUT THE BOY ON A TABLE. ELEVATE HIS LEGS AND LET HIM REST.

REEEEEE EEESSSSS.

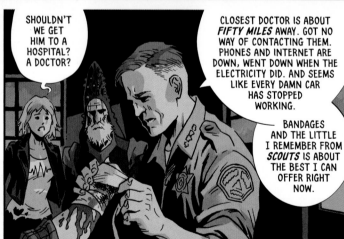

SHOULDN'T WE GET HIM TO A HOSPITAL? A DOCTOR?

CLOSEST DOCTOR IS ABOUT *FIFTY MILES* AWAY. GOT NO WAY OF CONTACTING THEM. PHONES AND INTERNET ARE DOWN, WENT DOWN WHEN THE ELECTRICITY DID. AND SEEMS LIKE EVERY DAMN CAR HAS STOPPED WORKING.

BANDAGES AND THE LITTLE I REMEMBER FROM *SCOUTS* IS ABOUT THE BEST I CAN OFFER RIGHT NOW.

I CAN HELP.

YOU'VE DONE **ENOUGH** ALREADY, YA **BASTARD!**

IT'S **YOUR FAULT** HE AIN'T GOT HIS HAND NO MORE.

THOUGH, HE DID TRY TO **KILL** ME.

THAT IS **TRUE.**

YEAH, WELL, STILL A GOOD CHANCE--

BILL, IF HE CAN HELP, THEN LET HIM.

REMOVE THE BANDAGES.

PUT HIS HAND BACK IN PLACE.

WHAT **THE HELL** ARE YOU--

TIME IS **NOT** ON OUR SIDE, DO IT AND MAKE SURE IT'S IN THE CORRECT POSITION.

NO. FUCK NO, GET THAT THING **AWAY** FROM ME!

STAY STILL.

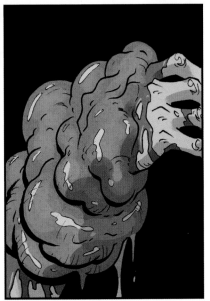

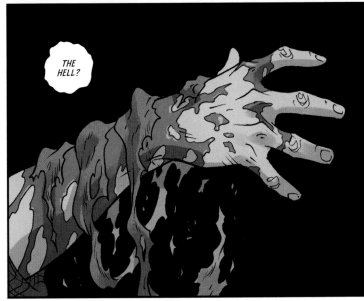

THE HELL?

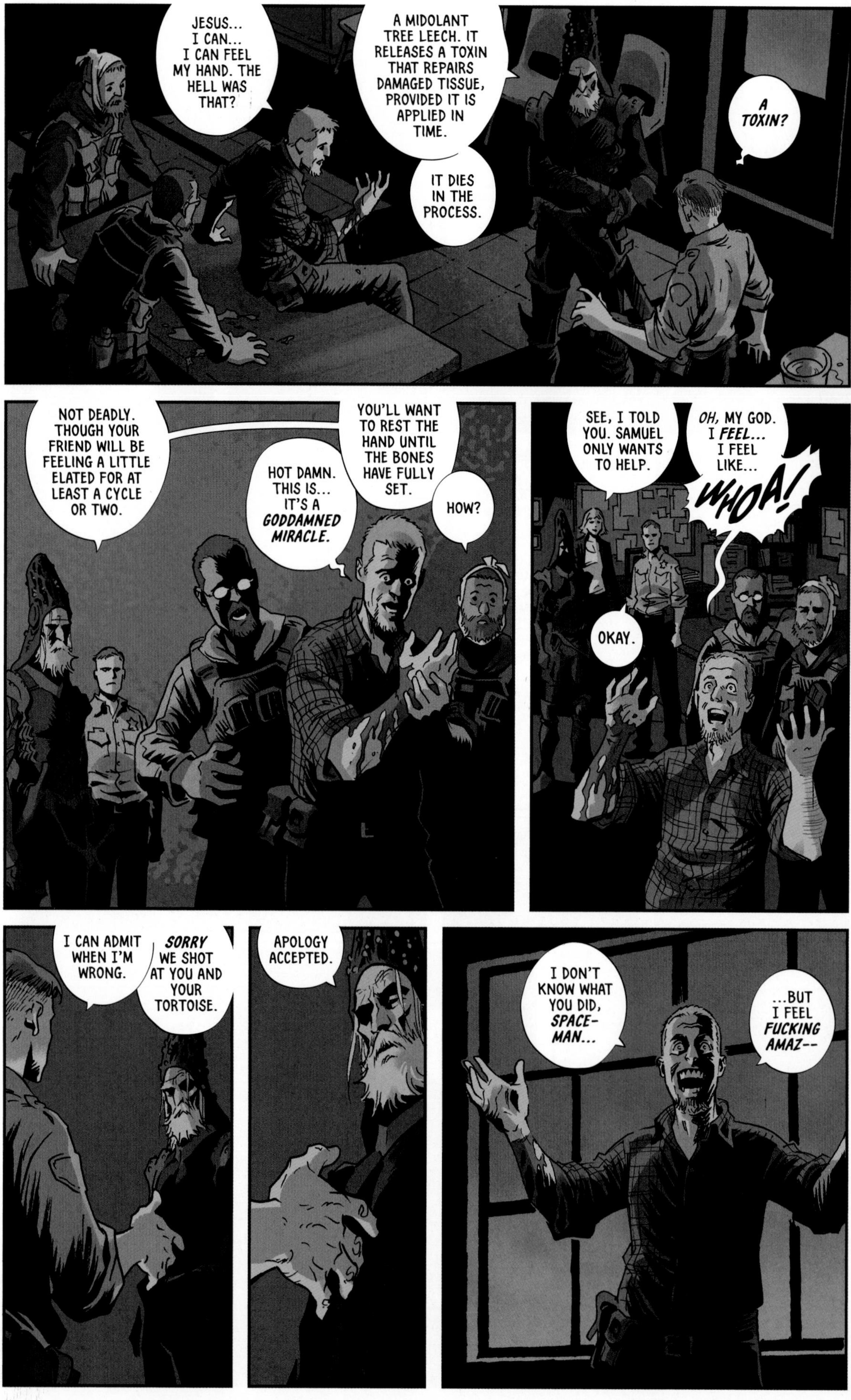
JESUS... I CAN... I CAN FEEL MY HAND. THE HELL WAS THAT?
A MIDOLANT TREE LEECH. IT RELEASES A TOXIN THAT REPAIRS DAMAGED TISSUE, PROVIDED IT IS APPLIED IN TIME.
IT DIES IN THE PROCESS.
A TOXIN?
NOT DEADLY. THOUGH YOUR FRIEND WILL BE FEELING A LITTLE ELATED FOR AT LEAST A CYCLE OR TWO.
YOU'LL WANT TO REST THE HAND UNTIL THE BONES HAVE FULLY SET.
HOT DAMN. THIS IS... IT'S A GODDAMNED MIRACLE.
HOW?
SEE, I TOLD YOU. SAMUEL ONLY WANTS TO HELP.
OH, MY GOD. I FEEL... I FEEL LIKE...
WHOA!
OKAY.
I CAN ADMIT WHEN I'M WRONG.
SORRY WE SHOT AT YOU AND YOUR TORTOISE.
APOLOGY ACCEPTED.
I DON'T KNOW WHAT YOU DID, SPACE-MAN...
...BUT I FEEL FUCKING AMAZ--

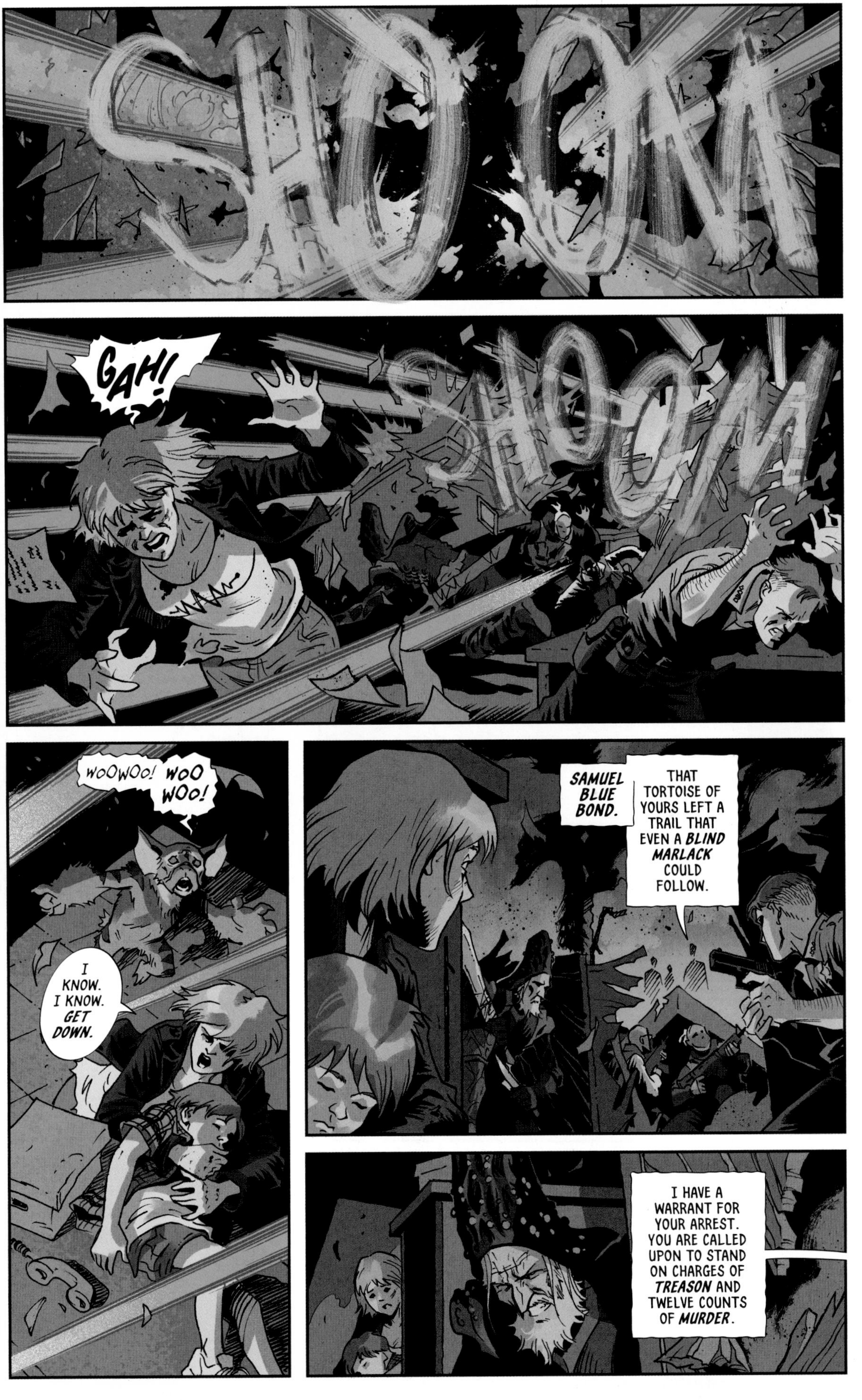
SHOOOM
GAH!
SHOOOM
WOOWOO! WOO WOO!
I KNOW. I KNOW. GET DOWN.
SAMUEL BLUE BOND.
THAT TORTOISE OF YOURS LEFT A TRAIL THAT EVEN A BLIND MARLACK COULD FOLLOW.
I HAVE A WARRANT FOR YOUR ARREST. YOU ARE CALLED UPON TO STAND ON CHARGES OF TREASON AND TWELVE COUNTS OF MURDER.

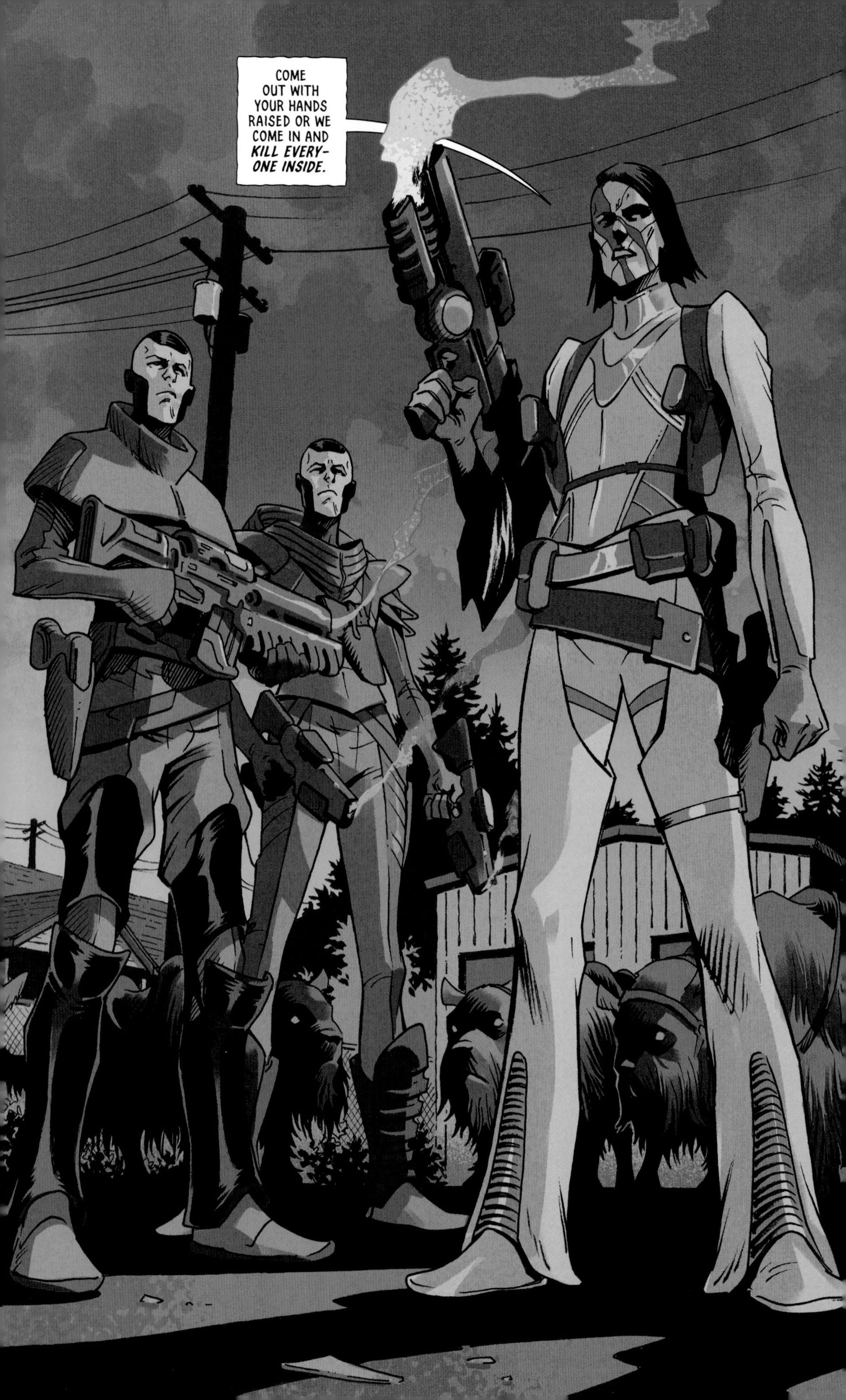
COME OUT WITH YOUR HANDS RAISED OR WE COME IN AND ***KILL EVERYONE INSIDE.***

3

LONG DAY'S RIDE 'TIL TOMORROW

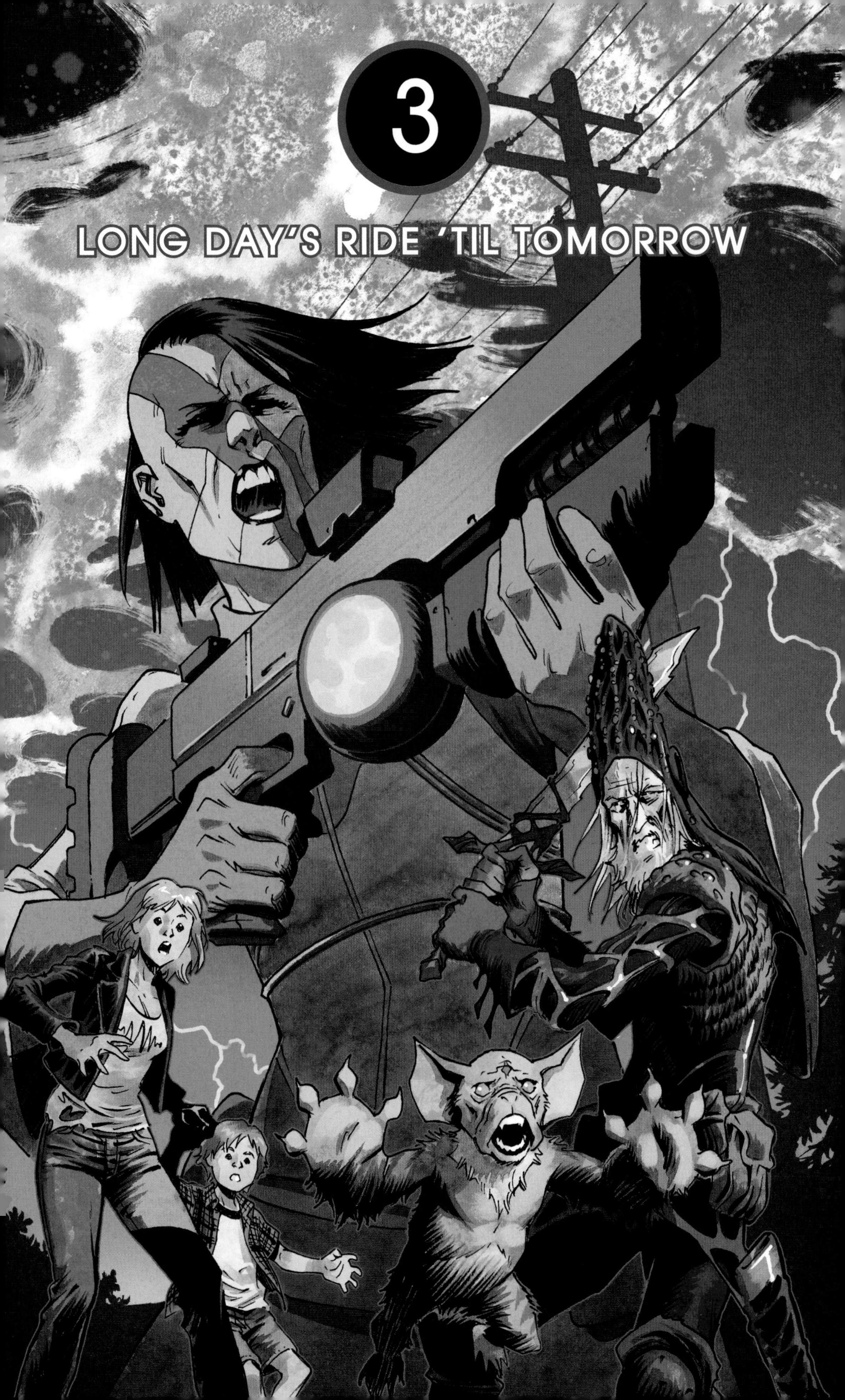

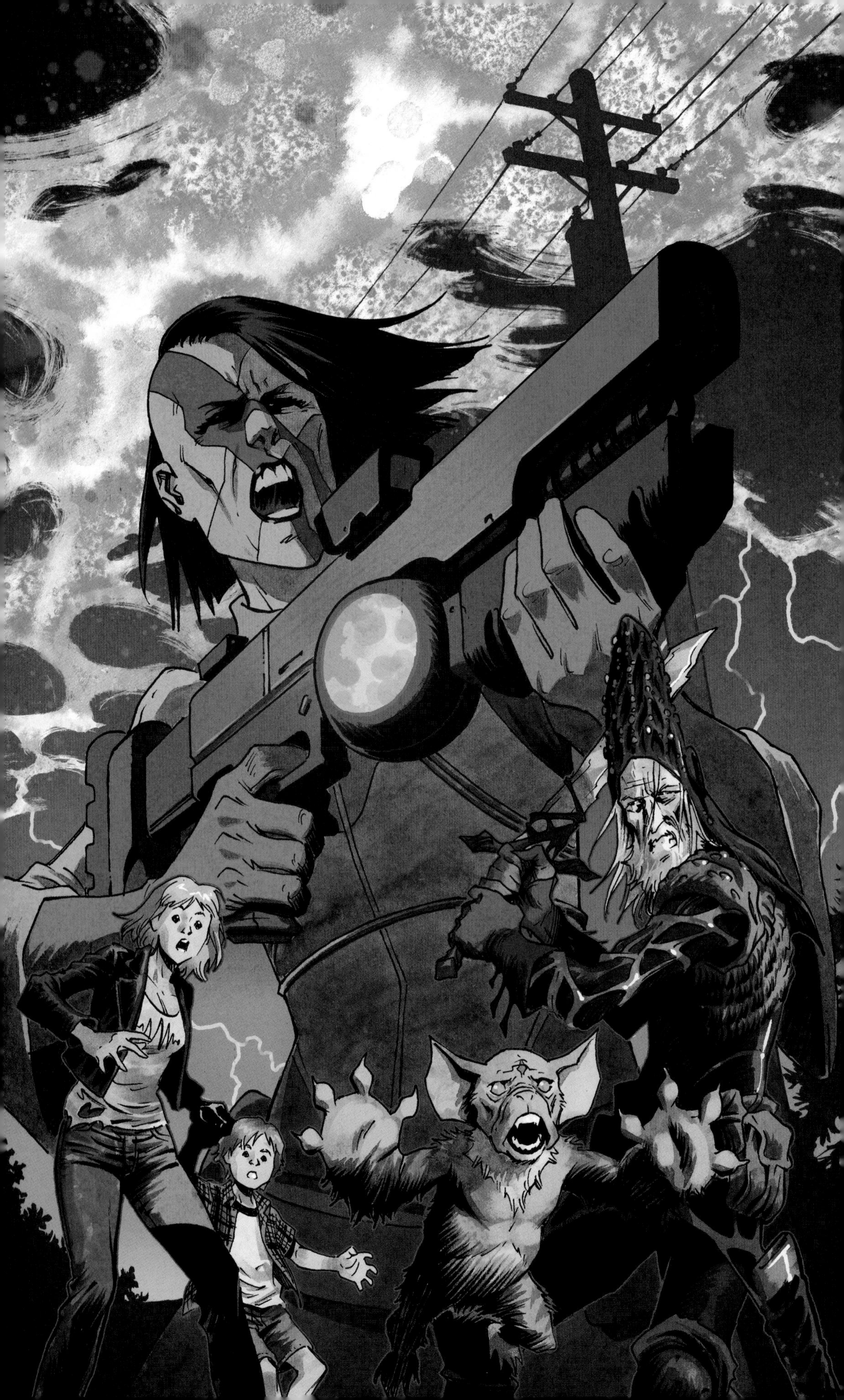

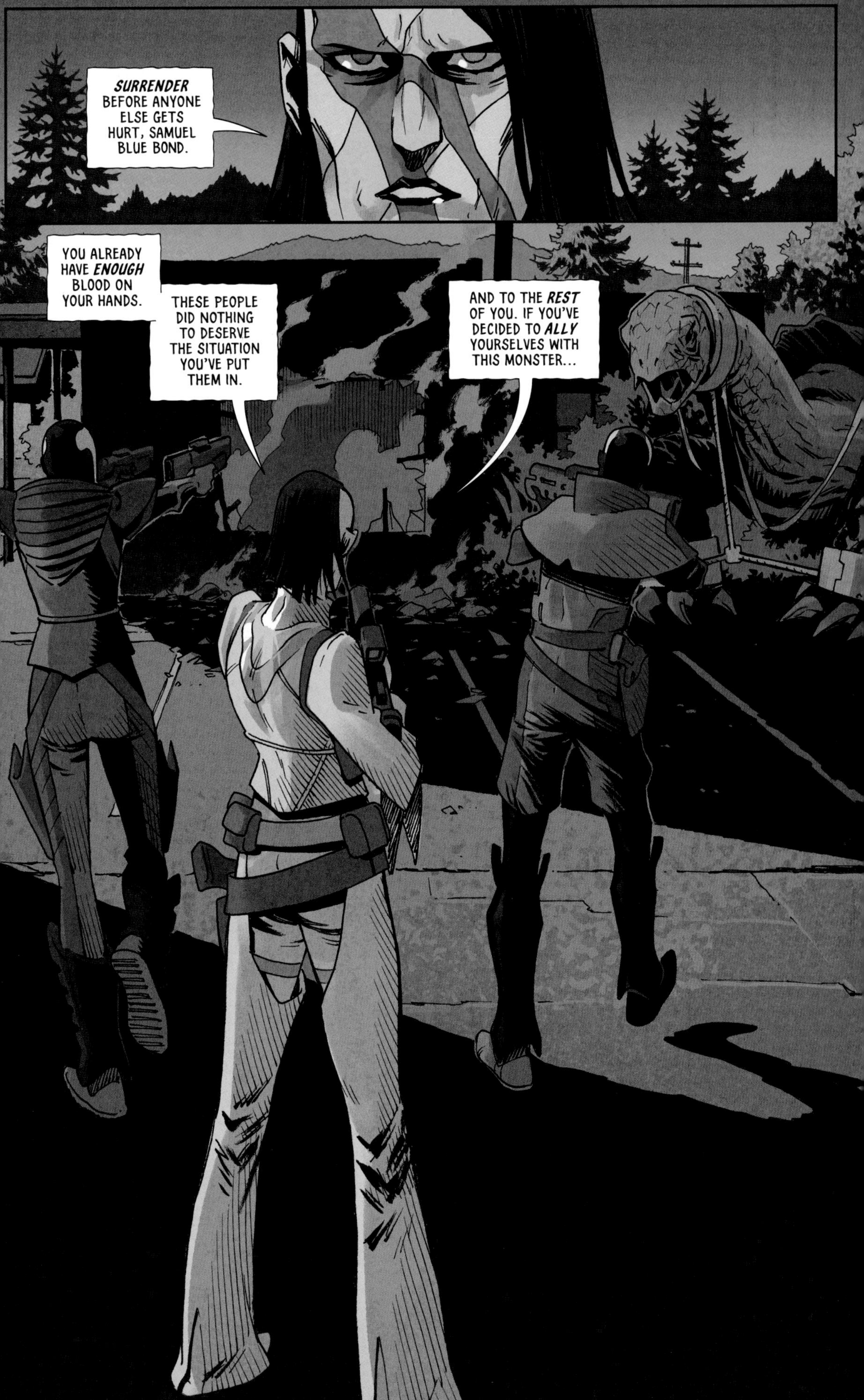
SURRENDER BEFORE ANYONE ELSE GETS HURT, SAMUEL BLUE BOND.
YOU ALREADY HAVE ENOUGH BLOOD ON YOUR HANDS.
THESE PEOPLE DID NOTHING TO DESERVE THE SITUATION YOU'VE PUT THEM IN.
AND TO THE REST OF YOU. IF YOU'VE DECIDED TO ALLY YOURSELVES WITH THIS MONSTER...

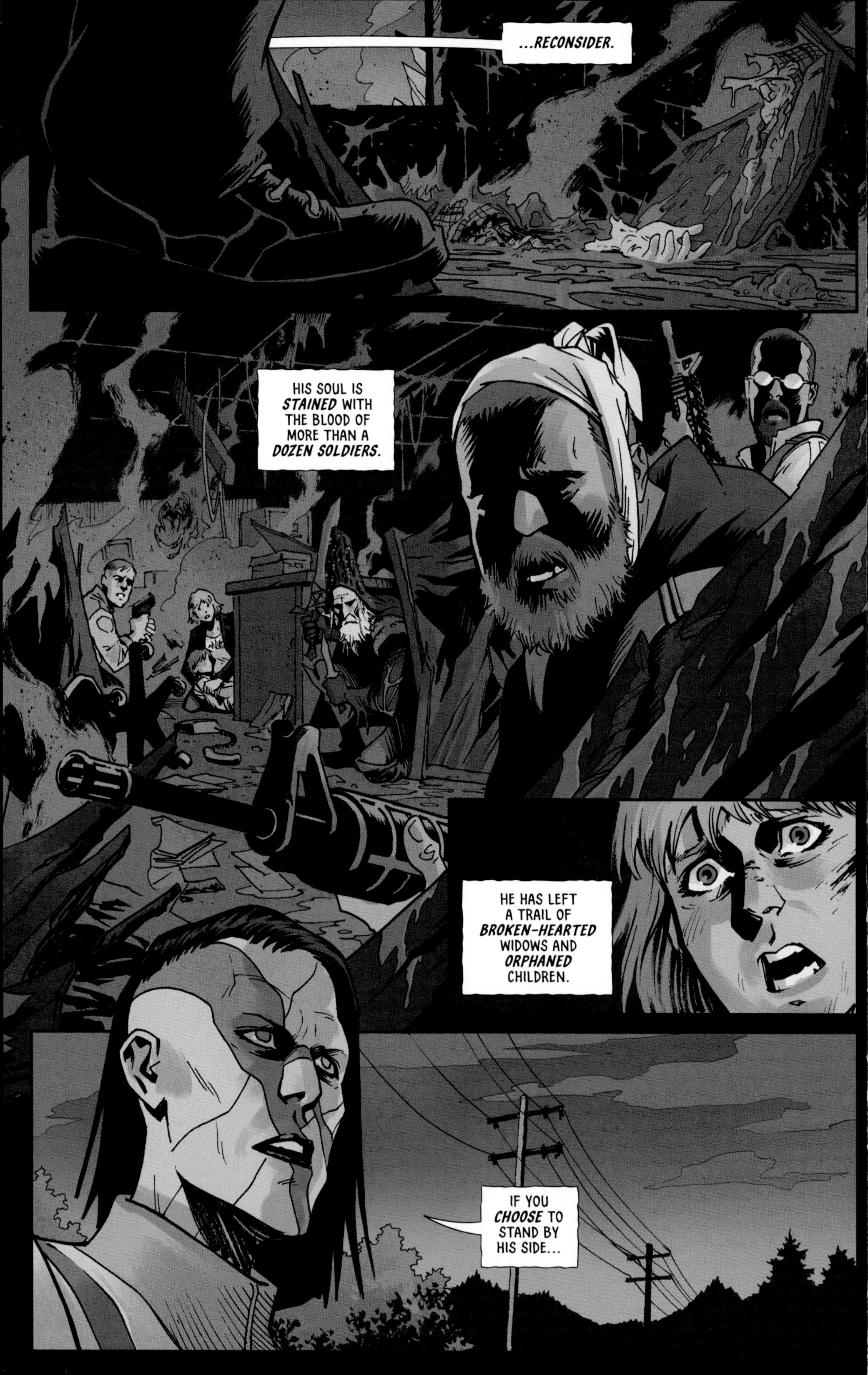
...RECONSIDER.
HIS SOUL IS STAINED WITH THE BLOOD OF MORE THAN A DOZEN SOLDIERS.
HE HAS LEFT A TRAIL OF BROKEN-HEARTED WIDOWS AND ORPHANED CHILDREN.
IF YOU CHOOSE TO STAND BY HIS SIDE...

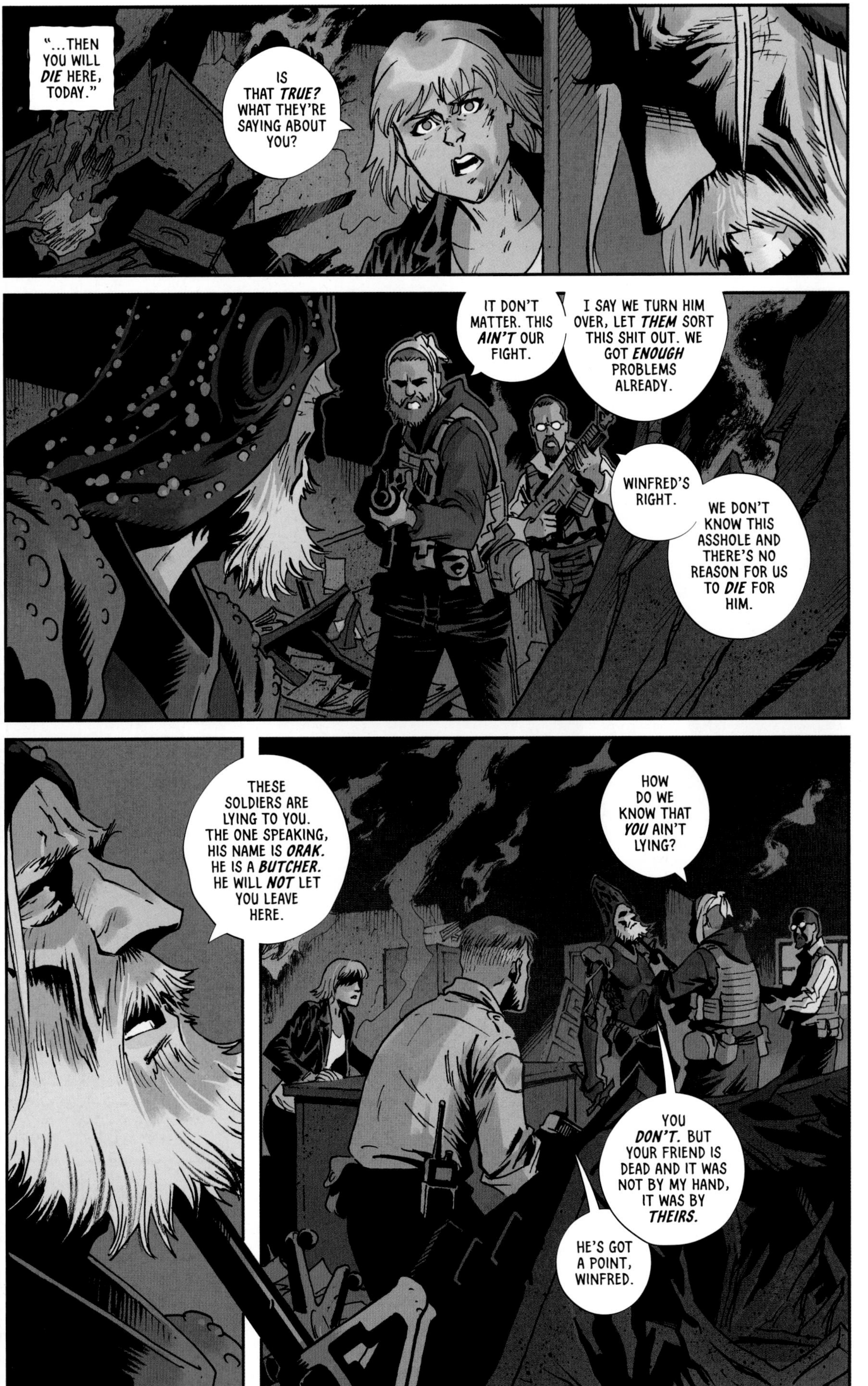
"...THEN YOU WILL *DIE* HERE, TODAY."
IS THAT *TRUE?* WHAT THEY'RE SAYING ABOUT YOU?
IT DON'T MATTER. THIS *AIN'T* OUR FIGHT.
I SAY WE TURN HIM OVER, LET *THEM* SORT THIS SHIT OUT. WE GOT *ENOUGH* PROBLEMS ALREADY.
WINFRED'S RIGHT.
WE DON'T KNOW THIS ASSHOLE AND THERE'S NO REASON FOR US TO *DIE* FOR HIM.
THESE SOLDIERS ARE LYING TO YOU. THE ONE SPEAKING, HIS NAME IS *ORAK.* HE IS A *BUTCHER.* HE WILL *NOT* LET YOU LEAVE HERE.
HOW DO WE KNOW THAT *YOU* AIN'T LYING?
YOU *DON'T.* BUT YOUR FRIEND IS DEAD AND IT WAS NOT BY MY HAND, IT WAS BY *THEIRS.*
HE'S GOT A POINT, WINFRED.

HOW LONG DO WE WAIT, ORAK?

LET'S GIVE THEM A LITTLE TIME TO TURN ON EACH OTHER, NORLO.

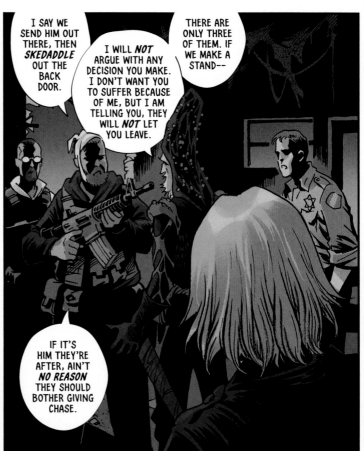

I SAY WE SEND HIM OUT THERE, THEN *SKEDADDLE* OUT THE BACK DOOR.

I WILL *NOT* ARGUE WITH ANY DECISION YOU MAKE. I DON'T WANT YOU TO SUFFER BECAUSE OF ME, BUT I AM TELLING YOU, THEY WILL *NOT* LET YOU LEAVE.

THERE ARE ONLY THREE OF THEM. IF WE MAKE A STAND--

IF IT'S HIM THEY'RE AFTER, AIN'T *NO REASON* THEY SHOULD BOTHER GIVING CHASE.

YOU ACTUALLY *BELIEVE* THOSE... THOSE THINGS?

SAMUEL *SAVED* MY LIFE.

HE SAVED ME, AND HE SAVED DOUGIE.

HE'S PROVEN THAT HE *CAN* BE TRUSTED. THAT HE'S *NOT* A KILLER.

BUT *THOSE* THINGS?!

THEY JUST *KILLED* YOUR FRIEND. THE SAME FRIEND THAT SAMUEL JUST *SAVED.*

VANESSA'S *RIGHT.*

THEY BROUGHT A CHILD HERE FOR MEDICAL ATTENTION. DON'T SOUND TOO MUCH LIKE A MURDERER TO ME.

BUT IF WE HAND HIM OVER, THAT'S EXACTLY WHAT WE'LL BE. *MURDERERS.*

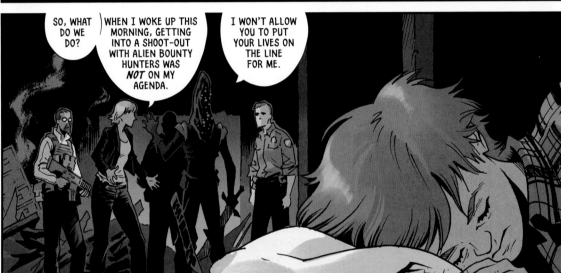

SO, WHAT DO WE DO?

WHEN I WOKE UP THIS MORNING, GETTING INTO A SHOOT-OUT WITH ALIEN BOUNTY HUNTERS WAS *NOT* ON MY AGENDA.

I WON'T ALLOW YOU TO PUT YOUR LIVES ON THE LINE FOR ME.

MAYBE...MAYBE WINFRED WAS RIGHT.

IF I CAN HOLD THEM OFF, PERHAPS THE REST OF YOU CAN LEAVE THROUGH THE BACK EXIT UNNOTICED.

I WILL STALL FOR AS LONG AS I CAN.

SAMUEL, YOU CAN'T JUST--

I DIDN'T SAVE THE BOY'S LIFE JUST TO HAVE HIM SLAUGHTERED.

WAAAAAAA!

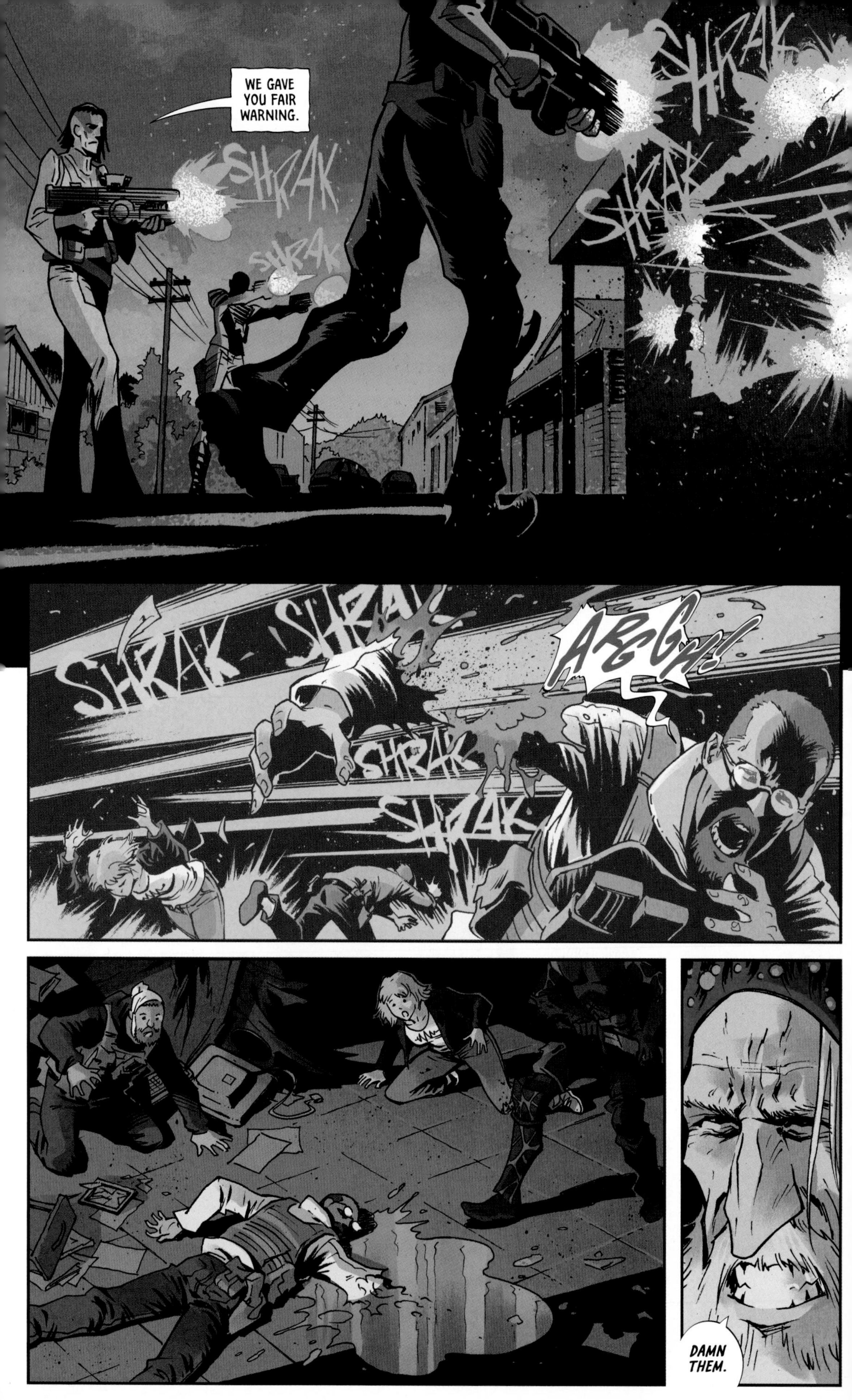
WE GAVE YOU FAIR WARNING.
SHRAK
SHRAK
SHRAK
SHRAK
SHRAK
SHRAK
ARGGH!
SHRAK
SHRAK
DAMN THEM.

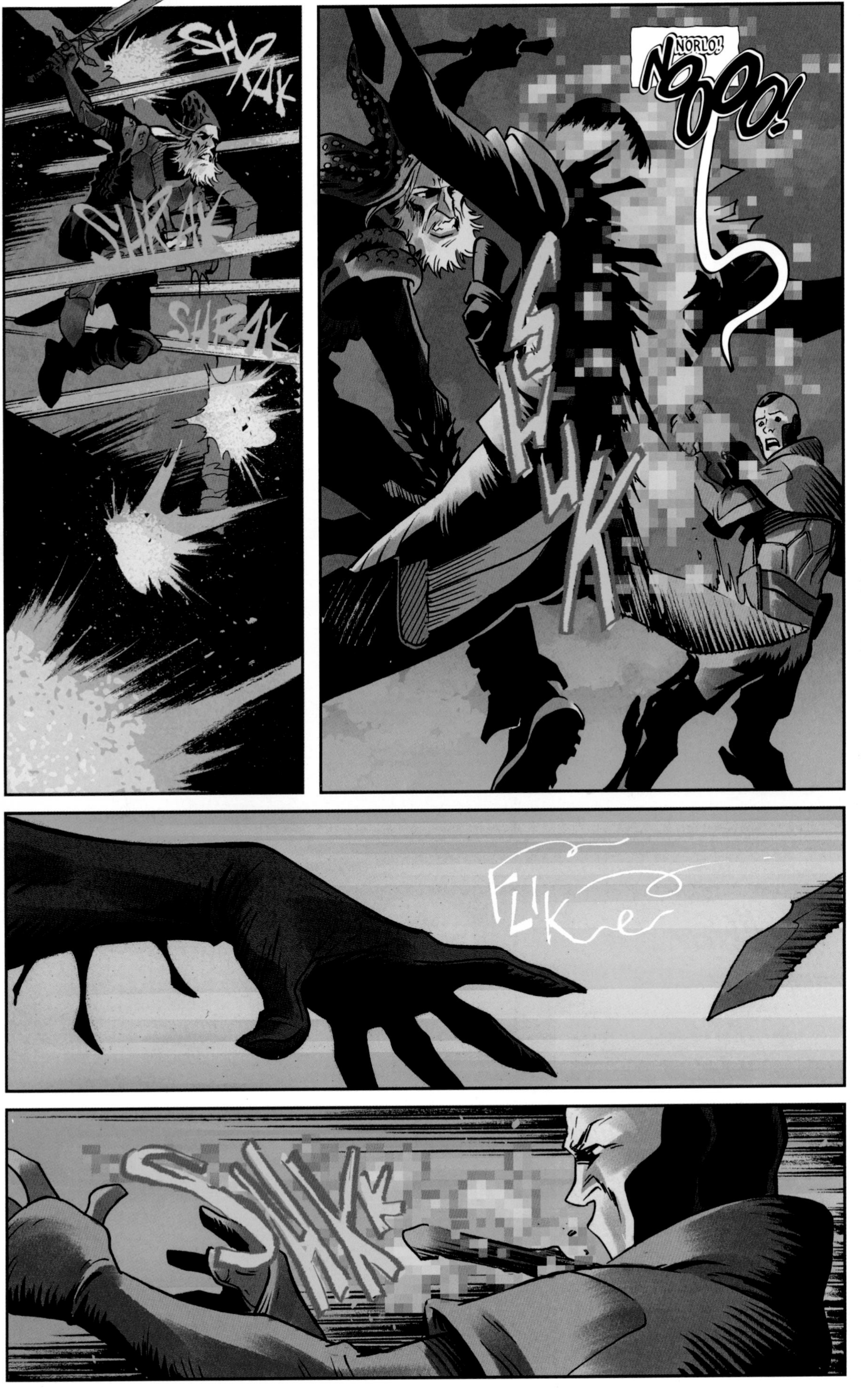
SHRAK
SHRAK
SHRAK
NORLO!
NOOOO!
SHUK
FLIK
SHK

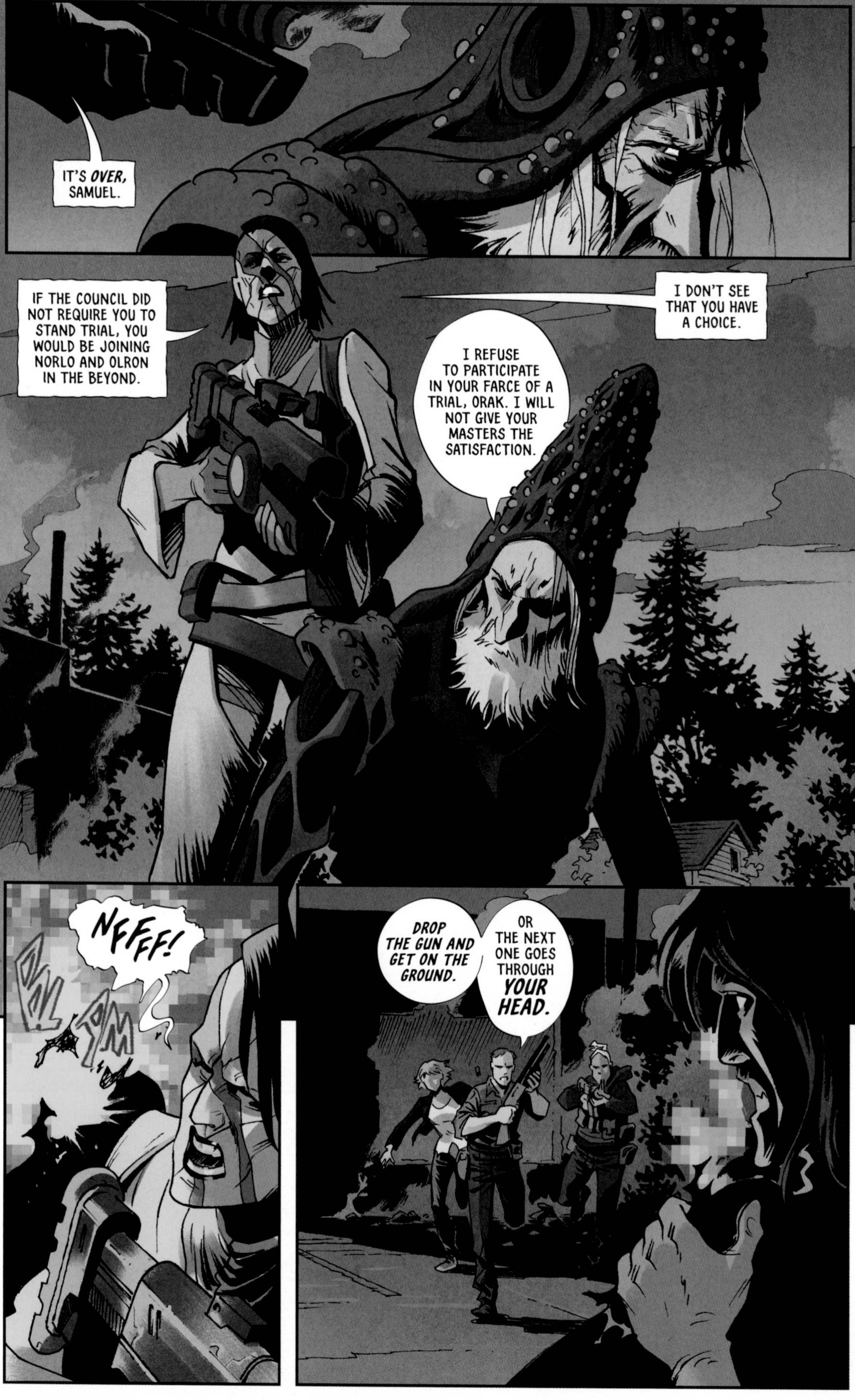
IT'S *OVER,* SAMUEL.
IF THE COUNCIL DID NOT REQUIRE YOU TO STAND TRIAL, YOU WOULD BE JOINING NORLO AND OLRON IN THE BEYOND.
I REFUSE TO PARTICIPATE IN YOUR FARCE OF A TRIAL, ORAK. I WILL NOT GIVE YOUR MASTERS THE SATISFACTION.
I DON'T SEE THAT YOU HAVE A CHOICE.
NFFFF!
BLAM
DROP THE GUN AND GET ON THE GROUND.
OR THE NEXT ONE GOES THROUGH ***YOUR HEAD.***

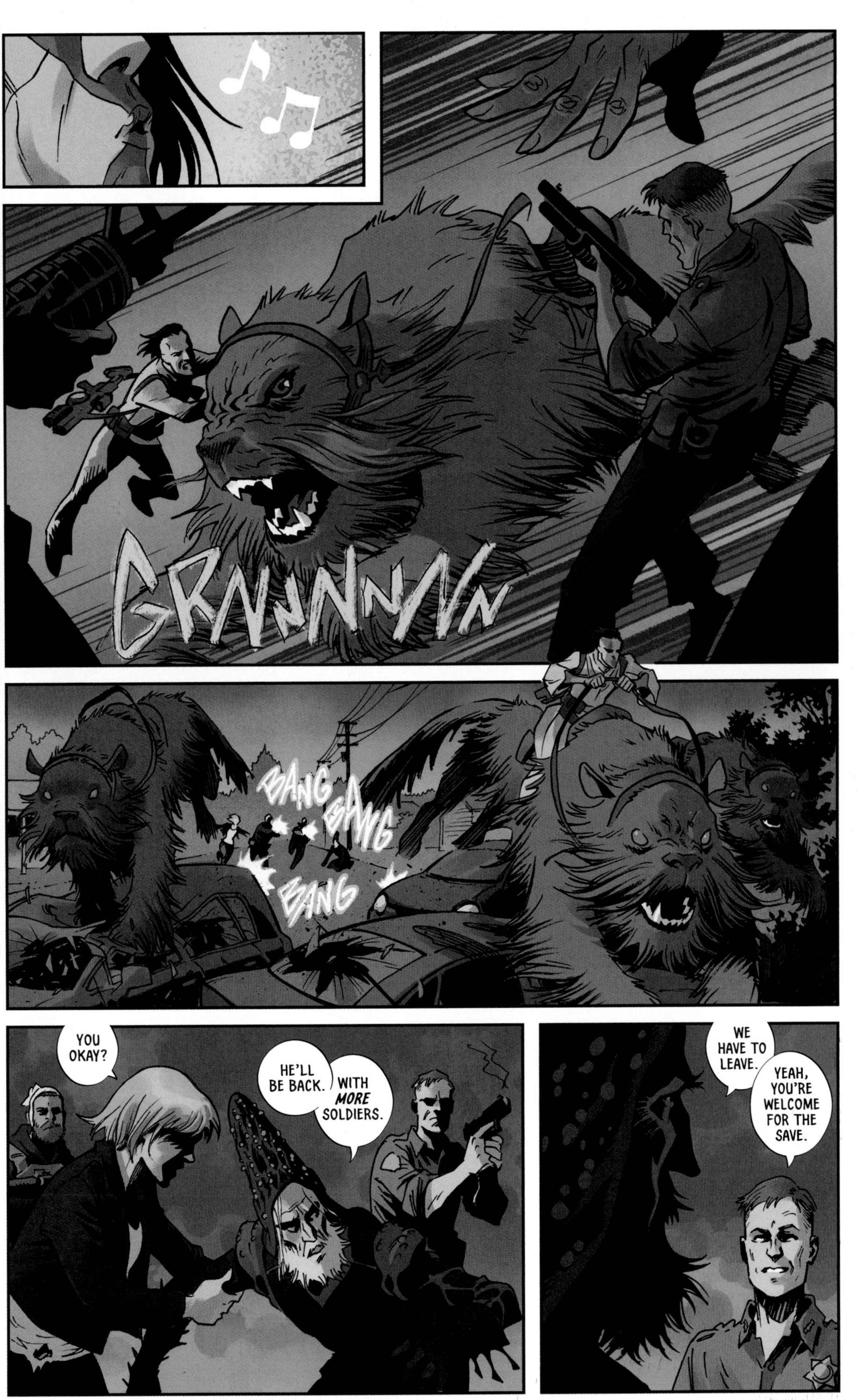
GRNNNNNN
BANG
BANG
BANG
YOU OKAY?
HE'LL BE BACK.
WITH *MORE* SOLDIERS.
WE HAVE TO LEAVE.
YEAH, YOU'RE WELCOME FOR THE SAVE.

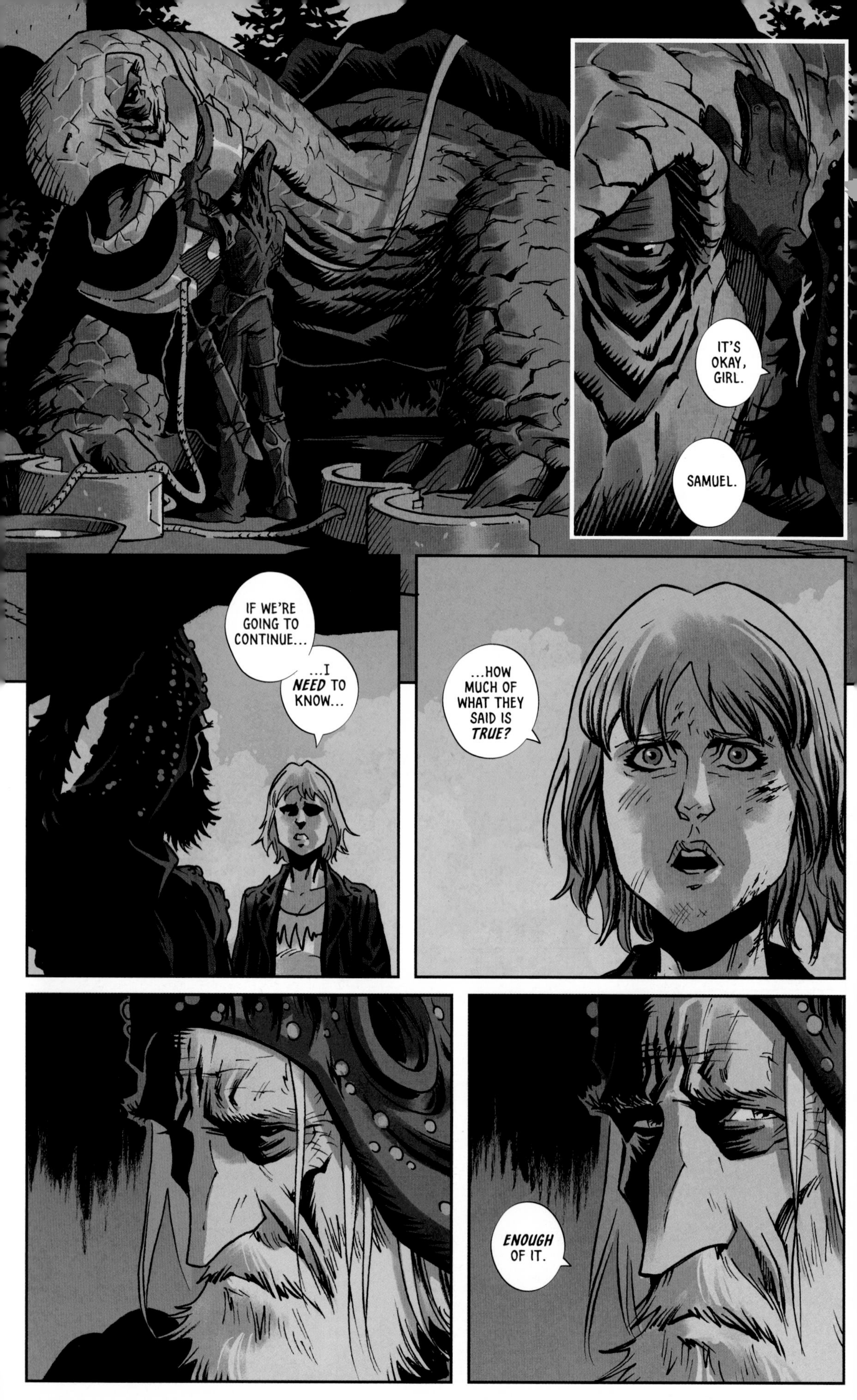
IT'S OKAY, GIRL.
SAMUEL.
IF WE'RE GOING TO CONTINUE...
...I *NEED* TO KNOW...
...HOW MUCH OF WHAT THEY SAID IS *TRUE?*
ENOUGH OF IT.

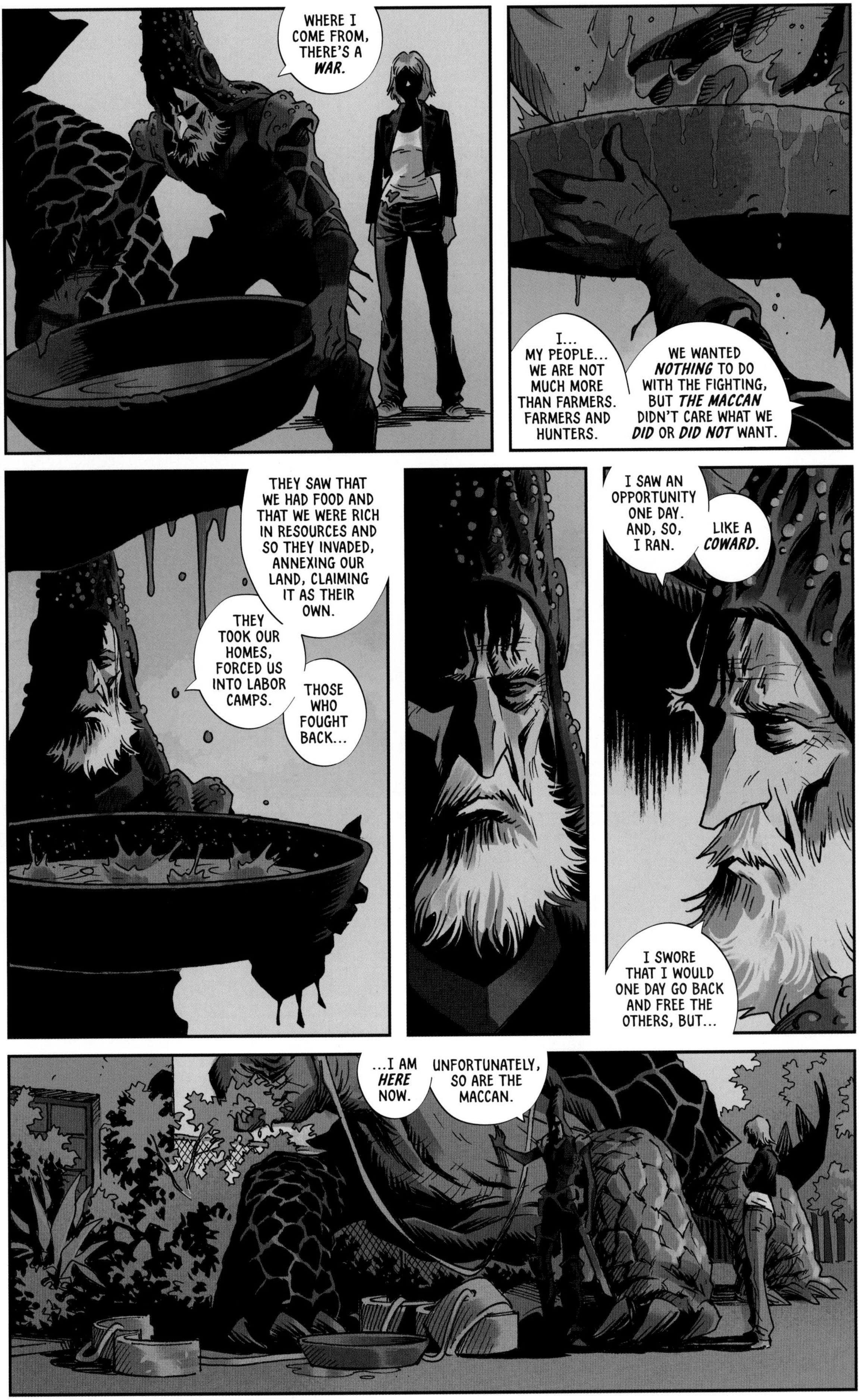
WHERE I COME FROM, THERE'S A *WAR.*
I... MY PEOPLE... WE ARE NOT MUCH MORE THAN FARMERS. FARMERS AND HUNTERS.
WE WANTED *NOTHING* TO DO WITH THE FIGHTING, BUT *THE MACCAN* DIDN'T CARE WHAT WE *DID* OR *DID NOT* WANT.
THEY SAW THAT WE HAD FOOD AND THAT WE WERE RICH IN RESOURCES AND SO THEY INVADED, ANNEXING OUR LAND, CLAIMING IT AS THEIR OWN.
THEY TOOK OUR HOMES, FORCED US INTO LABOR CAMPS.
THOSE WHO FOUGHT BACK...
I SAW AN OPPORTUNITY ONE DAY. AND, SO, I RAN.
LIKE A *COWARD.*
I SWORE THAT I WOULD ONE DAY GO BACK AND FREE THE OTHERS, BUT...
...I AM *HERE* NOW.
UNFORTUNATELY, SO ARE THE MACCAN.

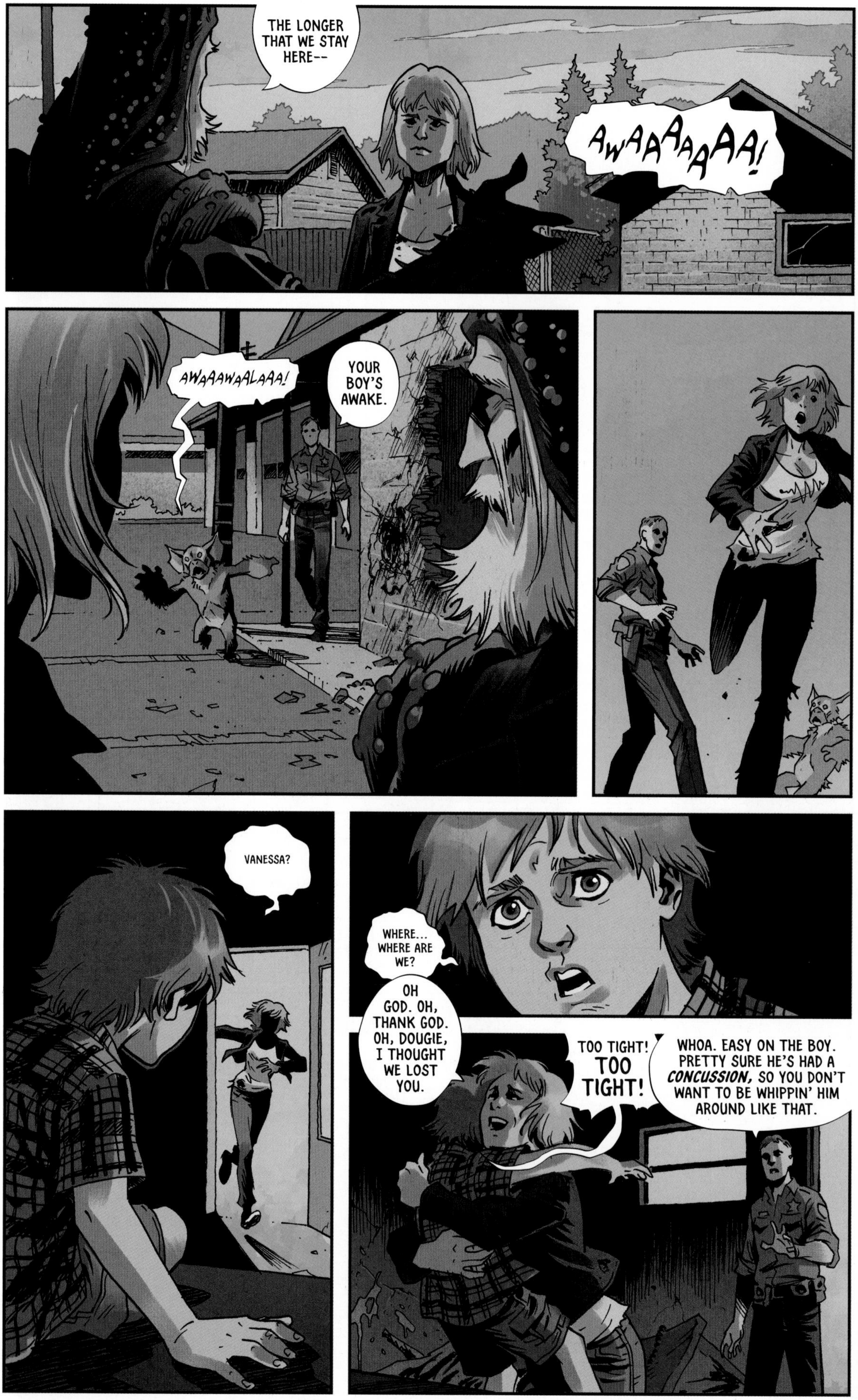
THE LONGER THAT WE STAY HERE--
AWAAAAAAA!
AWAAAWAALAAA!
YOUR BOY'S AWAKE.
VANESSA?
WHERE... WHERE ARE WE?
OH GOD. OH, THANK GOD. OH, DOUGIE, I THOUGHT WE LOST YOU.
TOO TIGHT! TOO TIGHT!
WHOA. EASY ON THE BOY. PRETTY SURE HE'S HAD A CONCUSSION, SO YOU DON'T WANT TO BE WHIPPIN' HIM AROUND LIKE THAT.

I'M SORRY. I'M JUST HAPPY TO SEE YOU. HOW ARE YOU FEELING? YOU HUNGRY? YOU WANT SOME--

WHO'S *THAT?*

THAT'S...

THIS IS SAMUEL. HE SAVED OUR LIVES.

PLEASURE TO MEET YOU, DOUGIE.

HI.

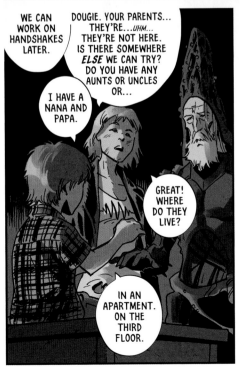

WE CAN WORK ON HANDSHAKES LATER.

DOUGIE. YOUR PARENTS... THEY'RE...*UHM...* THEY'RE NOT HERE. IS THERE SOMEWHERE *ELSE* WE CAN TRY? DO YOU HAVE ANY AUNTS OR UNCLES OR...

I HAVE A NANA AND PAPA.

GREAT! WHERE DO THEY LIVE?

IN AN APARTMENT. ON THE THIRD FLOOR.

OKAY. THAT'S GOOD. THAT'S A GOOD START.

DO YOU KNOW *WHERE* THE APARTMENT IS? THE CITY? THE STREET EVEN?

YEAH, OF COURSE. IT'S THE SAME CITY I LIVE IN.

OKAY, AND WHAT CITY IS THAT?

TWIN FALLS...

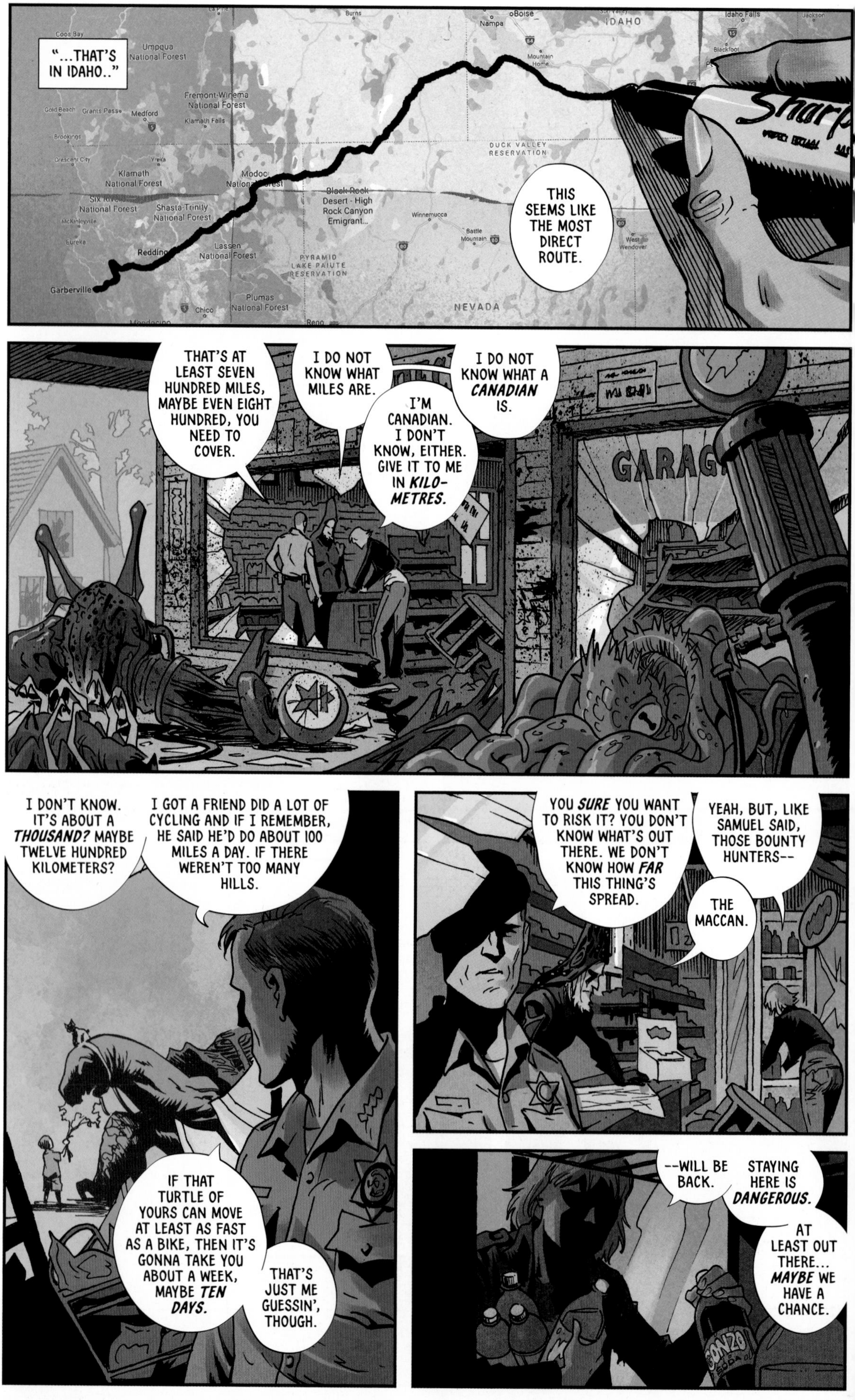

"...THAT'S IN IDAHO.."
Umpqua National Forest
Coos Bay
Fremont-Winema National Forest
Gold Beach
Grants Pass
Medford
Klamath Falls
Brookings
Crescent City
Yreka
Klamath National Forest
Modoc
Six Rivers National Forest
Shasta-Trinity National Forest
McKinleyville
Eureka
Redding
Lassen National Forest
Garberville
Chico
Plumas National Forest
Black Rock Desert - High Rock Canyon Emigrant...
PYRAMID LAKE PAIUTE RESERVATION
Winnemucca
Battle Mountain
NEVADA
Reno
Burns
Boise
Nampa
IDAHO
Mountain Home
Idaho Falls
Blackfoot
Jackson
DUCK VALLEY RESERVATION
West Wendover
THIS SEEMS LIKE THE MOST DIRECT ROUTE.
THAT'S AT LEAST SEVEN HUNDRED MILES, MAYBE EVEN EIGHT HUNDRED, YOU NEED TO COVER.
I DO NOT KNOW WHAT MILES ARE.
I'M CANADIAN. I DON'T KNOW, EITHER. GIVE IT TO ME IN *KILO-METRES.*
I DO NOT KNOW WHAT A *CANADIAN* IS.
I DON'T KNOW. IT'S ABOUT A *THOUSAND?* MAYBE TWELVE HUNDRED KILOMETERS?
I GOT A FRIEND DID A LOT OF CYCLING AND IF I REMEMBER, HE SAID HE'D DO ABOUT 100 MILES A DAY. IF THERE WEREN'T TOO MANY HILLS.
IF THAT TURTLE OF YOURS CAN MOVE AT LEAST AS FAST AS A BIKE, THEN IT'S GONNA TAKE YOU ABOUT A WEEK, MAYBE *TEN DAYS.*
THAT'S JUST ME GUESSIN', THOUGH.
YOU *SURE* YOU WANT TO RISK IT? YOU DON'T KNOW WHAT'S OUT THERE. WE DON'T KNOW HOW *FAR* THIS THING'S SPREAD.
YEAH, BUT, LIKE SAMUEL SAID, THOSE BOUNTY HUNTERS--
THE MACCAN.
--WILL BE BACK.
STAYING HERE IS *DANGEROUS.*
AT LEAST OUT THERE... *MAYBE* WE HAVE A CHANCE.

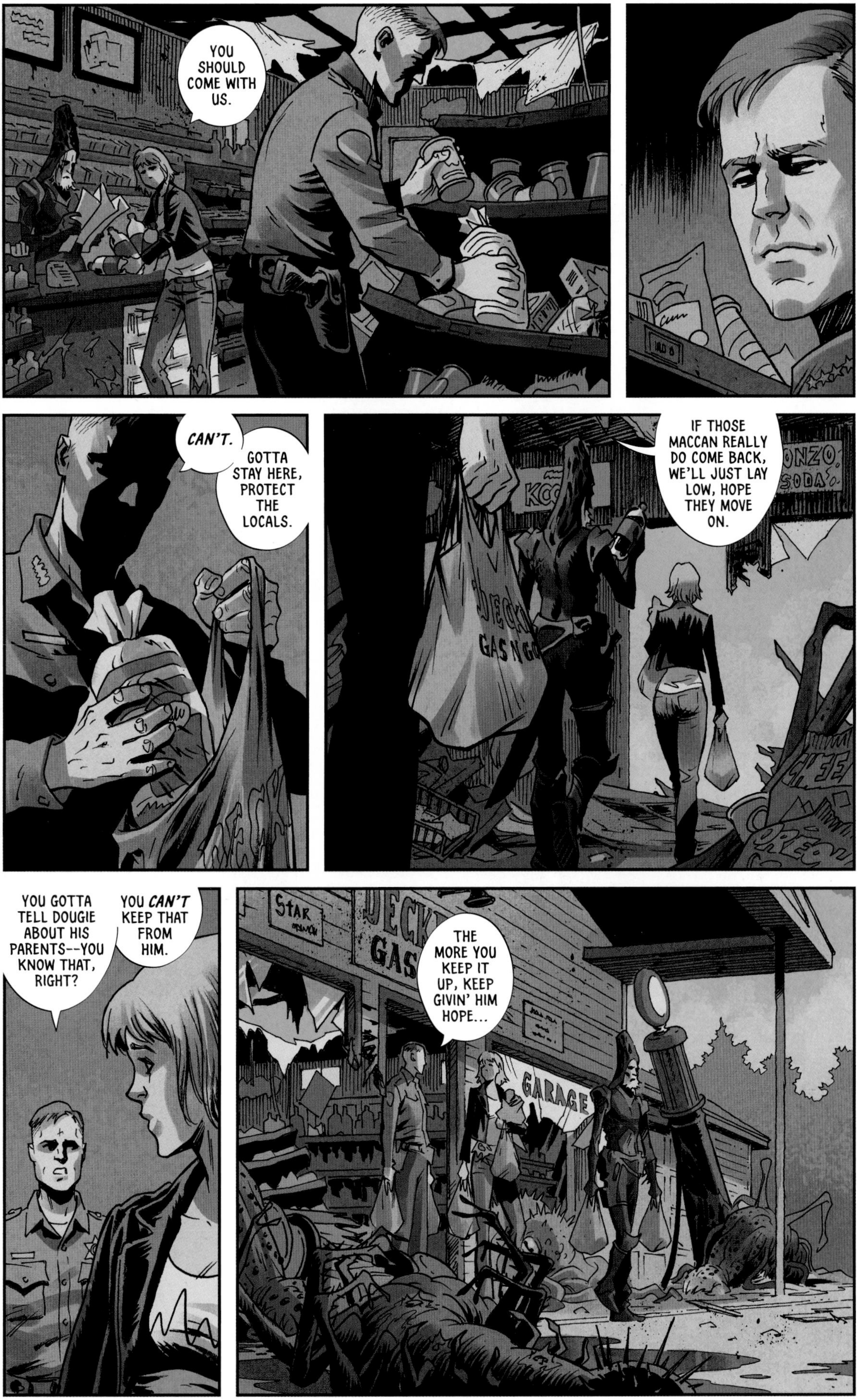
YOU SHOULD COME WITH US.
CAN'T.
GOTTA STAY HERE, PROTECT THE LOCALS.
IF THOSE MACCAN REALLY DO COME BACK, WE'LL JUST LAY LOW, HOPE THEY MOVE ON.
YOU GOTTA TELL DOUGIE ABOUT HIS PARENTS--YOU KNOW THAT, RIGHT?
YOU CAN'T KEEP THAT FROM HIM.
THE MORE YOU KEEP IT UP, KEEP GIVIN' HIM HOPE...

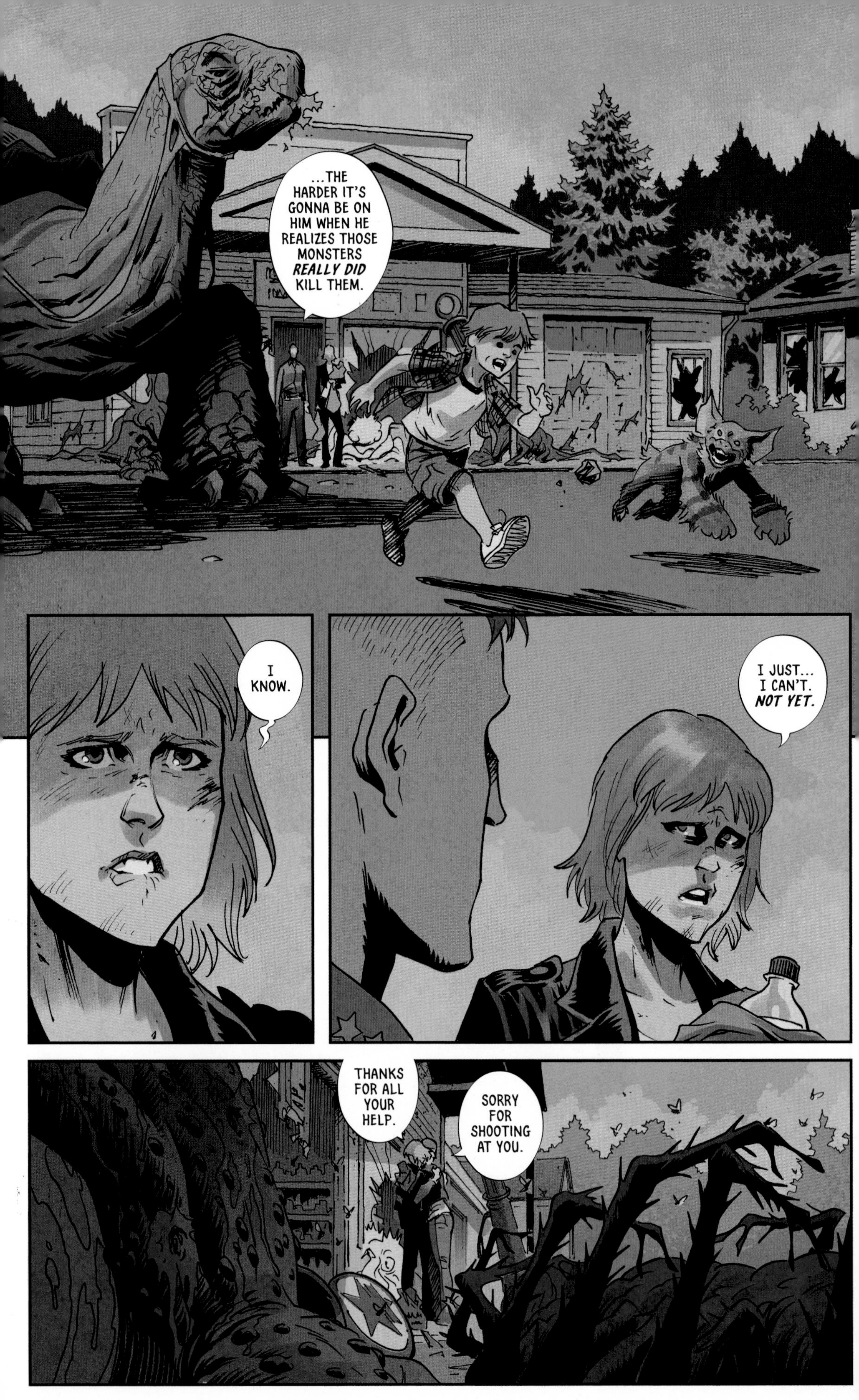
...THE HARDER IT'S GONNA BE ON HIM WHEN HE REALIZES THOSE MONSTERS *REALLY DID* KILL THEM.
I KNOW.
I JUST... I CAN'T. *NOT YET.*
THANKS FOR ALL YOUR HELP.
SORRY FOR SHOOTING AT YOU.

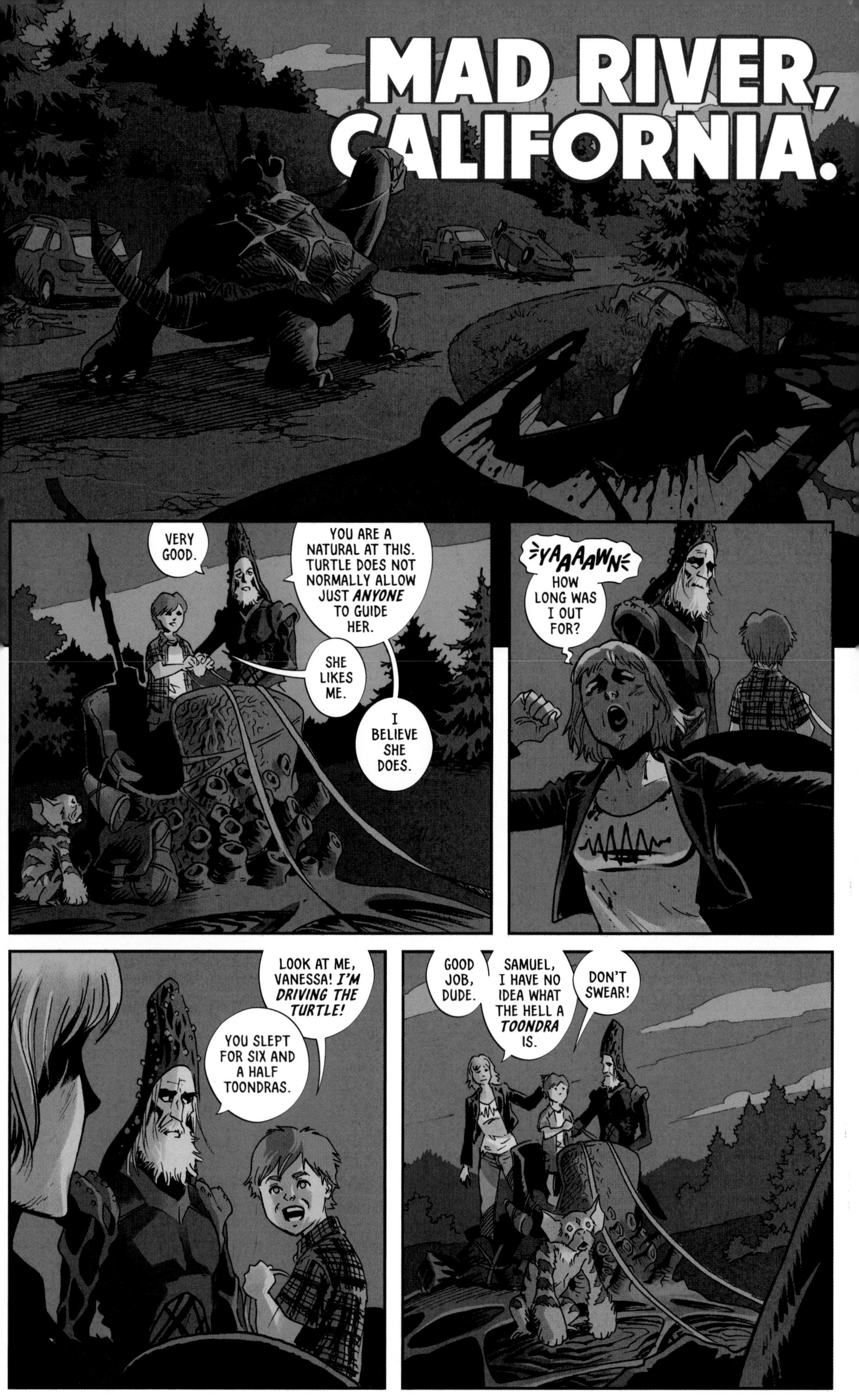
MAD RIVER, CALIFORNIA.
VERY GOOD.
YOU ARE A NATURAL AT THIS. TURTLE DOES NOT NORMALLY ALLOW JUST *ANYONE* TO GUIDE HER.
SHE LIKES ME.
I BELIEVE SHE DOES.
YAAAAWN
HOW LONG WAS I OUT FOR?
LOOK AT ME, VANESSA! *I'M DRIVING THE TURTLE!*
YOU SLEPT FOR SIX AND A HALF TOONDRAS.
GOOD JOB, DUDE.
SAMUEL, I HAVE NO IDEA WHAT THE HELL A *TOONDRA* IS.
DON'T SWEAR!

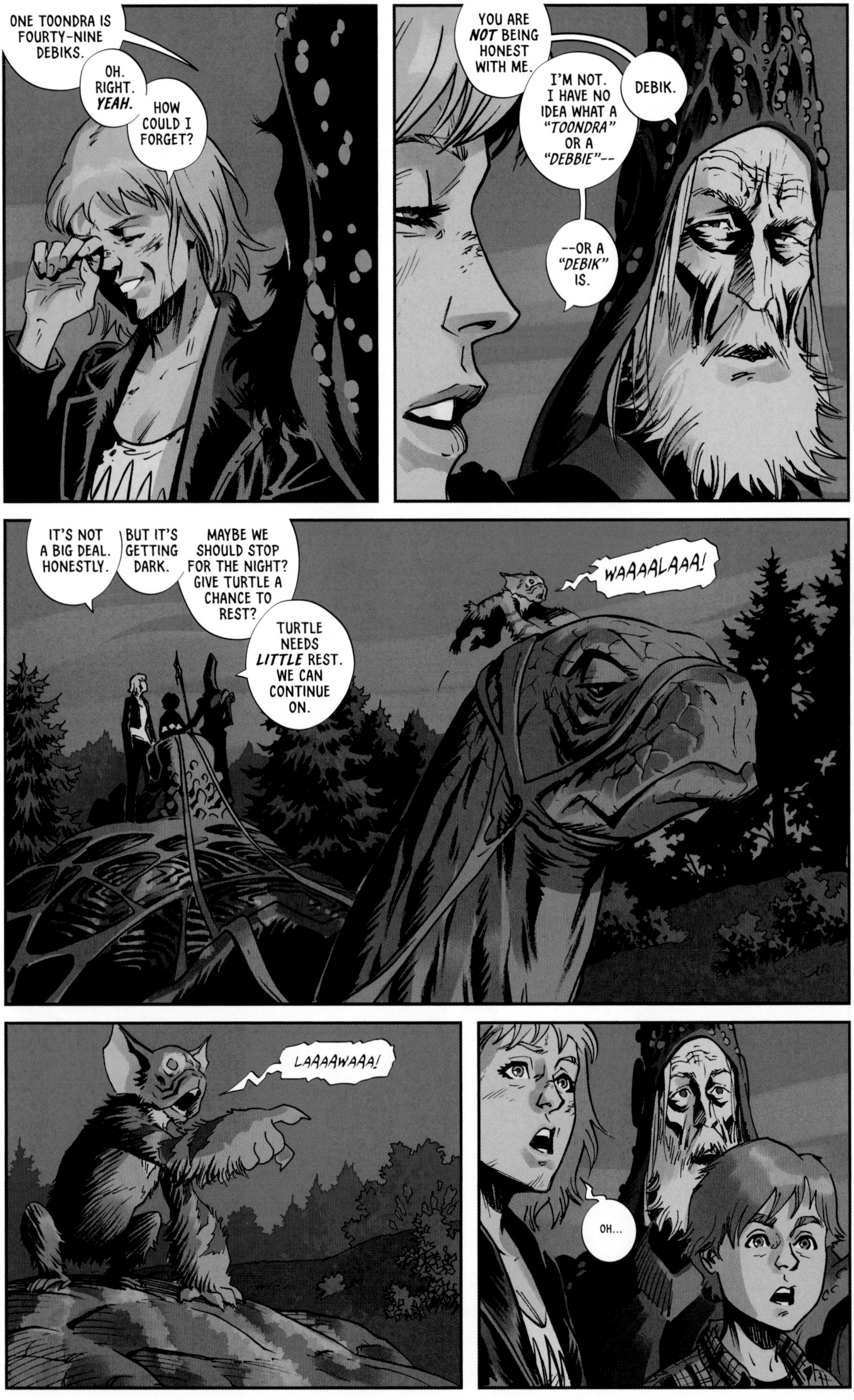
ONE TOONDRA IS FOURTY-NINE DEBIKS.
OH. RIGHT. *YEAH.*
HOW COULD I FORGET?
YOU ARE *NOT* BEING HONEST WITH ME.
I'M NOT. I HAVE NO IDEA WHAT A "*TOONDRA*" OR A "*DEBBIE*"--
DEBIK.
--OR A "*DEBIK*" IS.
IT'S NOT A BIG DEAL. HONESTLY.
BUT IT'S GETTING DARK.
MAYBE WE SHOULD STOP FOR THE NIGHT? GIVE TURTLE A CHANCE TO REST?
WAAAALAAA!
TURTLE NEEDS *LITTLE* REST. WE CAN CONTINUE ON.
LAAAAWAAA!
OH...

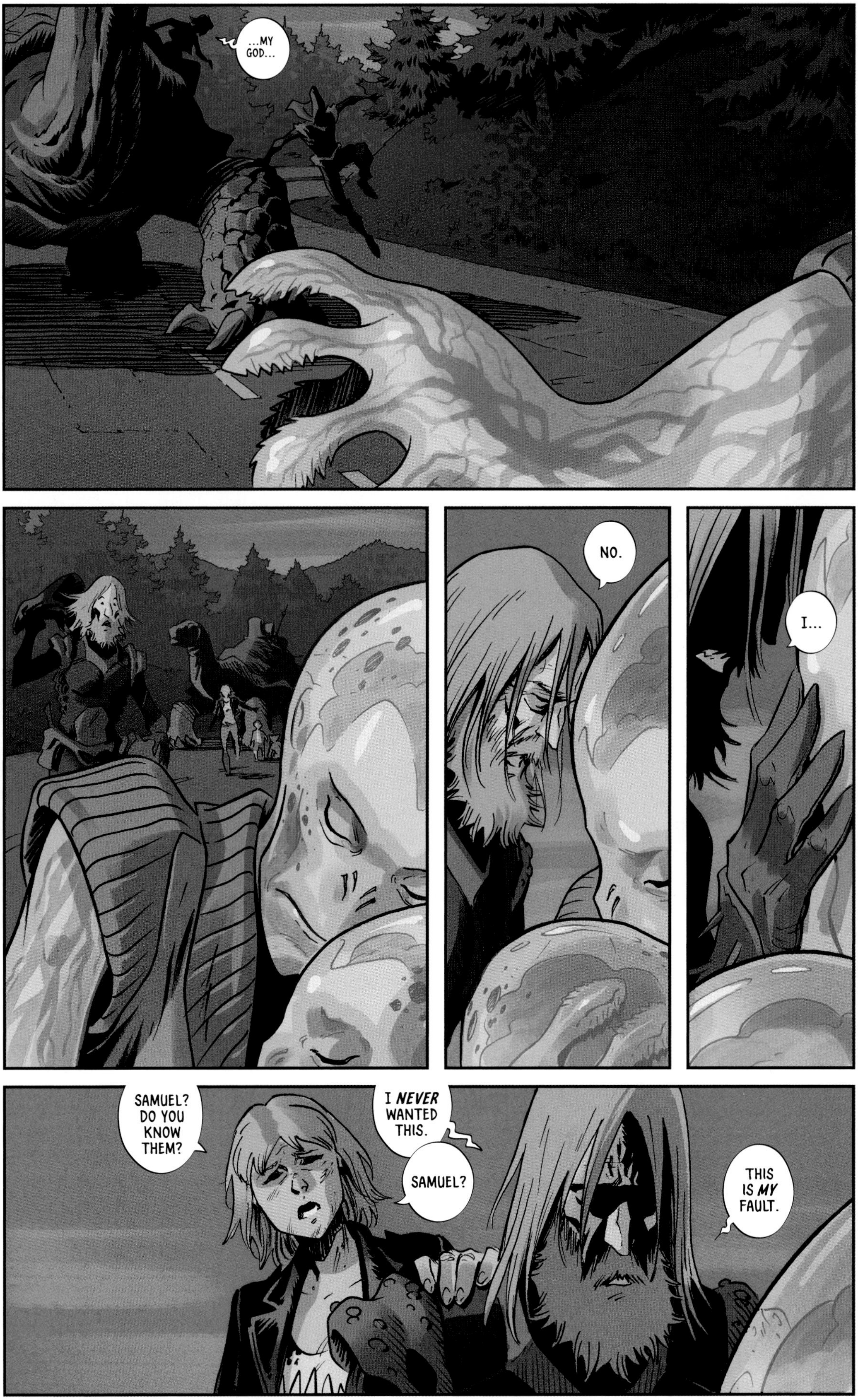
...MY GOD...
NO.
I...
SAMUEL? DO YOU KNOW THEM?
I NEVER WANTED THIS.
SAMUEL?
THIS IS MY FAULT.

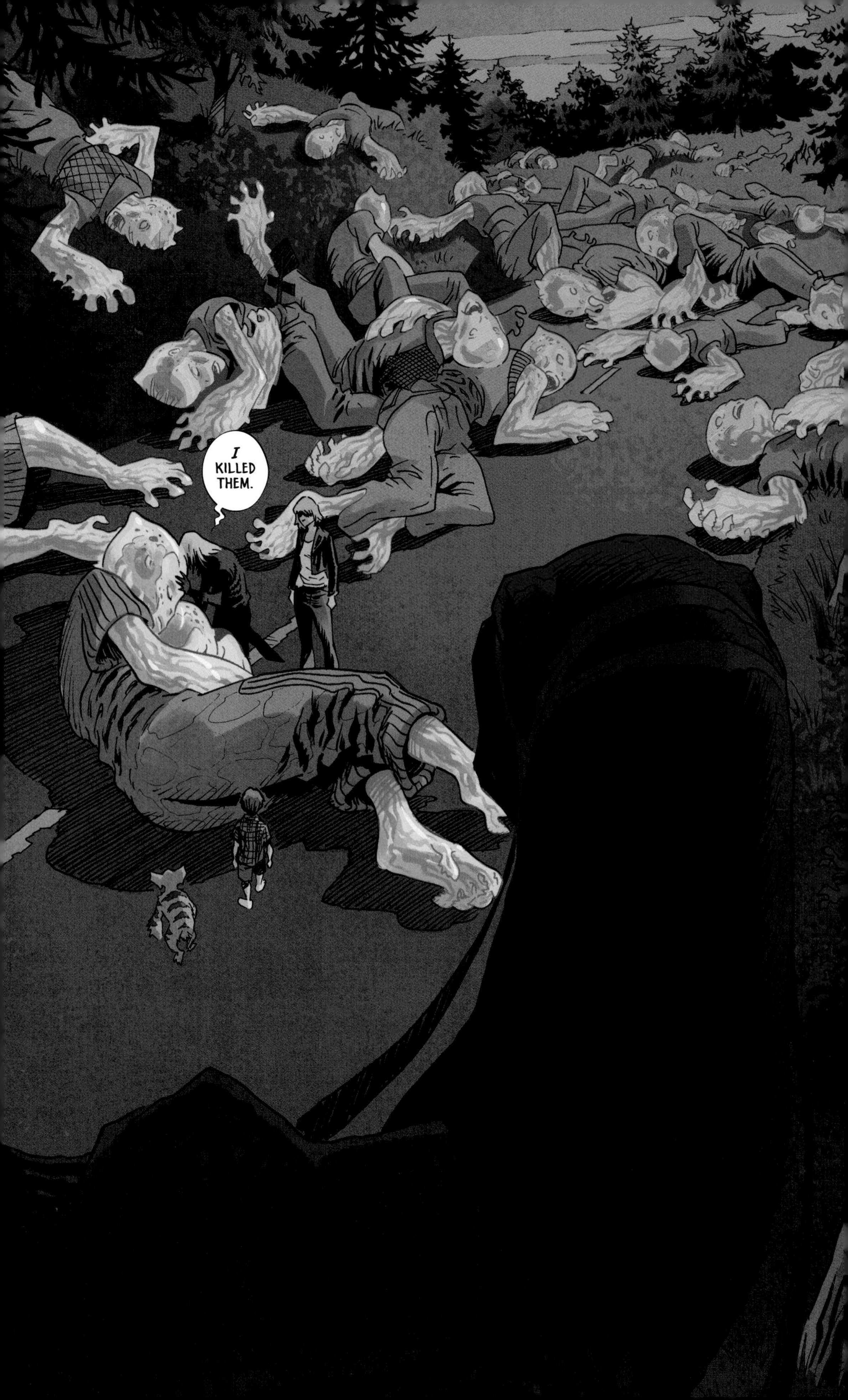
I KILLED THEM.

4

NEVER BE THE SAME

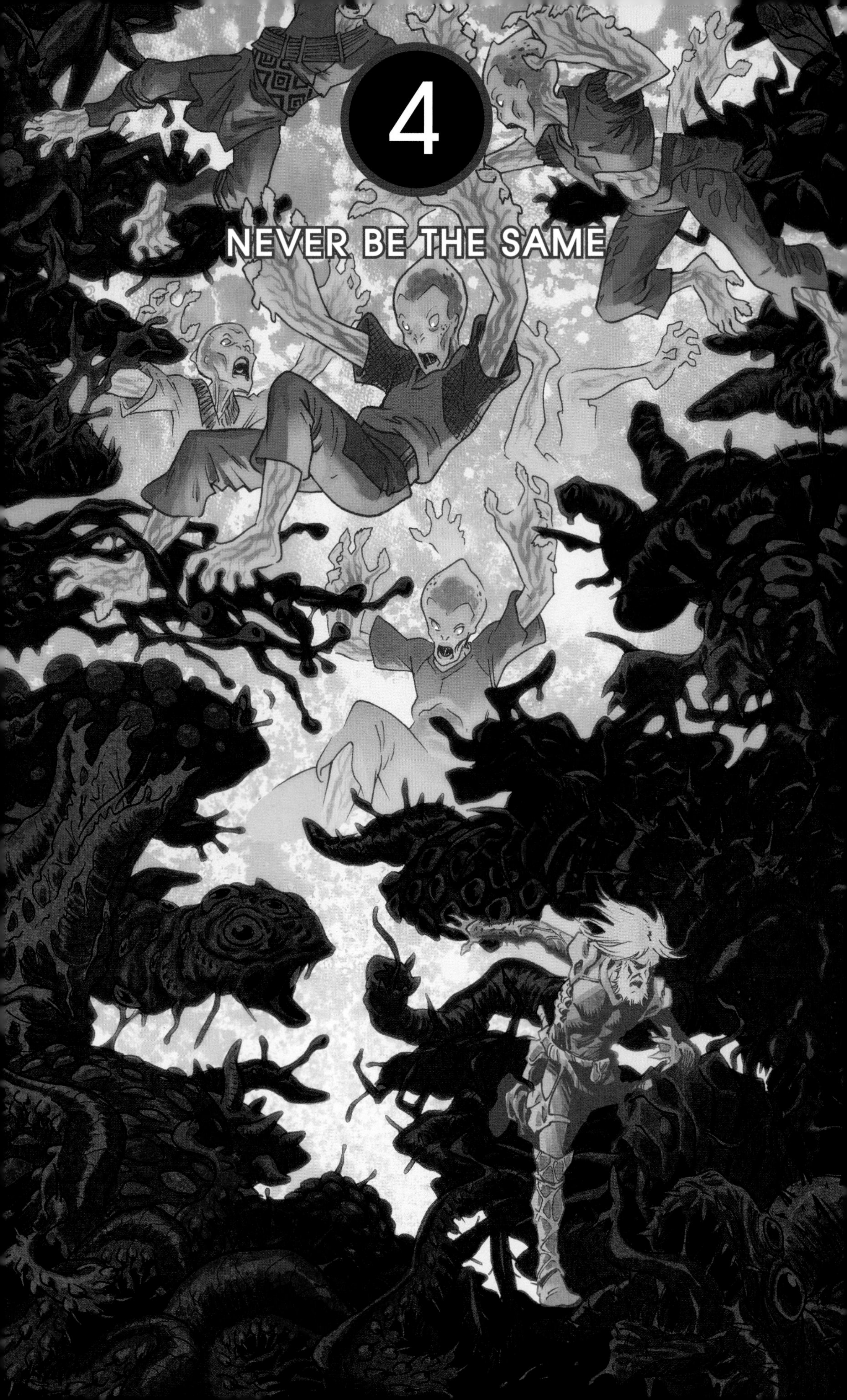

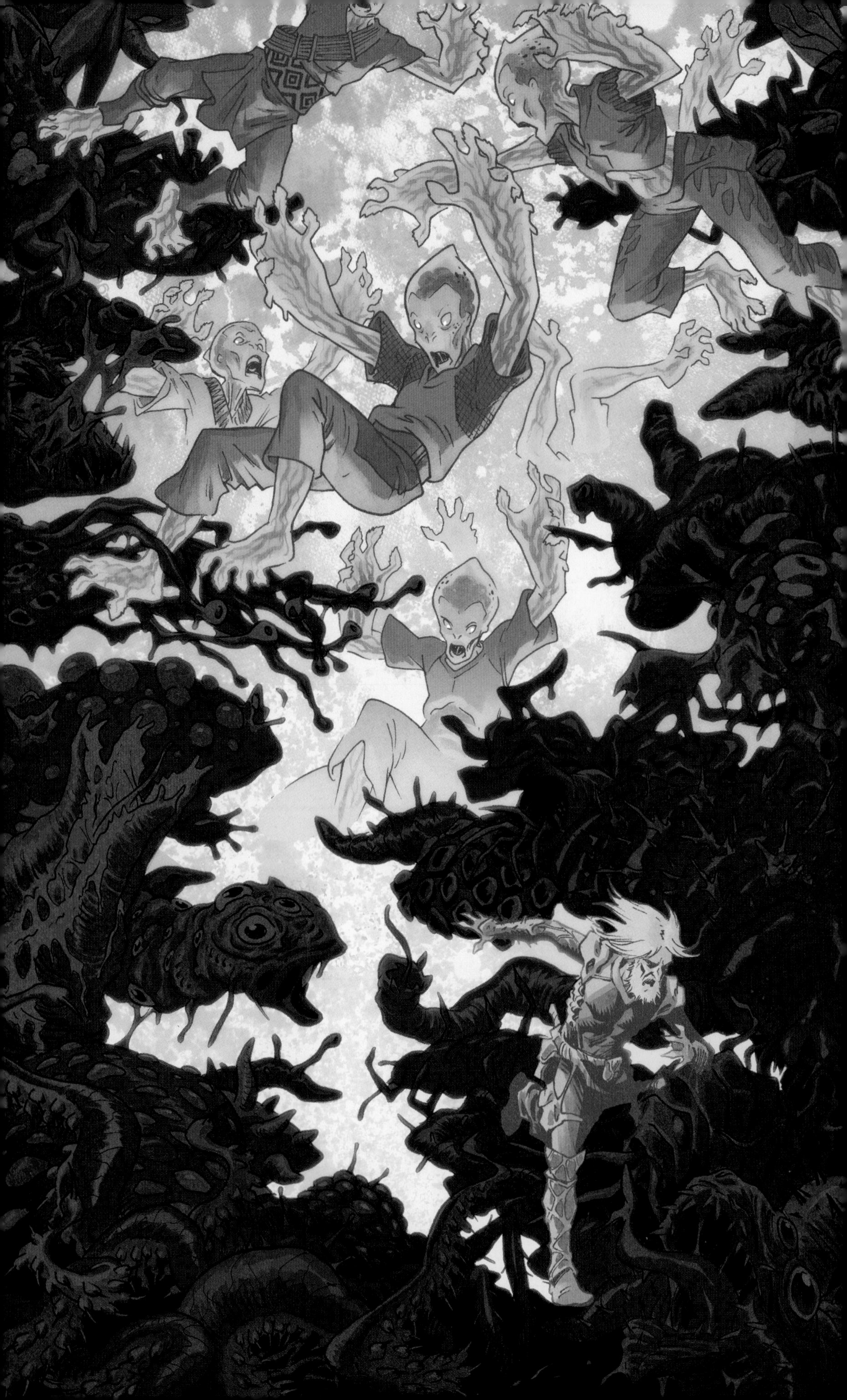

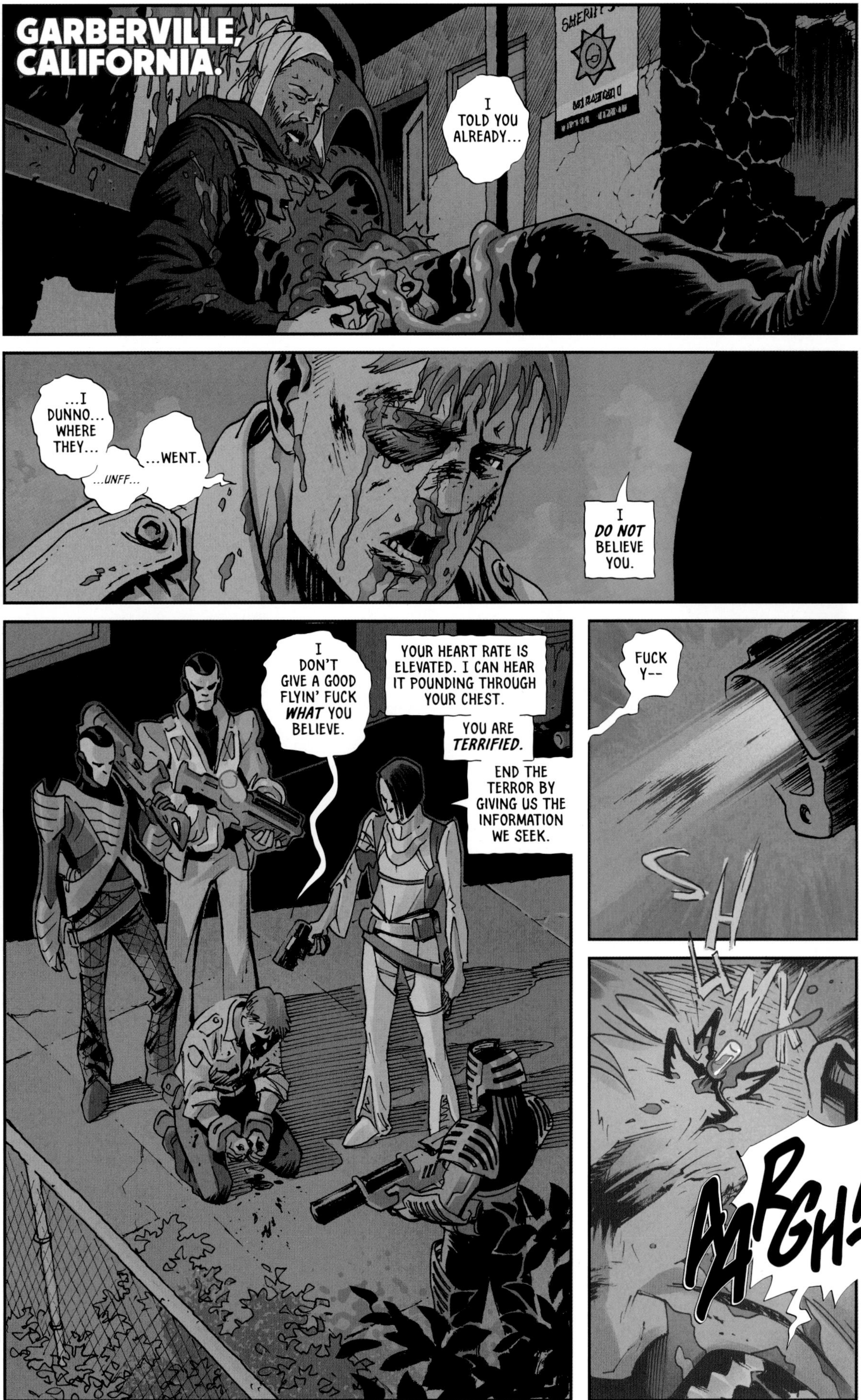
GARBERVILLE, CALIFORNIA.
I TOLD YOU ALREADY...
...I DUNNO... WHERE THEY...
...UNFF...
...WENT.
I *DO NOT* BELIEVE YOU.
I DON'T GIVE A GOOD FLYIN' FUCK *WHAT* YOU BELIEVE.
YOUR HEART RATE IS ELEVATED. I CAN HEAR IT POUNDING THROUGH YOUR CHEST.
YOU ARE *TERRIFIED.*
END THE TERROR BY GIVING US THE INFORMATION WE SEEK.
FUCK Y--
SHUNK
AARGH!

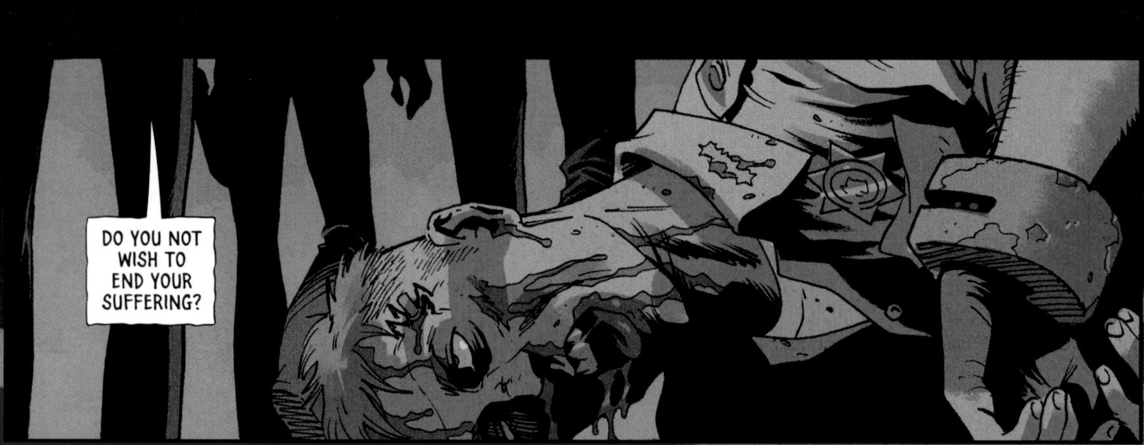
DO YOU NOT WISH TO END YOUR SUFFERING?

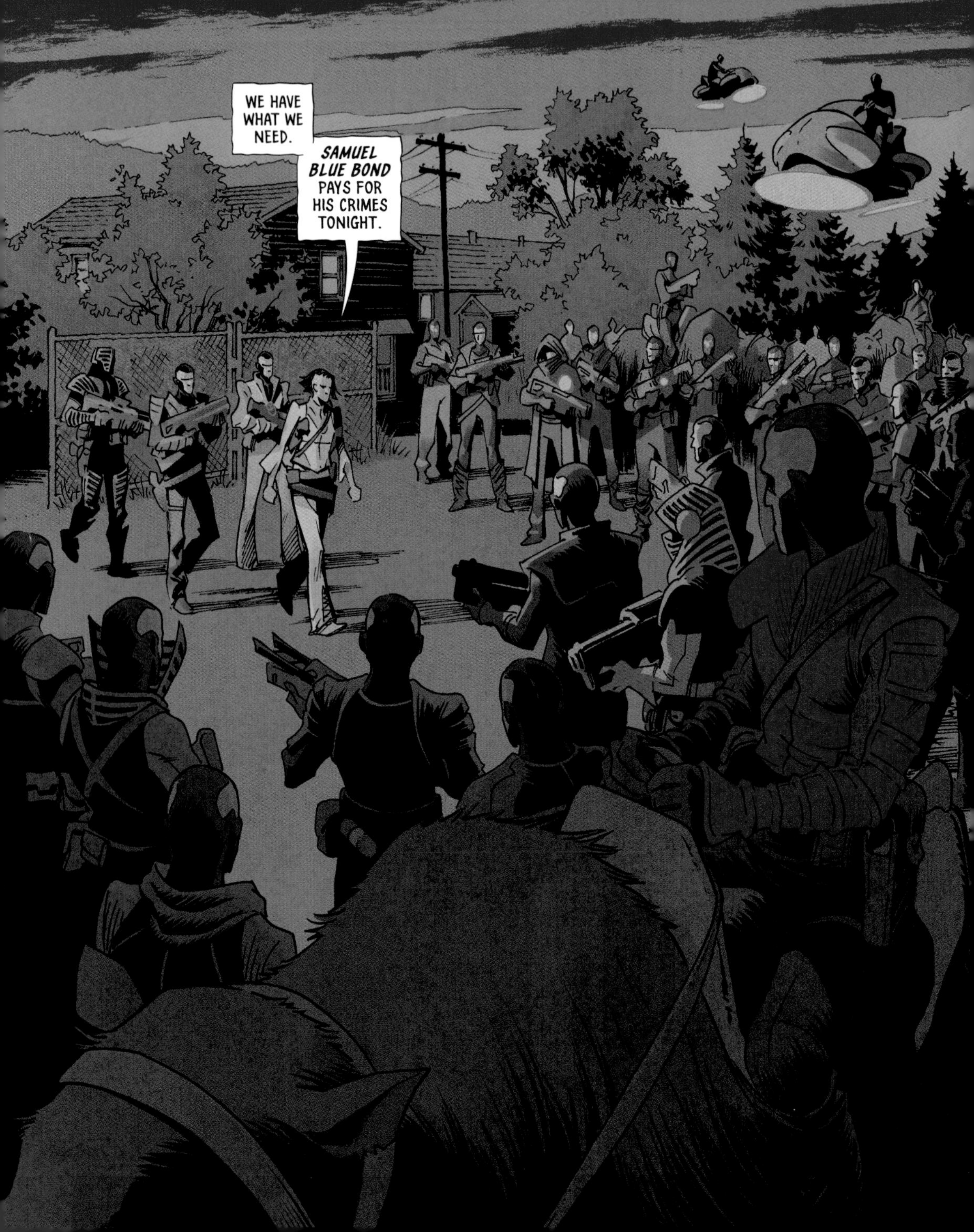
WE HAVE WHAT WE NEED.
SAMUEL BLUE BOND PAYS FOR HIS CRIMES TONIGHT.

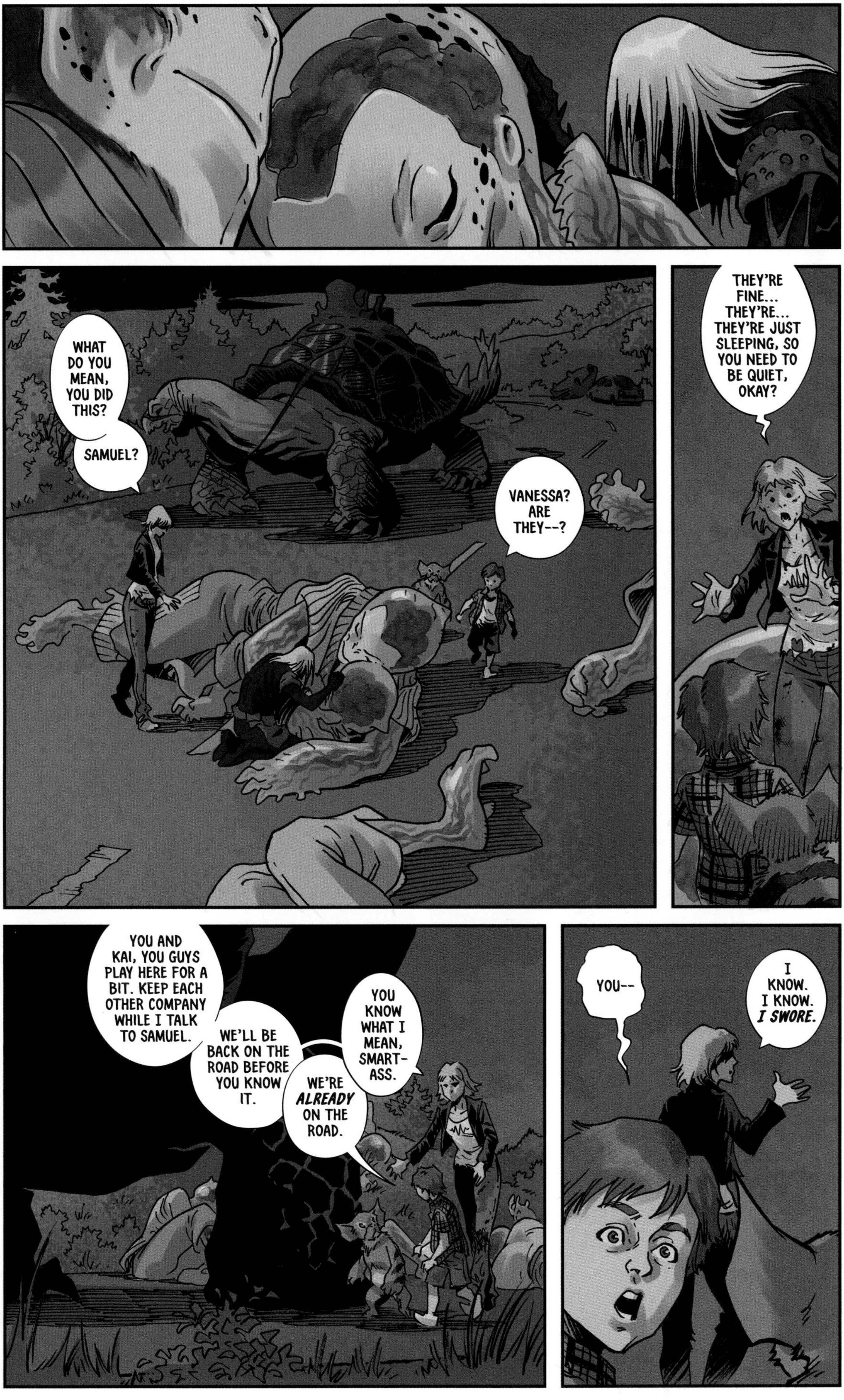
WHAT DO YOU MEAN, YOU DID THIS?
SAMUEL?
VANESSA? ARE THEY--?
THEY'RE FINE... THEY'RE... THEY'RE JUST SLEEPING, SO YOU NEED TO BE QUIET, OKAY?
YOU AND KAI, YOU GUYS PLAY HERE FOR A BIT. KEEP EACH OTHER COMPANY WHILE I TALK TO SAMUEL.
WE'LL BE BACK ON THE ROAD BEFORE YOU KNOW IT.
WE'RE *ALREADY* ON THE ROAD.
YOU KNOW WHAT I MEAN, SMART-ASS.
YOU--
I KNOW. I KNOW. ***I SWORE.***

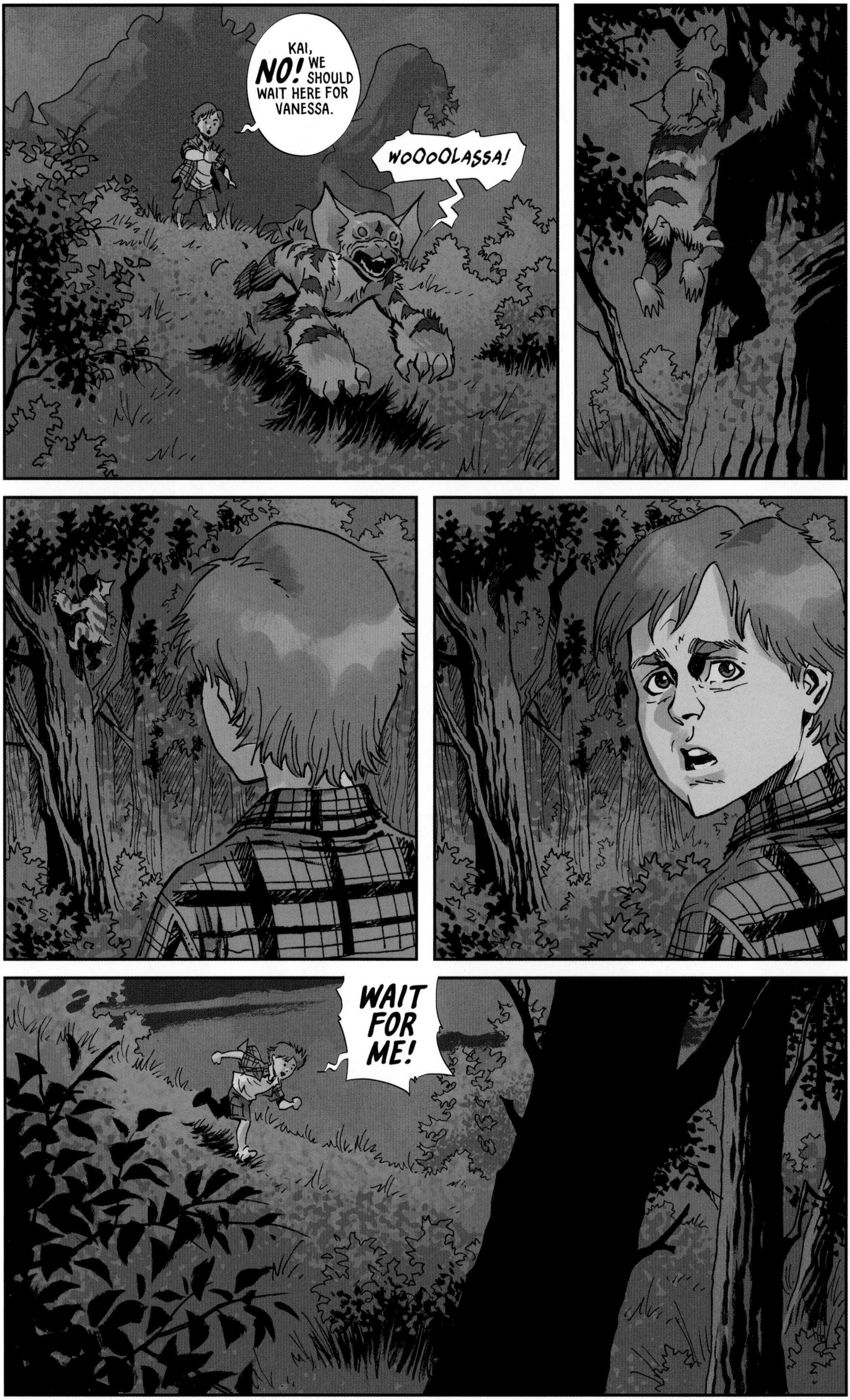
KAI, NO! WE SHOULD WAIT HERE FOR VANESSA.
WOOOOLASSA!
WAIT FOR ME!

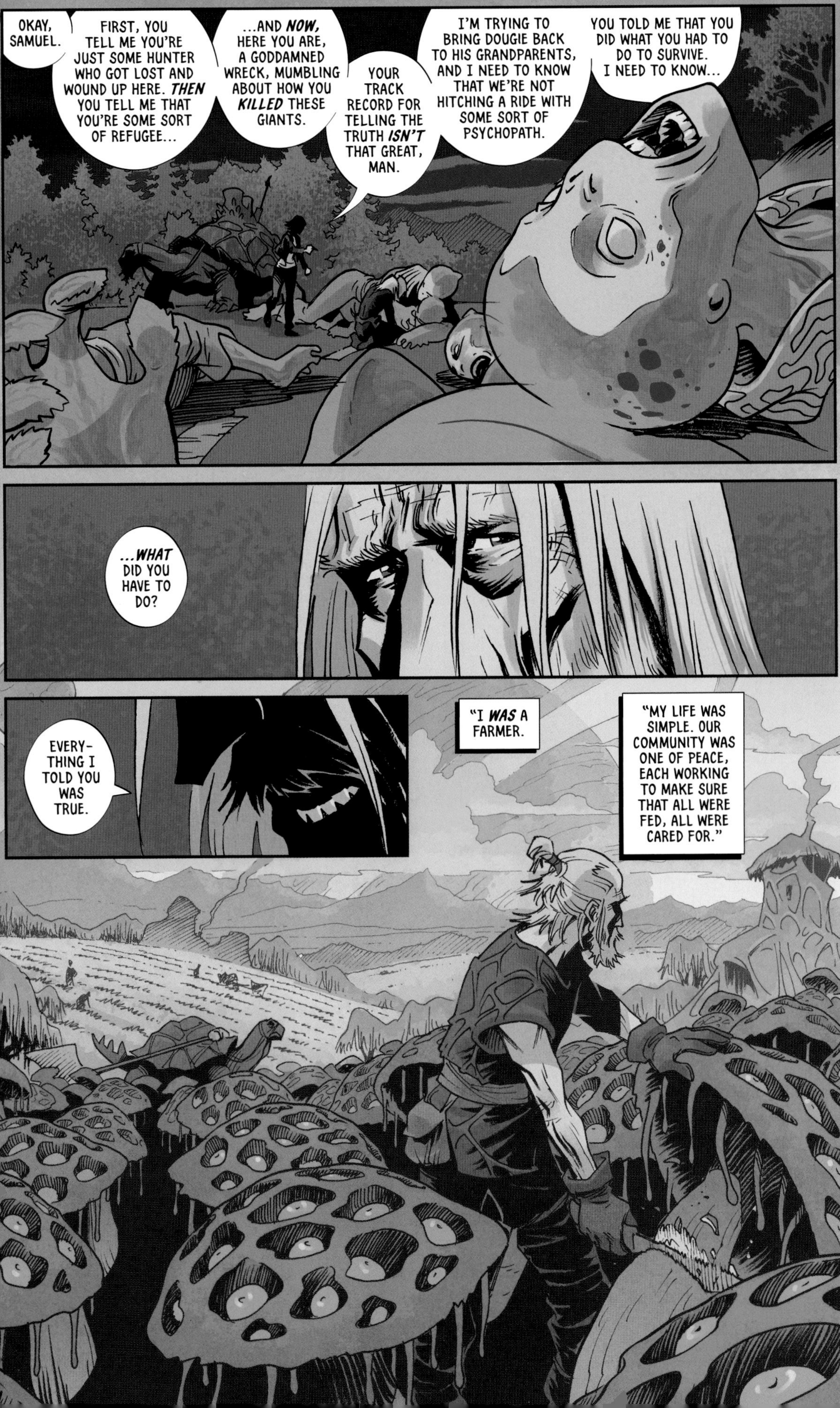
OKAY, SAMUEL.
FIRST, YOU TELL ME YOU'RE JUST SOME HUNTER WHO GOT LOST AND WOUND UP HERE. *THEN* YOU TELL ME THAT YOU'RE SOME SORT OF REFUGEE...
...AND *NOW,* HERE YOU ARE, A GODDAMNED WRECK, MUMBLING ABOUT HOW YOU *KILLED* THESE GIANTS.
YOUR TRACK RECORD FOR TELLING THE TRUTH *ISN'T* THAT GREAT, MAN.
I'M TRYING TO BRING DOUGIE BACK TO HIS GRANDPARENTS, AND I NEED TO KNOW THAT WE'RE NOT HITCHING A RIDE WITH SOME SORT OF PSYCHOPATH.
YOU TOLD ME THAT YOU DID WHAT YOU HAD TO DO TO SURVIVE. I NEED TO KNOW...
...*WHAT* DID YOU HAVE TO DO?
EVERY-THING I TOLD YOU WAS TRUE.
"I *WAS* A FARMER.
"MY LIFE WAS SIMPLE. OUR COMMUNITY WAS ONE OF PEACE, EACH WORKING TO MAKE SURE THAT ALL WERE FED, ALL WERE CARED FOR."

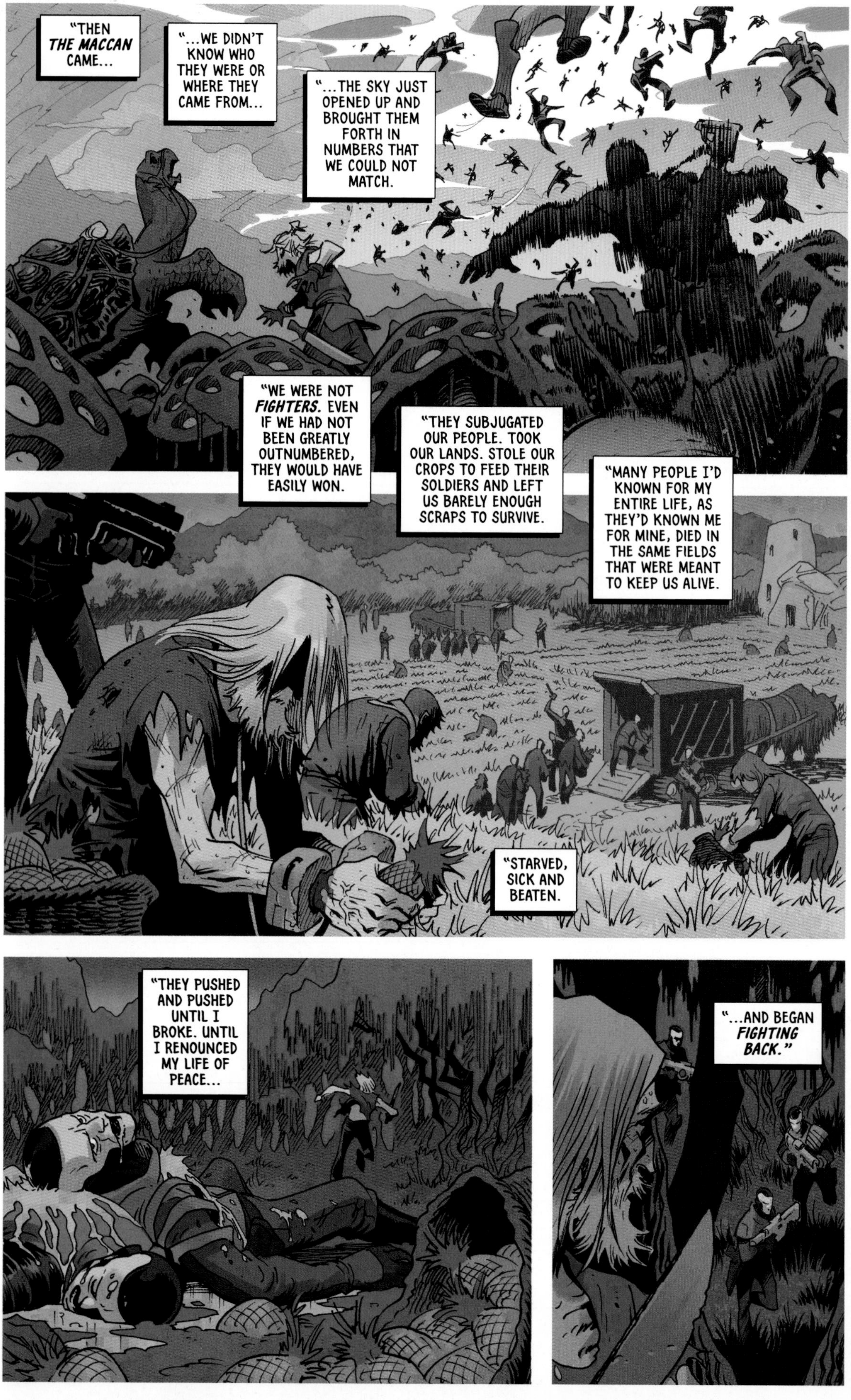
"THEN *THE MACCAN* CAME...
"...WE DIDN'T KNOW WHO THEY WERE OR WHERE THEY CAME FROM...
"...THE SKY JUST OPENED UP AND BROUGHT THEM FORTH IN NUMBERS THAT WE COULD NOT MATCH.
"WE WERE NOT *FIGHTERS.* EVEN IF WE HAD NOT BEEN GREATLY OUTNUMBERED, THEY WOULD HAVE EASILY WON.
"THEY SUBJUGATED OUR PEOPLE. TOOK OUR LANDS. STOLE OUR CROPS TO FEED THEIR SOLDIERS AND LEFT US BARELY ENOUGH SCRAPS TO SURVIVE.
"MANY PEOPLE I'D KNOWN FOR MY ENTIRE LIFE, AS THEY'D KNOWN ME FOR MINE, DIED IN THE SAME FIELDS THAT WERE MEANT TO KEEP US ALIVE.
"STARVED, SICK AND BEATEN.
"THEY PUSHED AND PUSHED UNTIL I BROKE. UNTIL I RENOUNCED MY LIFE OF PEACE...
"...AND BEGAN *FIGHTING BACK.*"

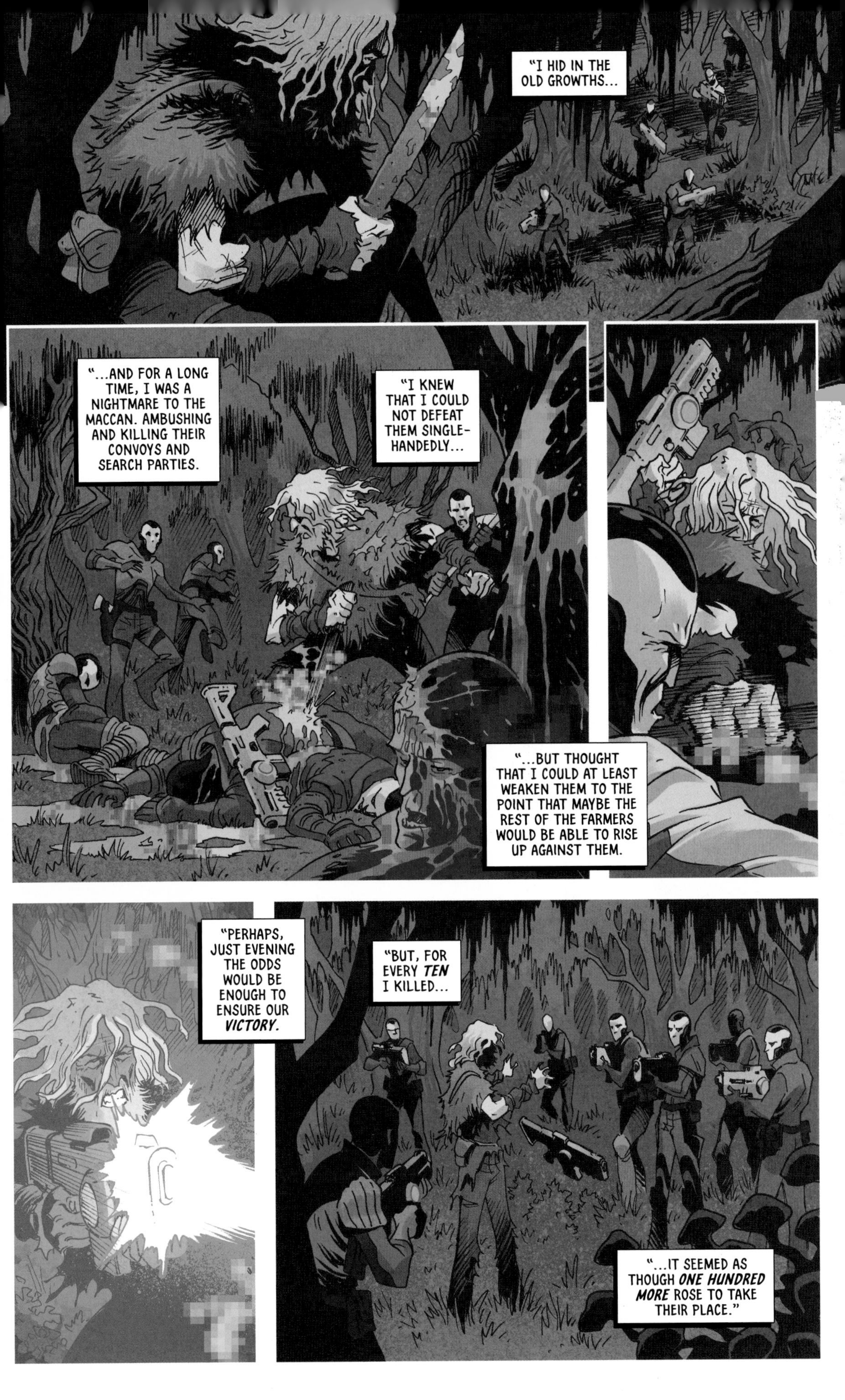
"I HID IN THE OLD GROWTHS...
"...AND FOR A LONG TIME, I WAS A NIGHTMARE TO THE MACCAN. AMBUSHING AND KILLING THEIR CONVOYS AND SEARCH PARTIES.
"I KNEW THAT I COULD NOT DEFEAT THEM SINGLE-HANDEDLY...
"...BUT THOUGHT THAT I COULD AT LEAST WEAKEN THEM TO THE POINT THAT MAYBE THE REST OF THE FARMERS WOULD BE ABLE TO RISE UP AGAINST THEM.
"PERHAPS, JUST EVENING THE ODDS WOULD BE ENOUGH TO ENSURE OUR *VICTORY*.
"BUT, FOR EVERY *TEN* I KILLED...
"...IT SEEMED AS THOUGH *ONE HUNDRED MORE* ROSE TO TAKE THEIR PLACE."

"THEY CHAINED ME IN THE CENTER OF TOWN AS A WARNING TO OTHERS WHO MIGHT HAVE HAD IDEAS OF REBELLION ON THEIR MIND.

"THEY BEAT ME, HUMILIATED ME, STARVED ME.

"LUCKILY, ONCE A FROST STAR TORTOISE HAS BONDED TO YOU, THAT BOND IS *FOR LIFE*.

"THEY TRIED TO STOP US...

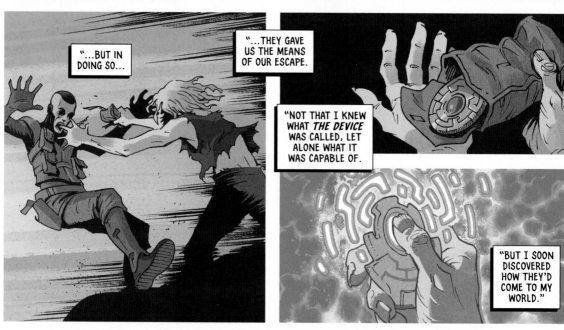

"...BUT IN DOING SO...

"...THEY GAVE US THE MEANS OF OUR ESCAPE.

"NOT THAT I KNEW WHAT *THE DEVICE* WAS CALLED, LET ALONE WHAT IT WAS CAPABLE OF.

"BUT I SOON DISCOVERED HOW THEY'D COME TO MY WORLD."

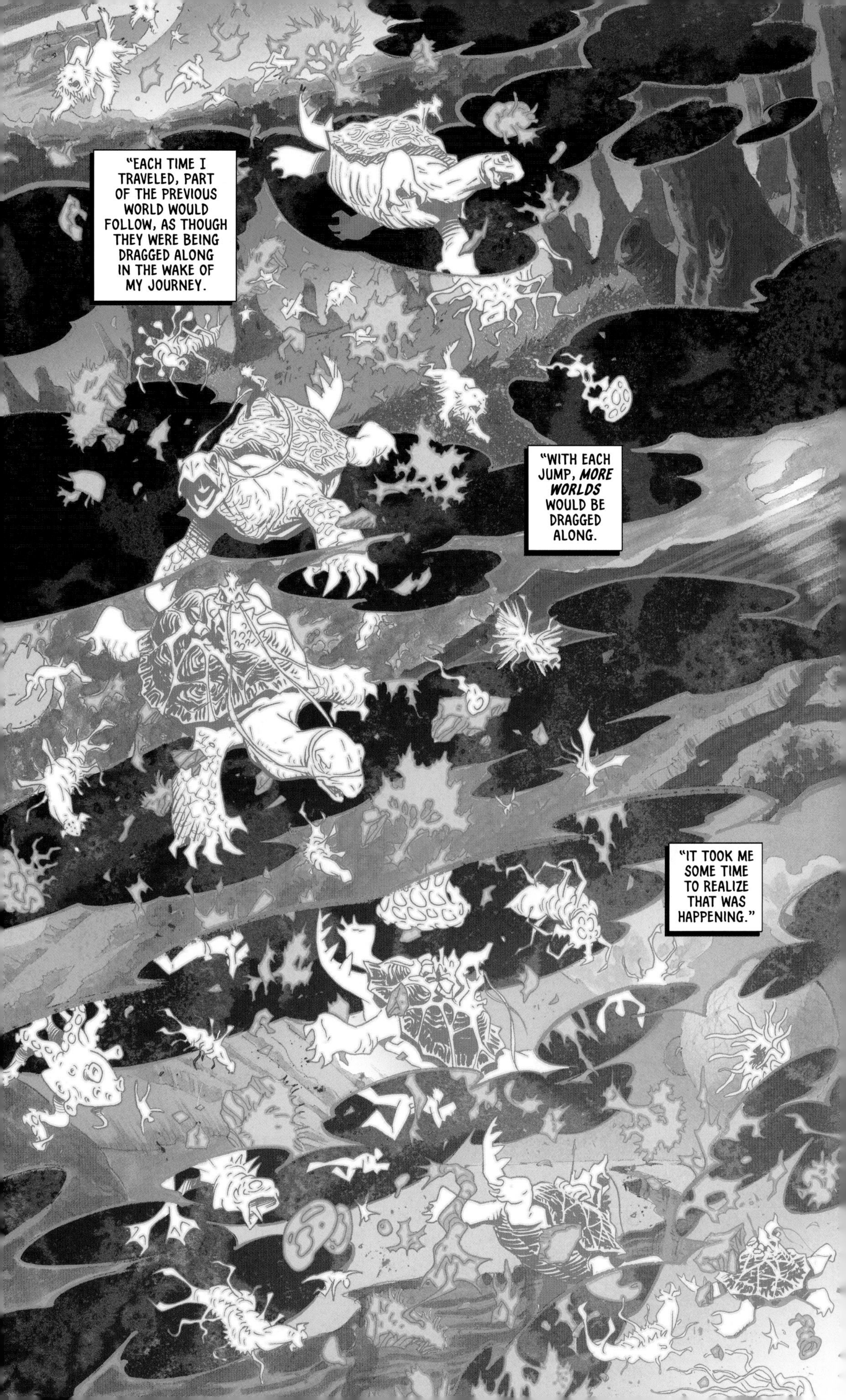
"EACH TIME I TRAVELED, PART OF THE PREVIOUS WORLD WOULD FOLLOW, AS THOUGH THEY WERE BEING DRAGGED ALONG IN THE WAKE OF MY JOURNEY.
"WITH EACH JUMP, *MORE WORLDS* WOULD BE DRAGGED ALONG.
"IT TOOK ME SOME TIME TO REALIZE THAT WAS HAPPENING."

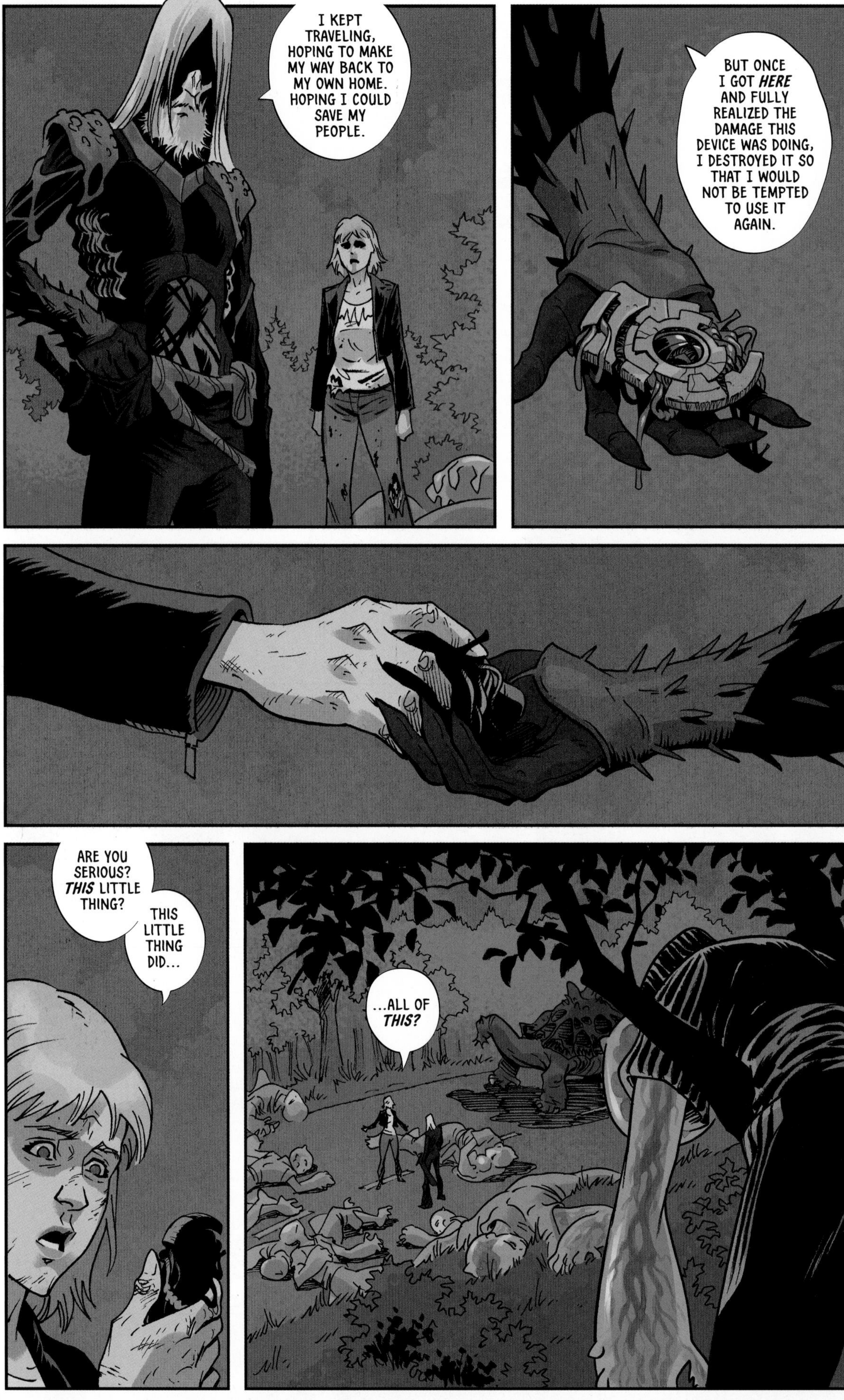
I KEPT TRAVELING, HOPING TO MAKE MY WAY BACK TO MY OWN HOME. HOPING I COULD SAVE MY PEOPLE.
BUT ONCE I GOT *HERE* AND FULLY REALIZED THE DAMAGE THIS DEVICE WAS DOING, I DESTROYED IT SO THAT I WOULD NOT BE TEMPTED TO USE IT AGAIN.
ARE YOU SERIOUS? *THIS* LITTLE THING?
THIS LITTLE THING DID...
...ALL OF *THIS?*

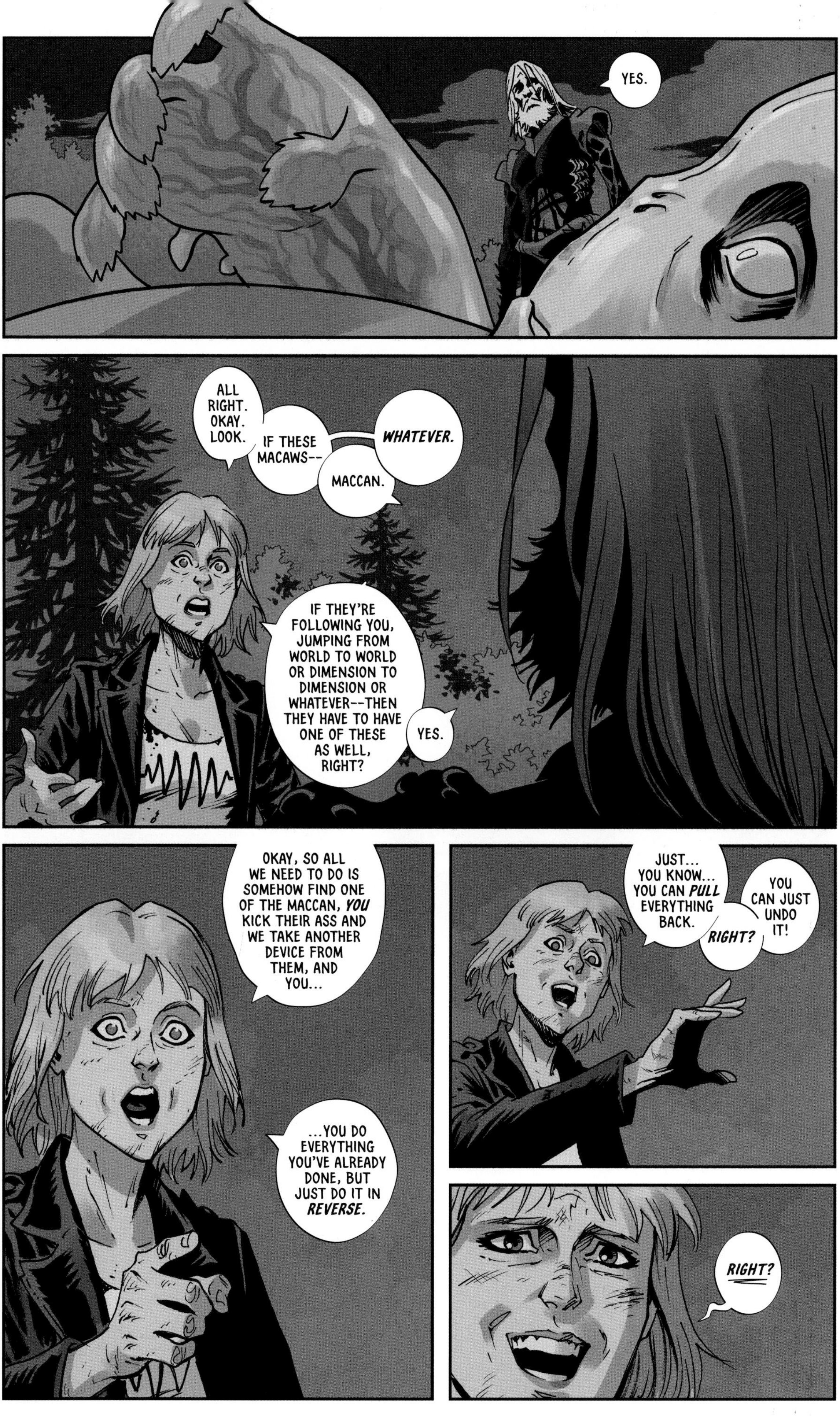
YES.
ALL RIGHT. OKAY. LOOK.
IF THESE MACAWS--
MACCAN.
WHATEVER.
IF THEY'RE FOLLOWING YOU, JUMPING FROM WORLD TO WORLD OR DIMENSION TO DIMENSION OR WHATEVER--THEN THEY HAVE TO HAVE ONE OF THESE AS WELL, RIGHT?
YES.
OKAY, SO ALL WE NEED TO DO IS SOMEHOW FIND ONE OF THE MACCAN, *YOU* KICK THEIR ASS AND WE TAKE ANOTHER DEVICE FROM THEM, AND YOU...
...YOU DO EVERYTHING YOU'VE ALREADY DONE, BUT JUST DO IT IN *REVERSE.*
JUST... YOU KNOW... YOU CAN *PULL* EVERYTHING BACK.
RIGHT?
YOU CAN JUST UNDO IT!
RIGHT?

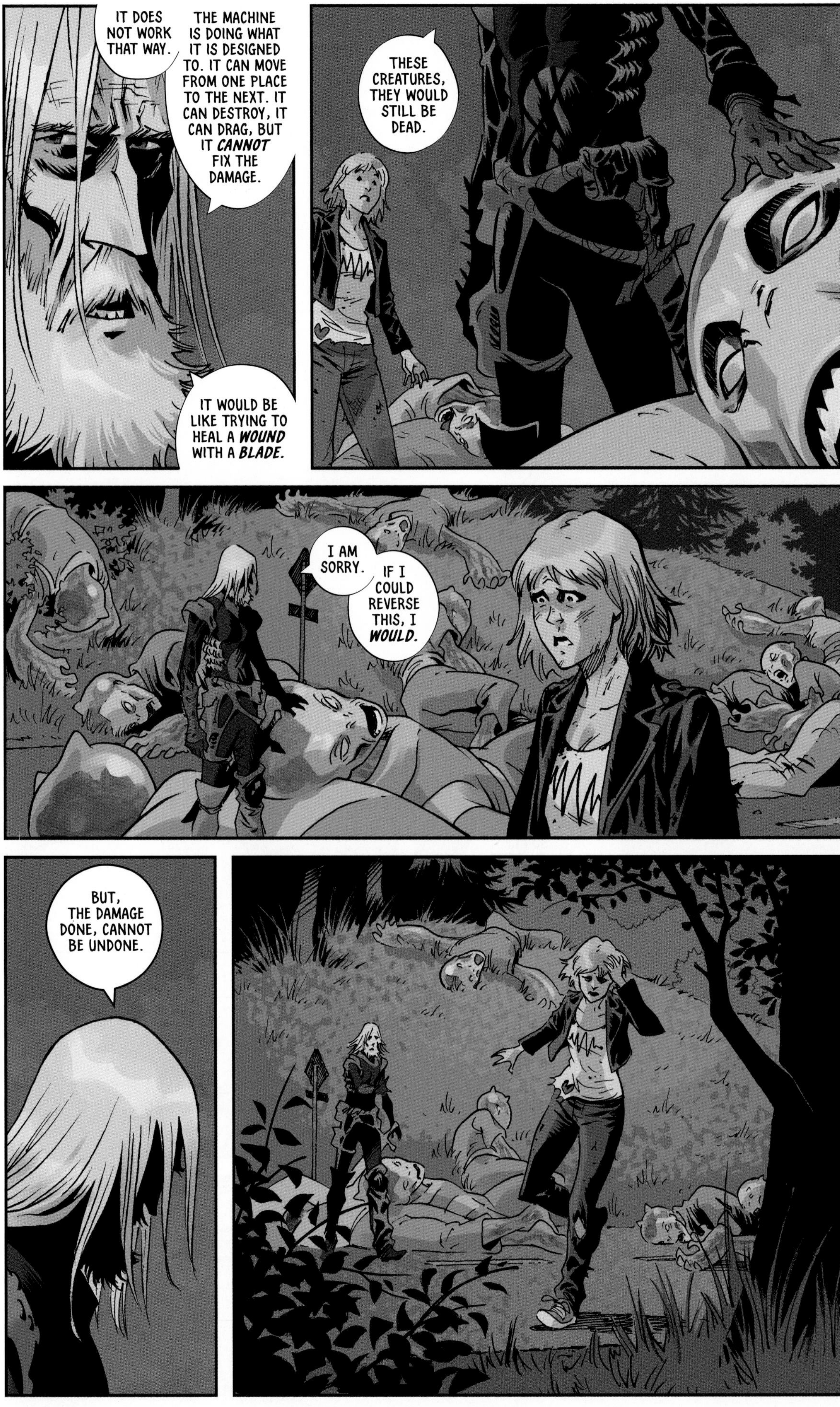
IT DOES NOT WORK THAT WAY.
THE MACHINE IS DOING WHAT IT IS DESIGNED TO. IT CAN MOVE FROM ONE PLACE TO THE NEXT. IT CAN DESTROY, IT CAN DRAG, BUT IT *CANNOT* FIX THE DAMAGE.
IT WOULD BE LIKE TRYING TO HEAL A ***WOUND*** WITH A ***BLADE.***
THESE CREATURES, THEY WOULD STILL BE DEAD.
I AM SORRY.
IF I COULD REVERSE THIS, I ***WOULD.***
BUT, THE DAMAGE DONE, CANNOT BE UNDONE.

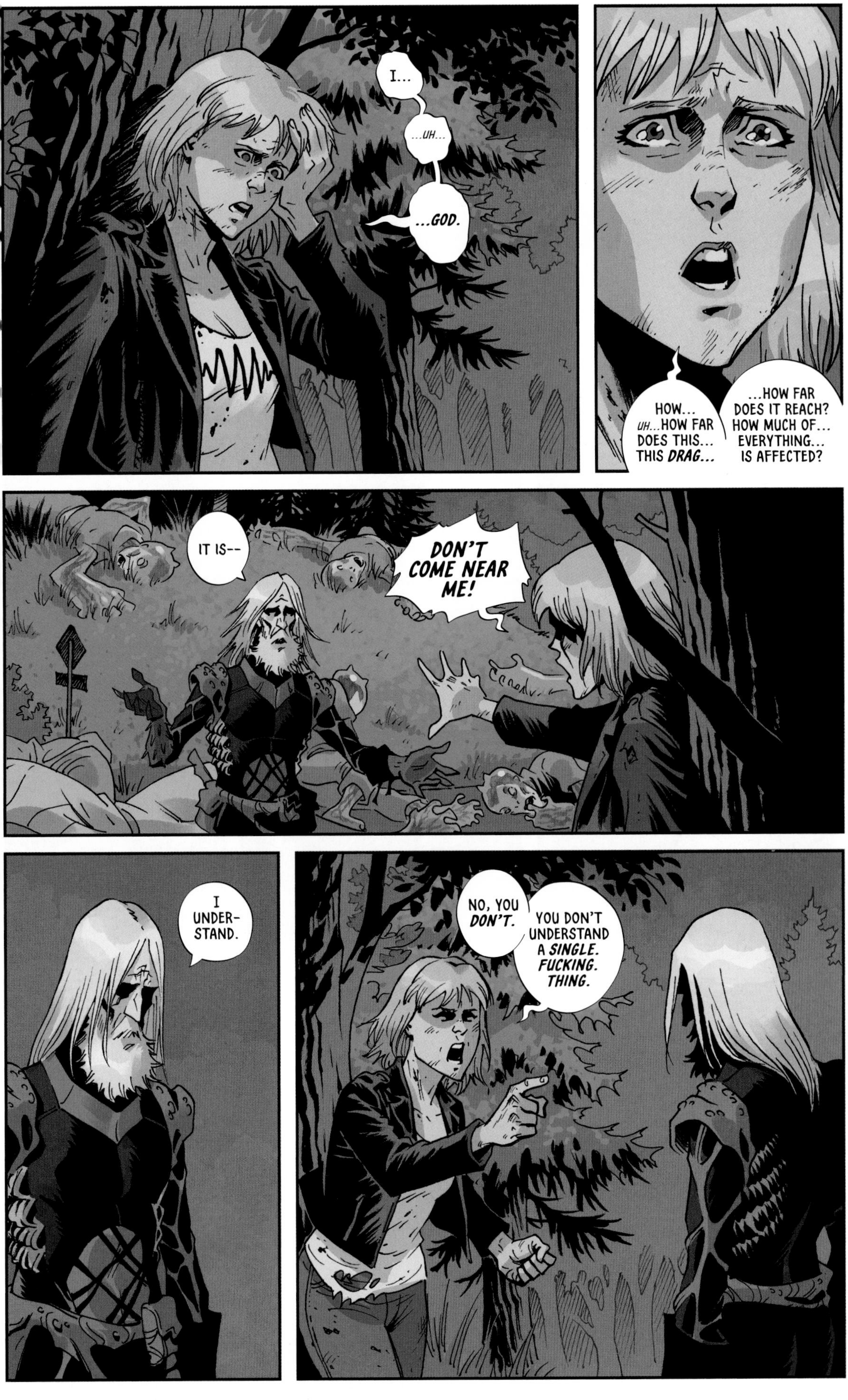
I...
...UH...
...GOD.
HOW... UH...HOW FAR DOES THIS... THIS DRAG...
...HOW FAR DOES IT REACH? HOW MUCH OF... EVERYTHING... IS AFFECTED?
IT IS--
DON'T COME NEAR ME!
I UNDER-STAND.
NO, YOU DON'T.
YOU DON'T UNDERSTAND A SINGLE. FUCKING. THING.

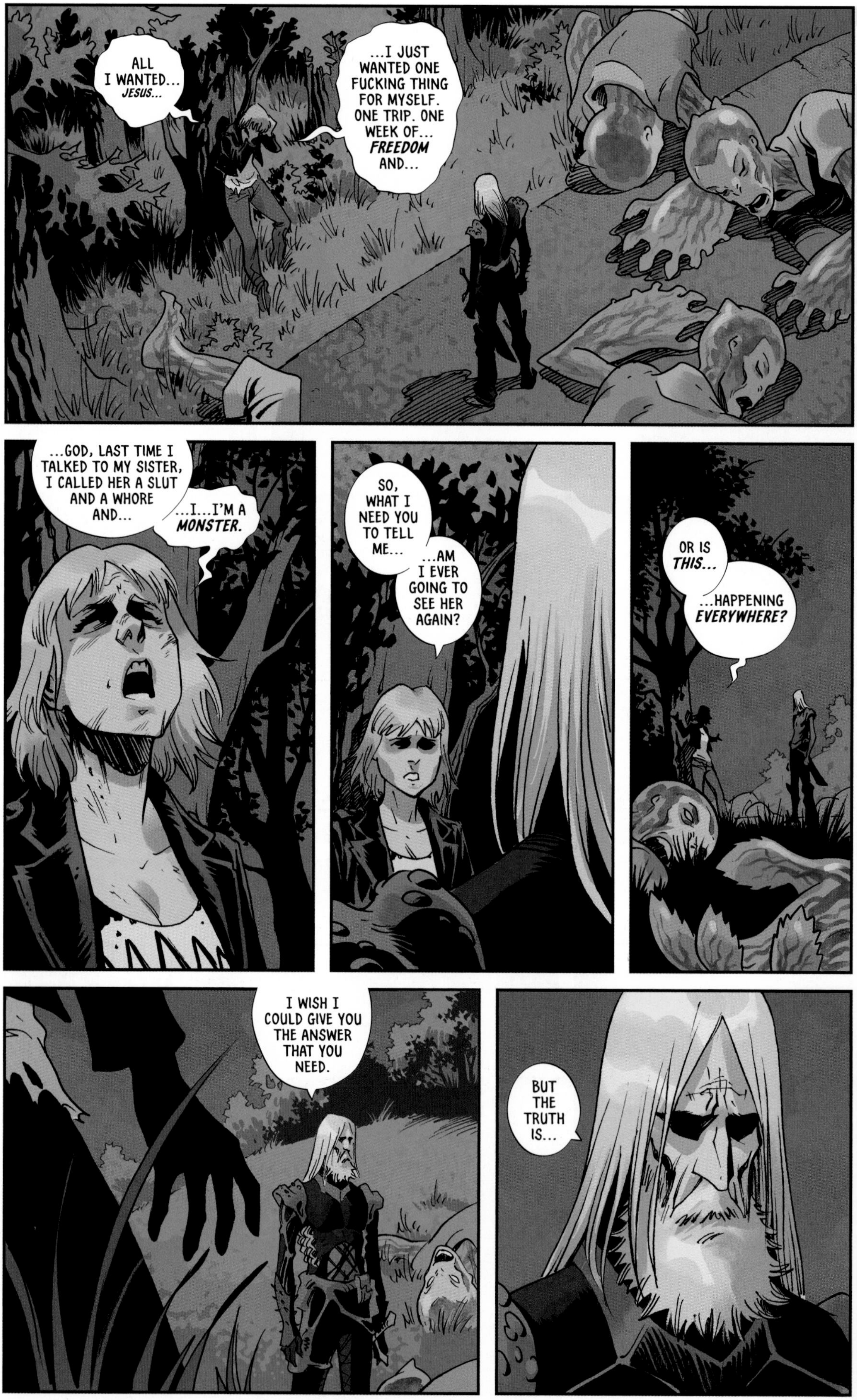

ALL I WANTED... JESUS...
...I JUST WANTED ONE FUCKING THING FOR MYSELF. ONE TRIP. ONE WEEK OF... FREEDOM AND...
...GOD, LAST TIME I TALKED TO MY SISTER, I CALLED HER A SLUT AND A WHORE AND...
...I...I'M A MONSTER.
SO, WHAT I NEED YOU TO TELL ME...
...AM I EVER GOING TO SEE HER AGAIN?
OR IS THIS...
...HAPPENING EVERYWHERE?
I WISH I COULD GIVE YOU THE ANSWER THAT YOU NEED.
BUT THE TRUTH IS...

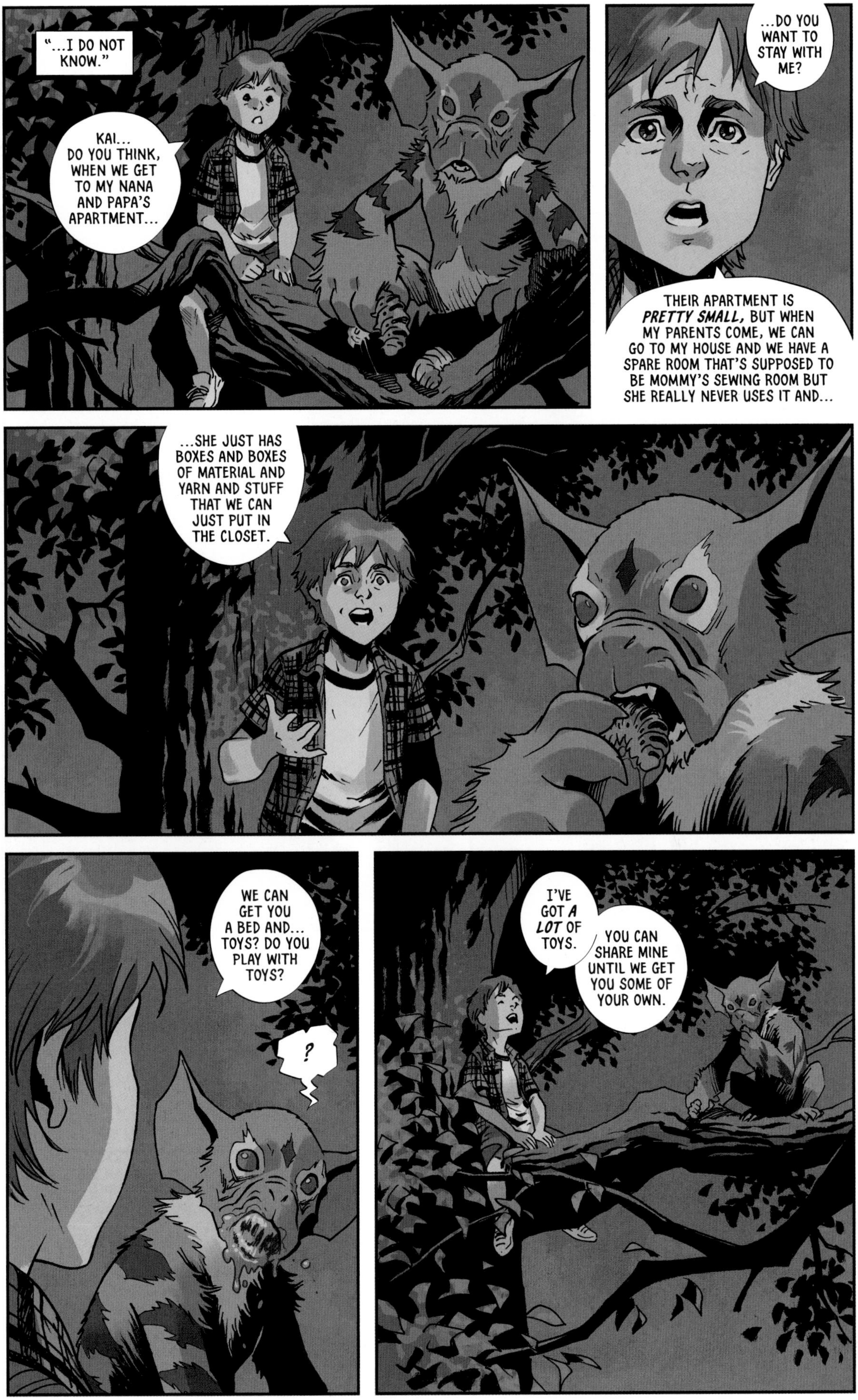
"...I DO NOT KNOW."
KAI... DO YOU THINK, WHEN WE GET TO MY NANA AND PAPA'S APARTMENT...
...DO YOU WANT TO STAY WITH ME?
THEIR APARTMENT IS ***PRETTY SMALL,*** BUT WHEN MY PARENTS COME, WE CAN GO TO MY HOUSE AND WE HAVE A SPARE ROOM THAT'S SUPPOSED TO BE MOMMY'S SEWING ROOM BUT SHE REALLY NEVER USES IT AND...
...SHE JUST HAS BOXES AND BOXES OF MATERIAL AND YARN AND STUFF THAT WE CAN JUST PUT IN THE CLOSET.
WE CAN GET YOU A BED AND... TOYS? DO YOU PLAY WITH TOYS?
?
I'VE GOT ***A LOT*** OF TOYS.
YOU CAN SHARE MINE UNTIL WE GET YOU SOME OF YOUR OWN.

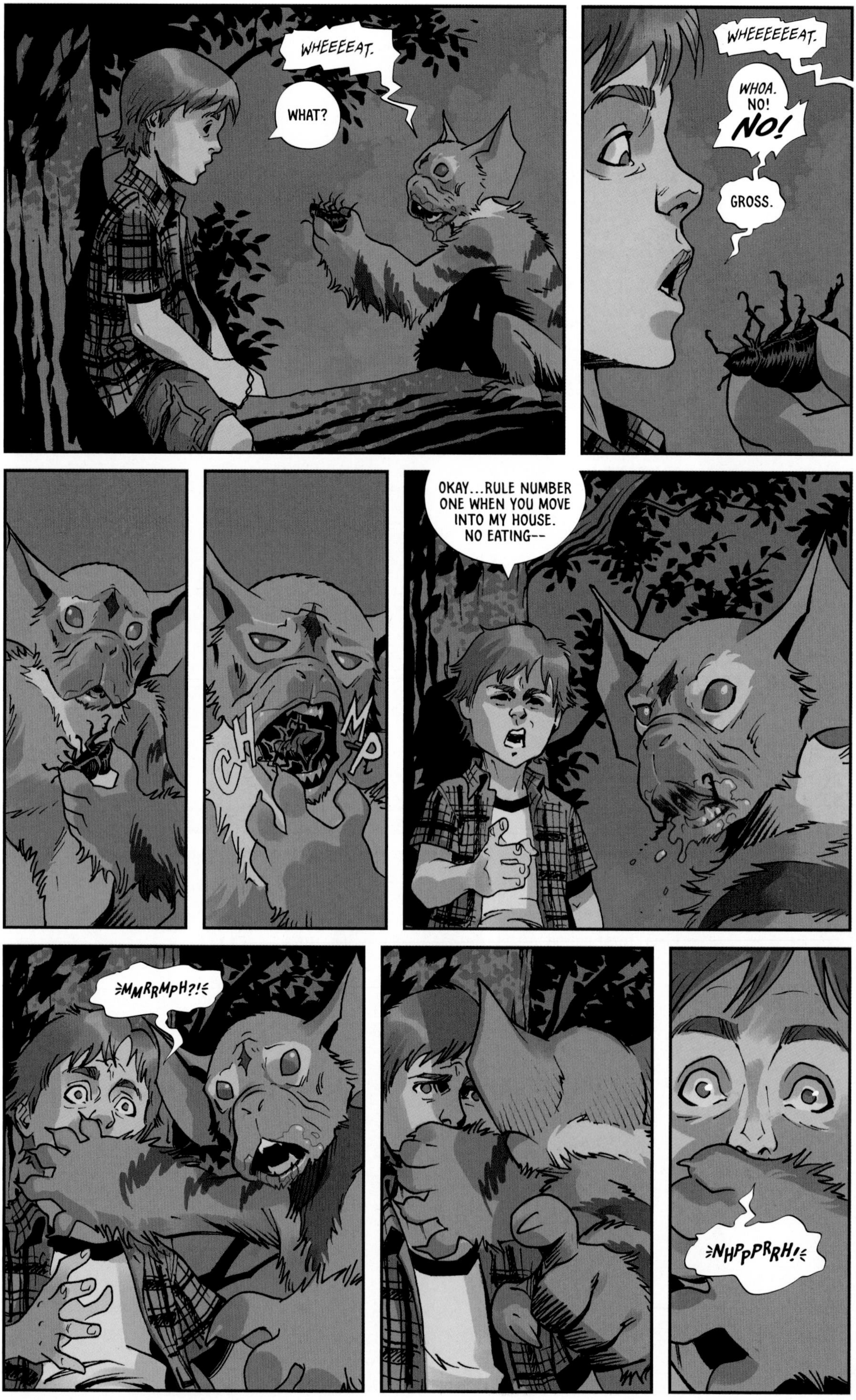
WHEEEEAT.
WHAT?
WHEEEEEEAT.
WHOA. NO! NO!
GROSS.
CH MP
OKAY...RULE NUMBER ONE WHEN YOU MOVE INTO MY HOUSE. NO EATING--
MMRRMPH?!
NHPPRRH!

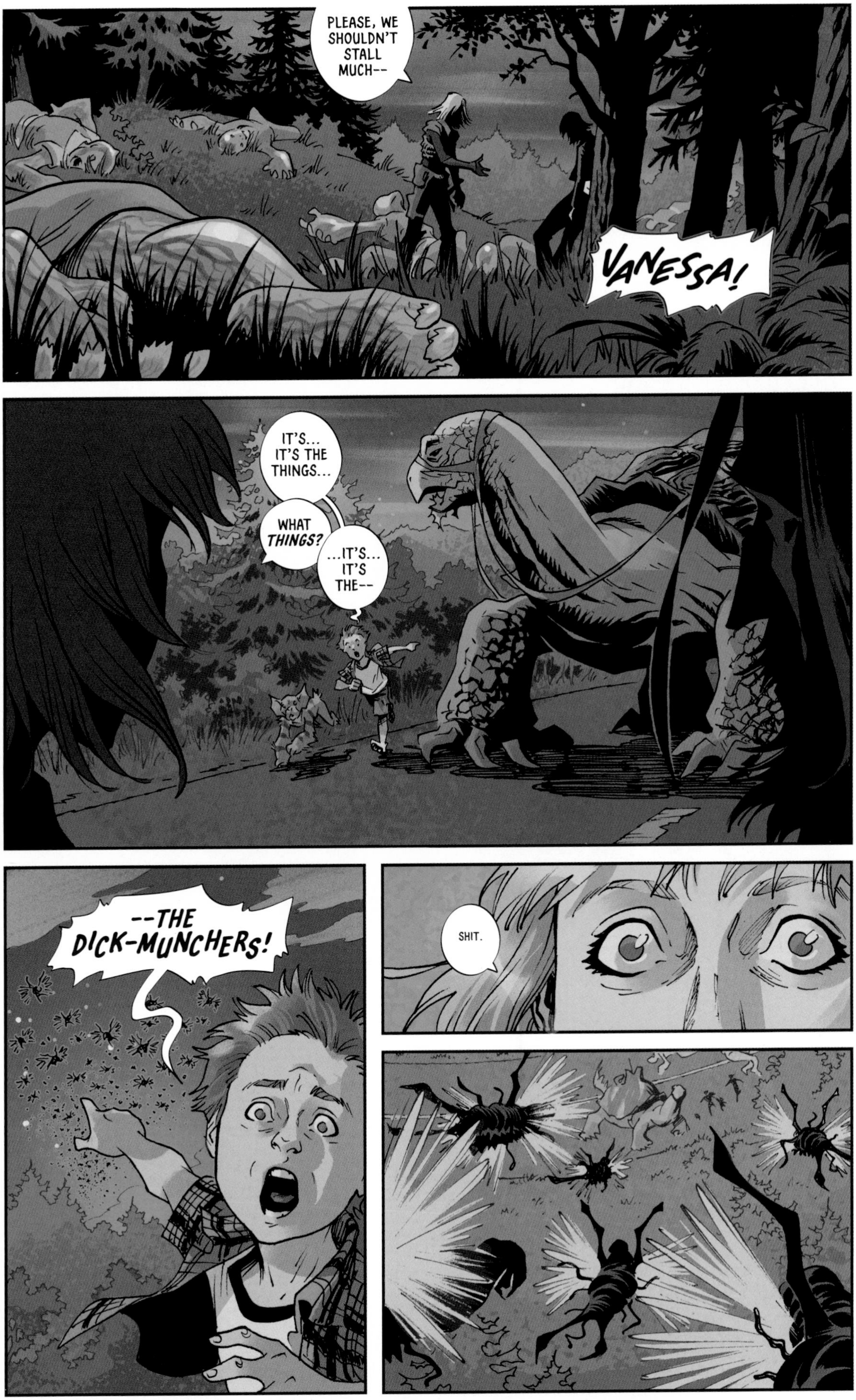
PLEASE, WE SHOULDN'T STALL MUCH--
VANESSA!
IT'S... IT'S THE THINGS...
WHAT THINGS?
...IT'S... IT'S THE--
--THE DICK-MUNCHERS!
SHIT.

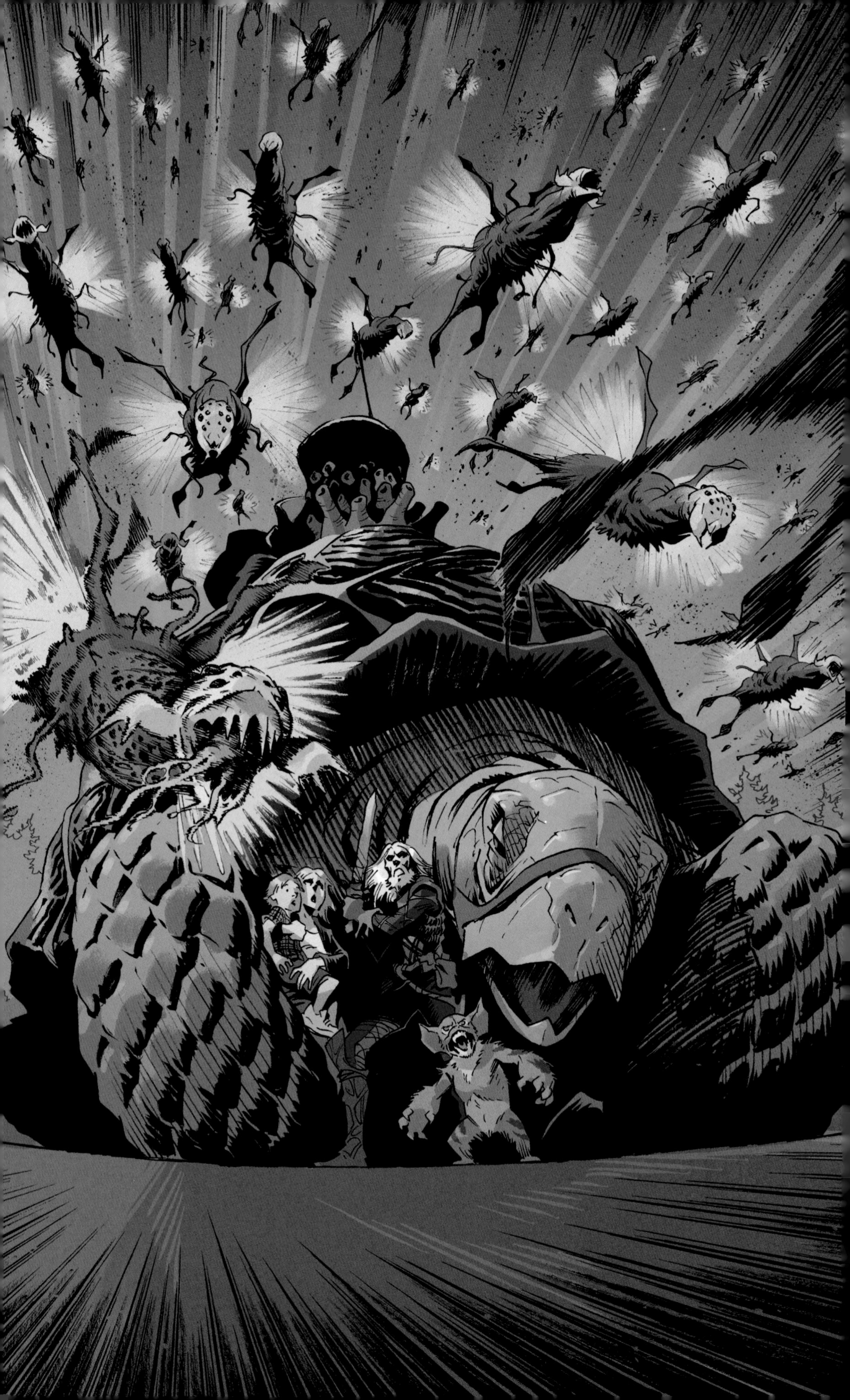

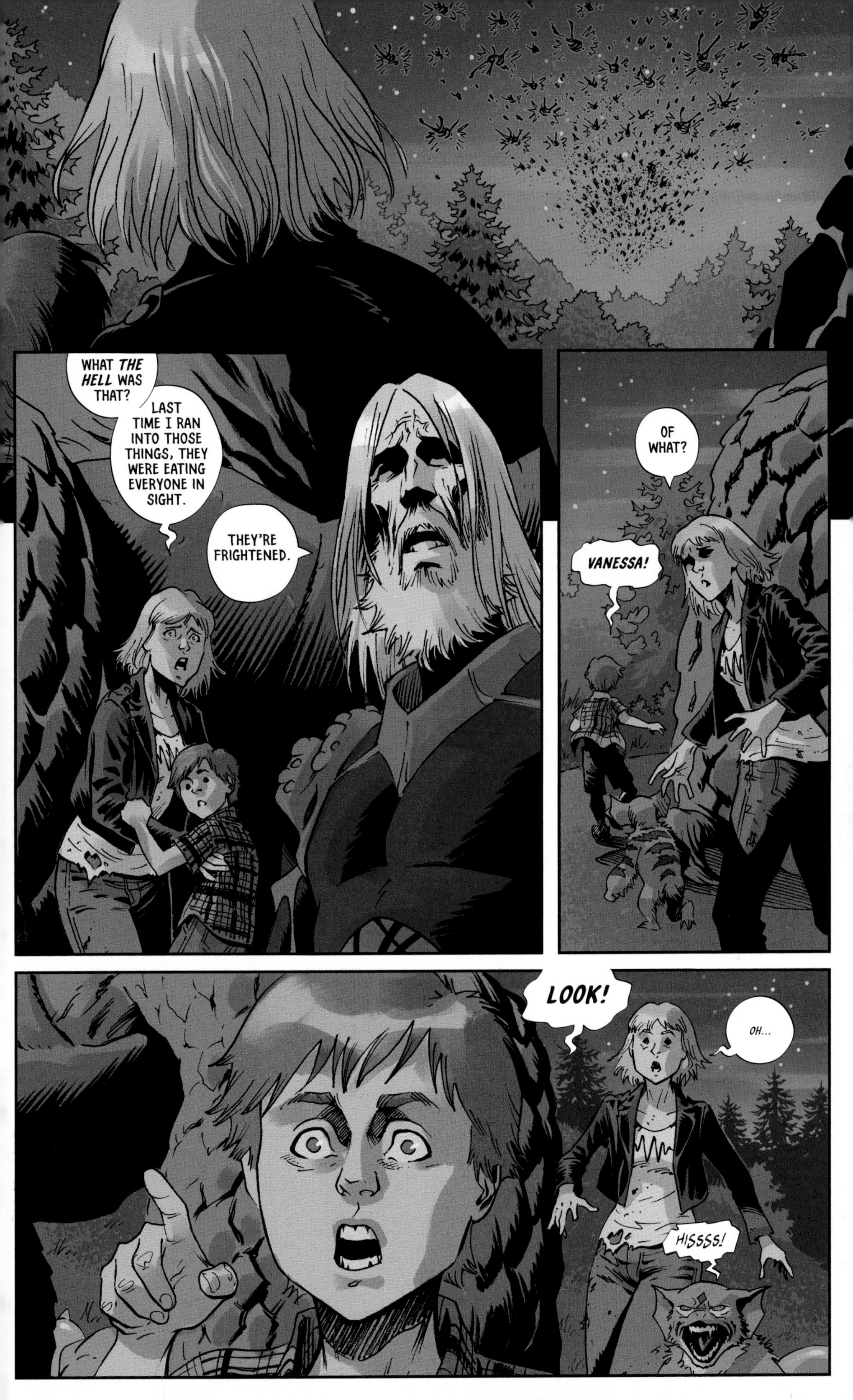
WHAT THE HELL WAS THAT?
LAST TIME I RAN INTO THOSE THINGS, THEY WERE EATING EVERYONE IN SIGHT.
THEY'RE FRIGHTENED.
OF WHAT?
VANESSA!
LOOK!
OH...
HISSSS!

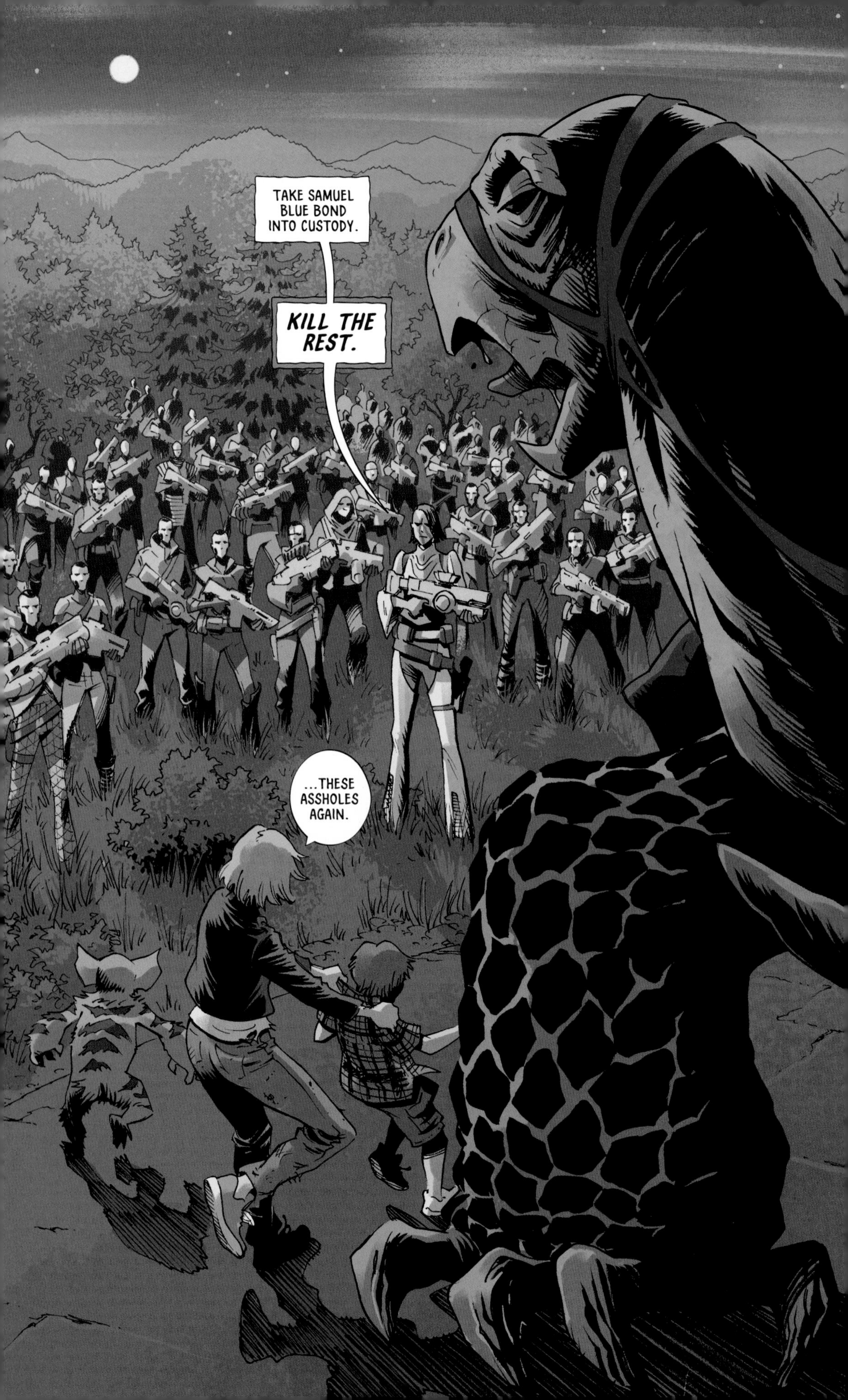
TAKE SAMUEL BLUE BOND INTO CUSTODY.
KILL THE REST.
...THESE ASSHOLES AGAIN.

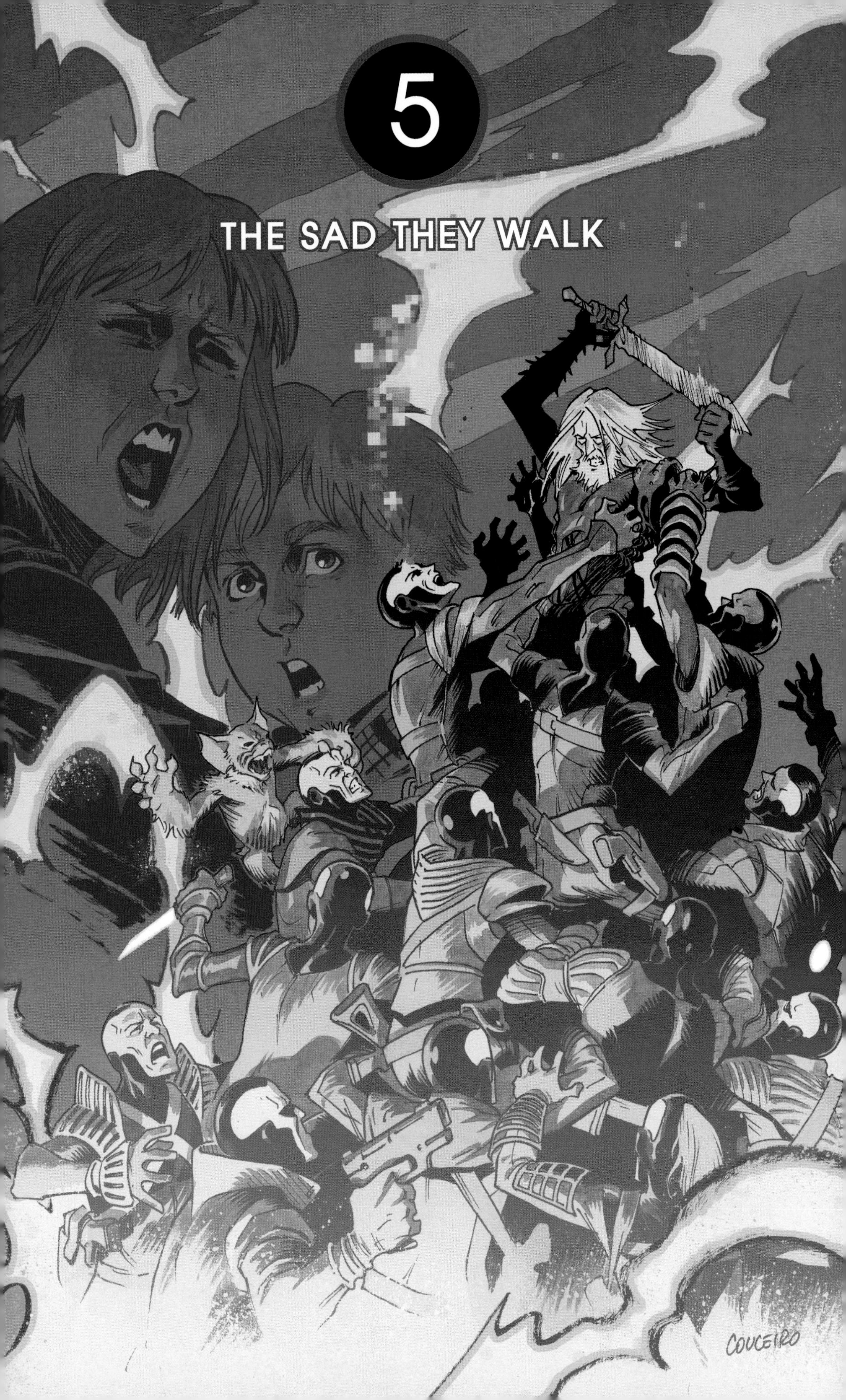
5
THE SAD THEY WALK
COUCEIRO

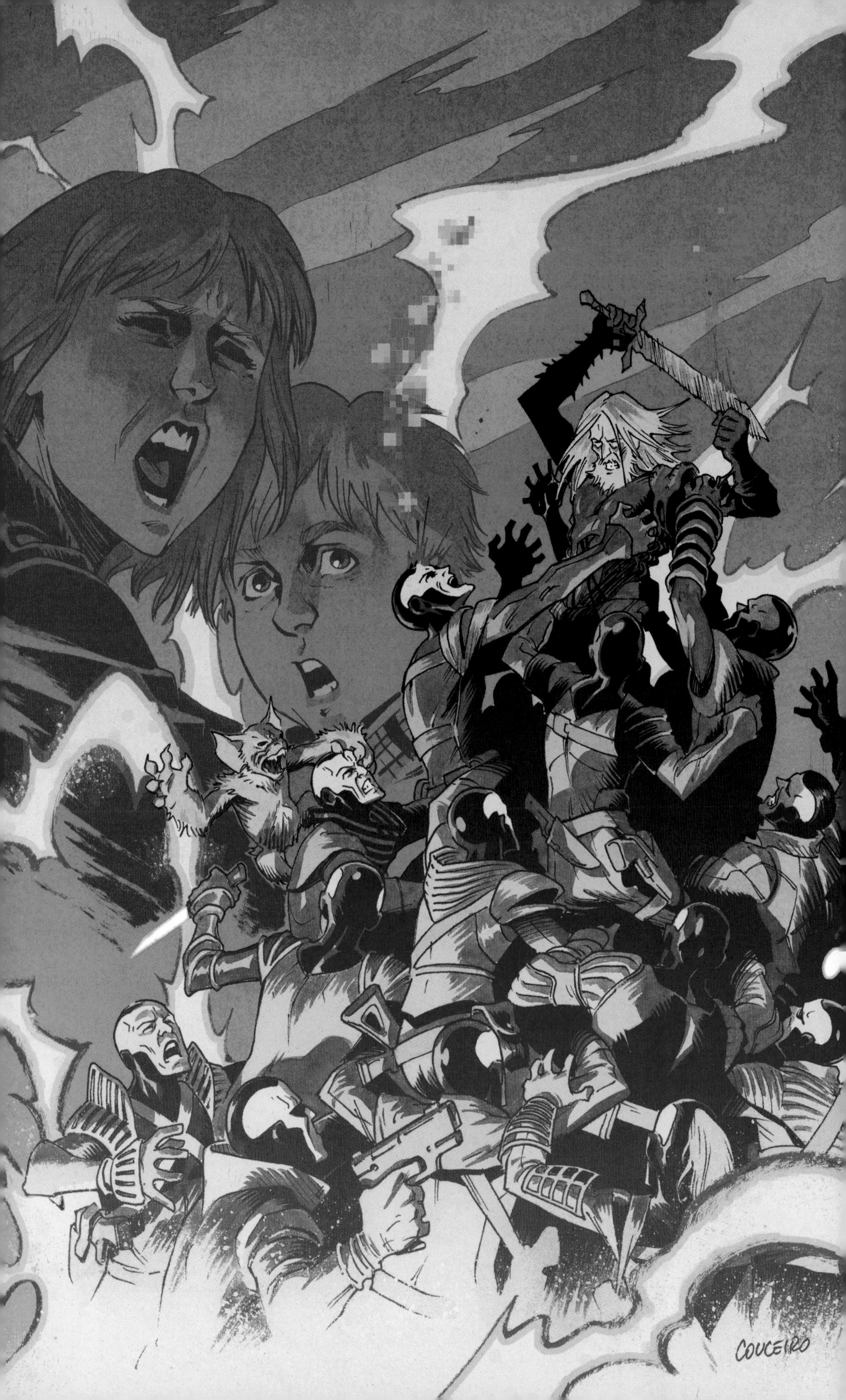
COUCEIRO

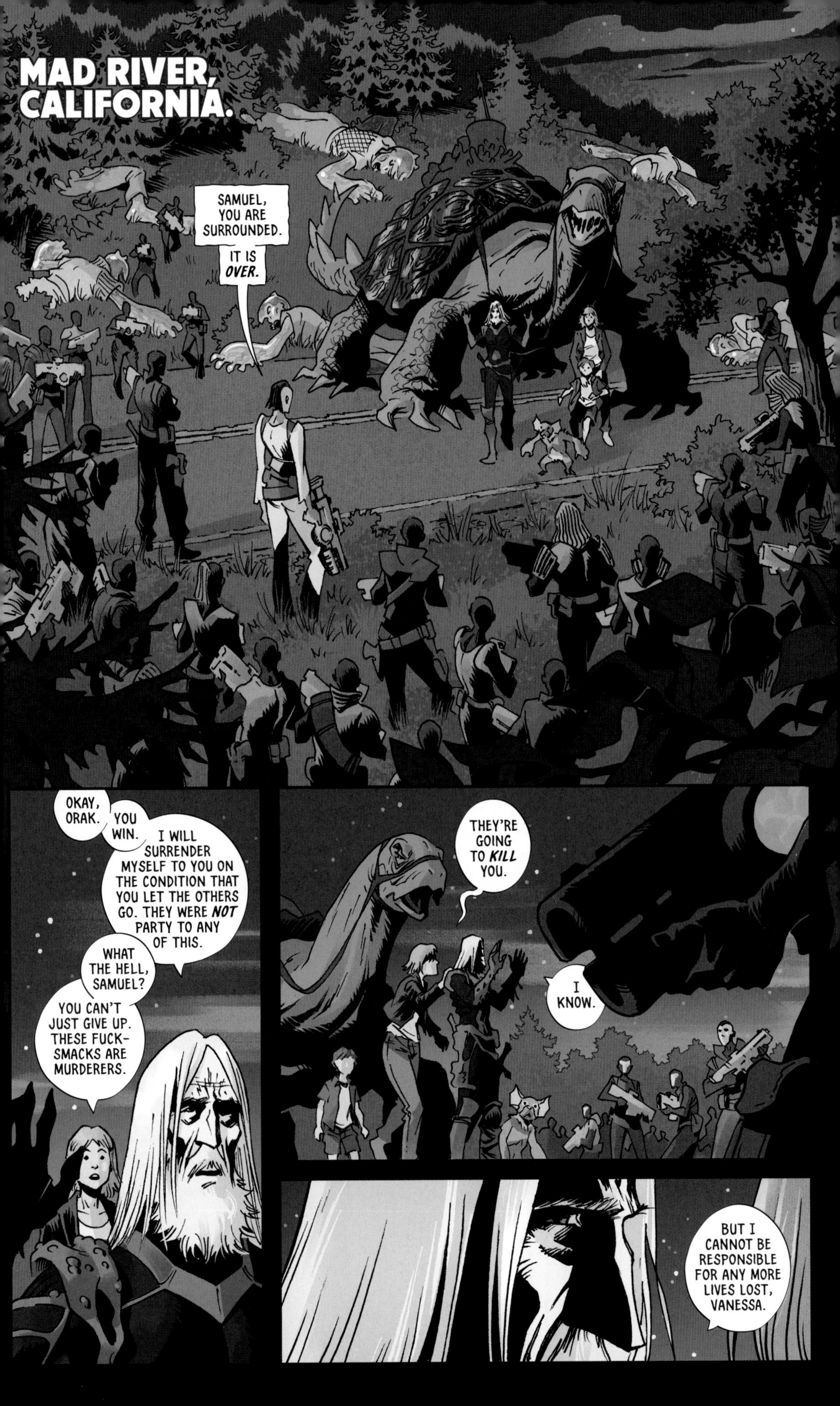
MAD RIVER, CALIFORNIA.
SAMUEL, YOU ARE SURROUNDED.
IT IS OVER.
OKAY, ORAK.
YOU WIN.
I WILL SURRENDER MYSELF TO YOU ON THE CONDITION THAT YOU LET THE OTHERS GO. THEY WERE NOT PARTY TO ANY OF THIS.
WHAT THE HELL, SAMUEL?
YOU CAN'T JUST GIVE UP. THESE FUCK-SMACKS ARE MURDERERS.
THEY'RE GOING TO KILL YOU.
I KNOW.
BUT I CANNOT BE RESPONSIBLE FOR ANY MORE LIVES LOST, VANESSA.

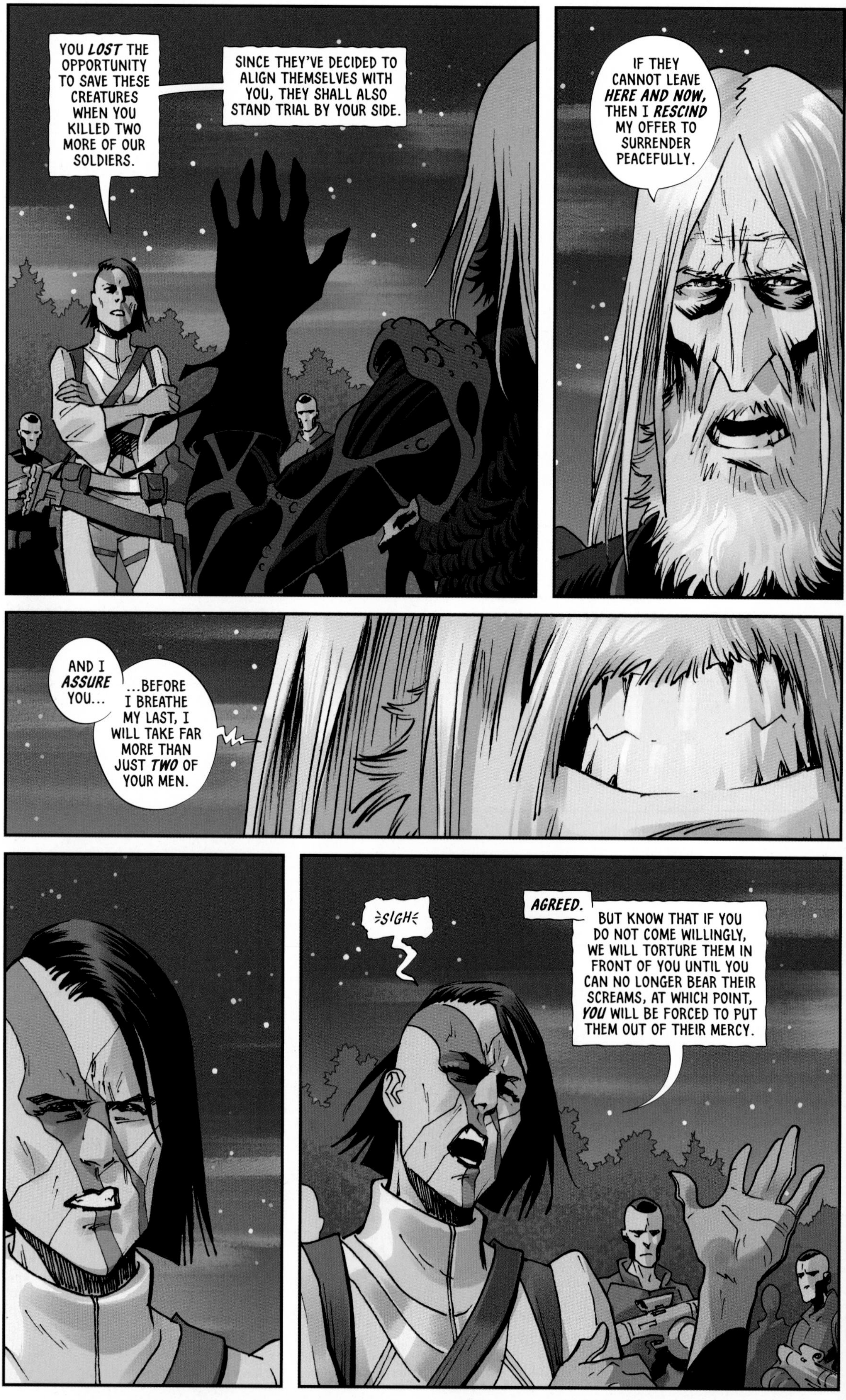
YOU LOST THE OPPORTUNITY TO SAVE THESE CREATURES WHEN YOU KILLED TWO MORE OF OUR SOLDIERS.
SINCE THEY'VE DECIDED TO ALIGN THEMSELVES WITH YOU, THEY SHALL ALSO STAND TRIAL BY YOUR SIDE.
IF THEY CANNOT LEAVE HERE AND NOW, THEN I RESCIND MY OFFER TO SURRENDER PEACEFULLY.
AND I ASSURE YOU...
...BEFORE I BREATHE MY LAST, I WILL TAKE FAR MORE THAN JUST TWO OF YOUR MEN.
SIGH
AGREED.
BUT KNOW THAT IF YOU DO NOT COME WILLINGLY, WE WILL TORTURE THEM IN FRONT OF YOU UNTIL YOU CAN NO LONGER BEAR THEIR SCREAMS, AT WHICH POINT, YOU WILL BE FORCED TO PUT THEM OUT OF THEIR MERCY.

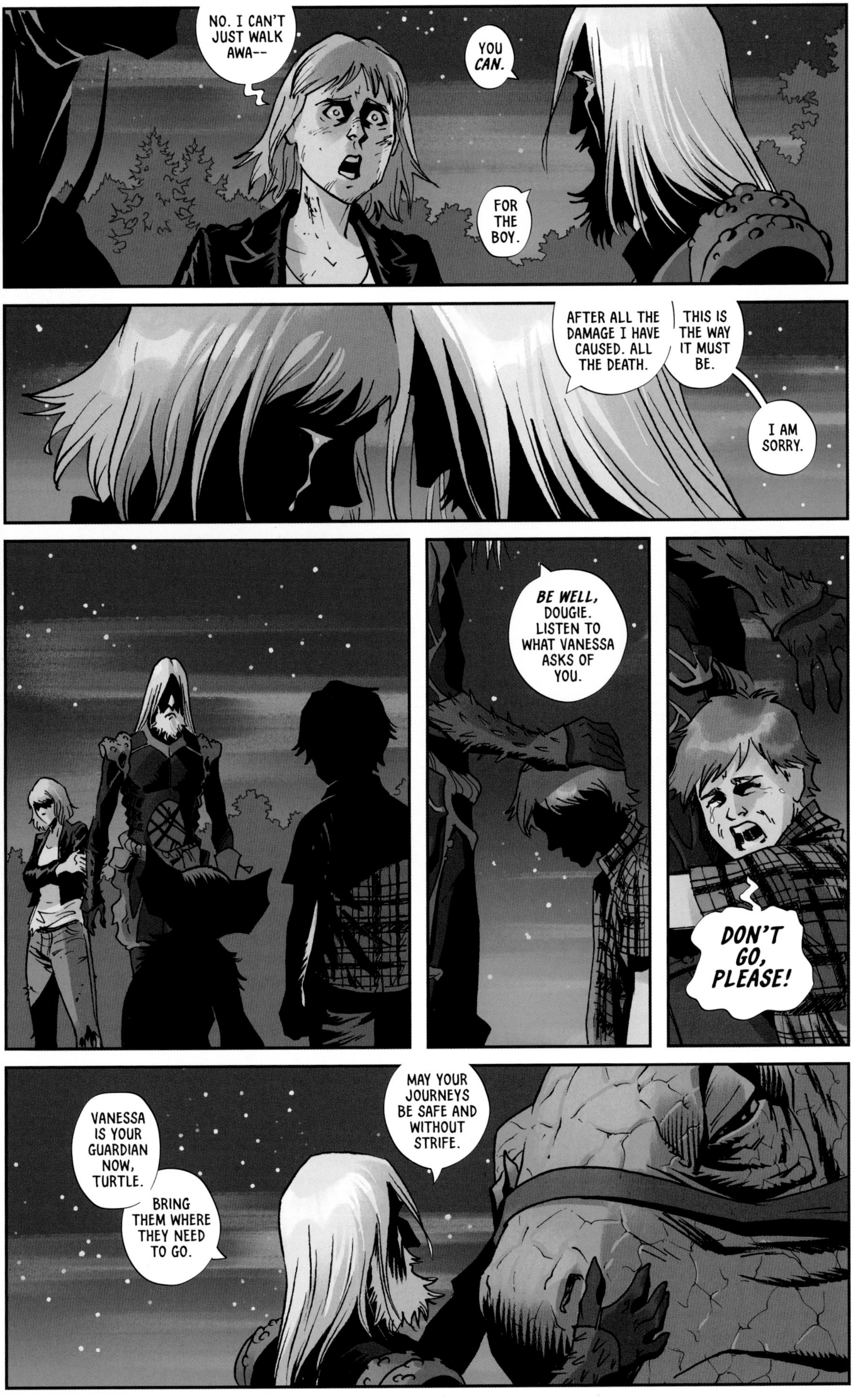
NO. I CAN'T JUST WALK AWA--
YOU *CAN.*
FOR THE BOY.
AFTER ALL THE DAMAGE I HAVE CAUSED. ALL THE DEATH.
THIS IS THE WAY IT MUST BE.
I AM SORRY.
BE WELL, DOUGIE. LISTEN TO WHAT VANESSA ASKS OF YOU.
DON'T GO, PLEASE!
VANESSA IS YOUR GUARDIAN NOW, TURTLE.
BRING THEM WHERE THEY NEED TO GO.
MAY YOUR JOURNEYS BE SAFE AND WITHOUT STRIFE.

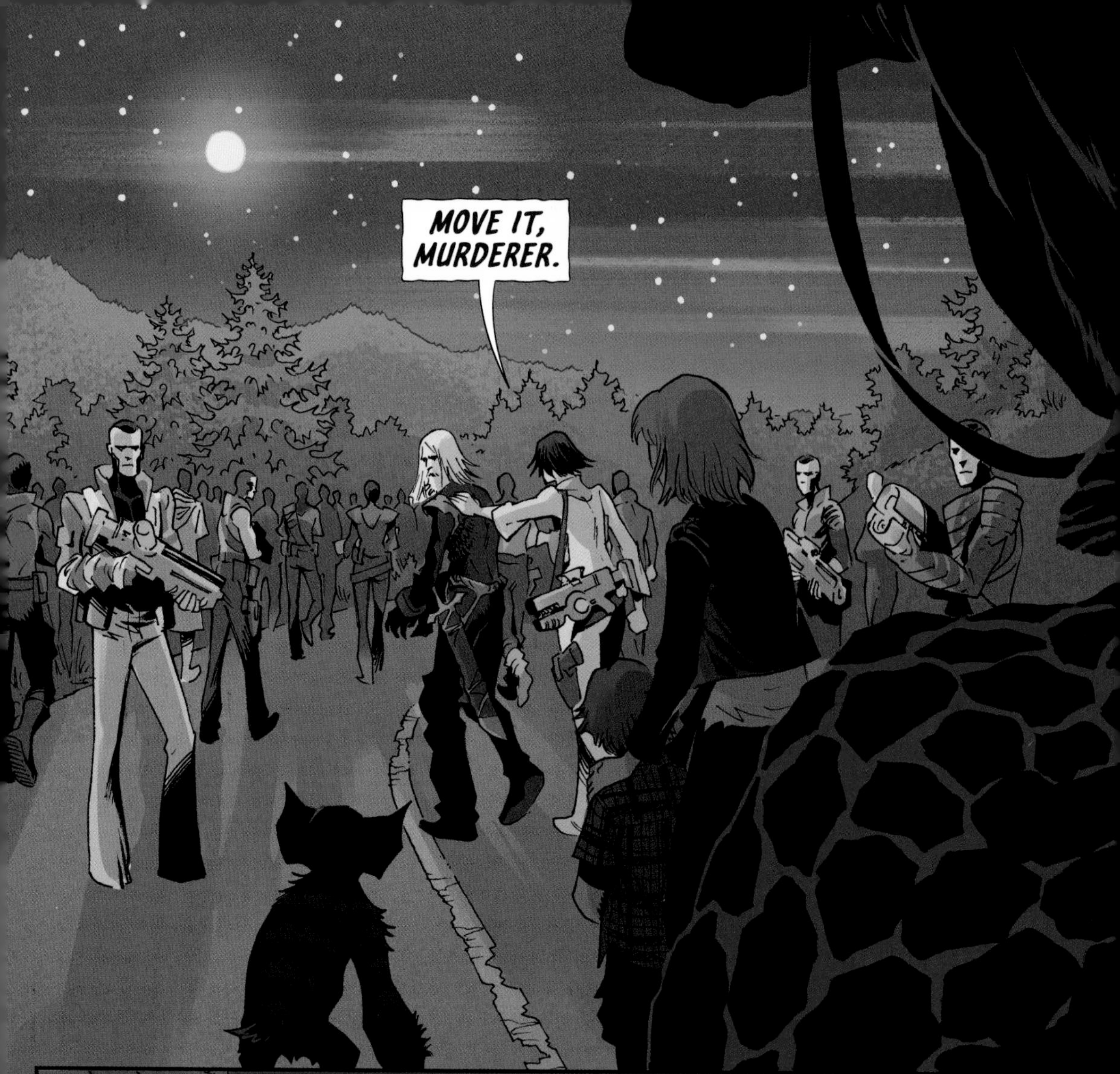
MOVE IT, MURDERER.

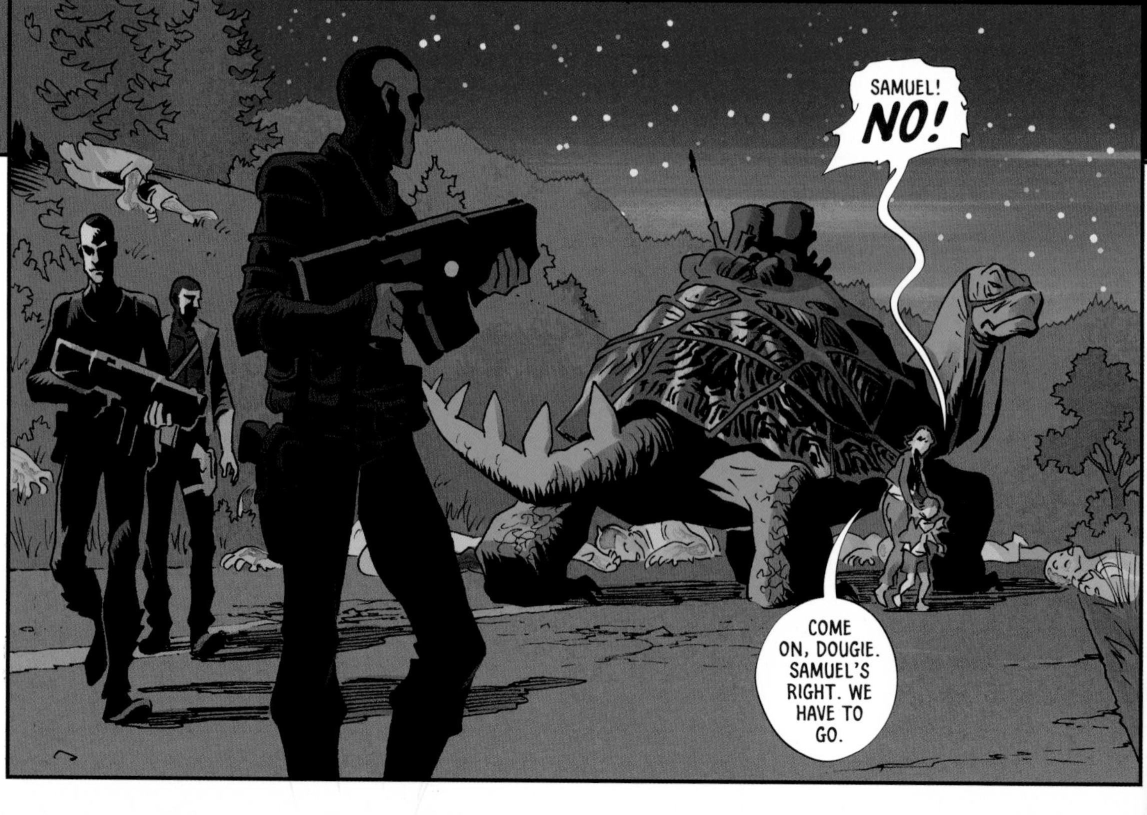
SAMUEL! NO!
COME ON, DOUGIE. SAMUEL'S RIGHT. WE HAVE TO GO.

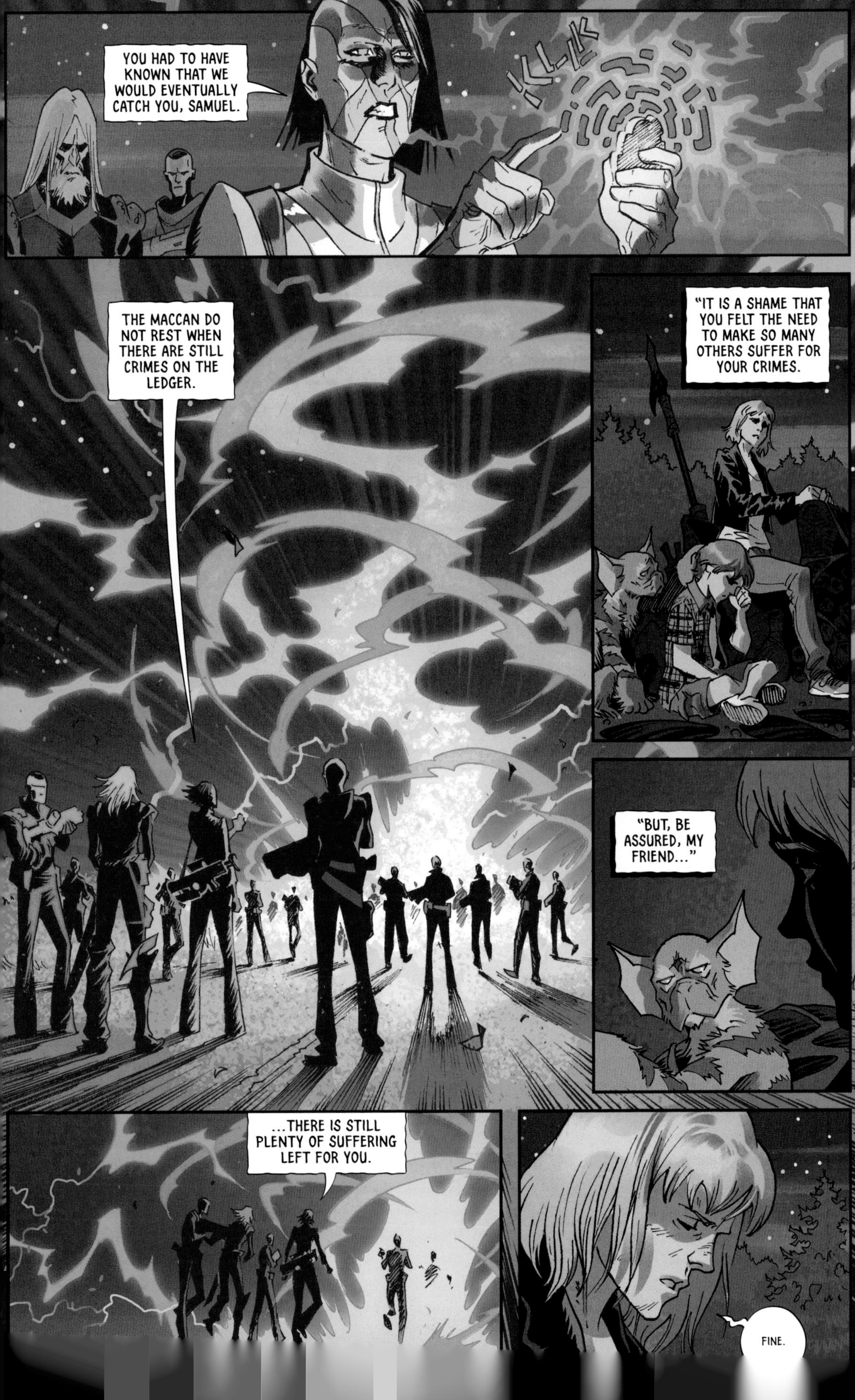
YOU HAD TO HAVE KNOWN THAT WE WOULD EVENTUALLY CATCH YOU, SAMUEL.
KLLK
THE MACCAN DO NOT REST WHEN THERE ARE STILL CRIMES ON THE LEDGER.
"IT IS A SHAME THAT YOU FELT THE NEED TO MAKE SO MANY OTHERS SUFFER FOR YOUR CRIMES.
"BUT, BE ASSURED, MY FRIEND..."
...THERE IS STILL PLENTY OF SUFFERING LEFT FOR YOU.
FINE.

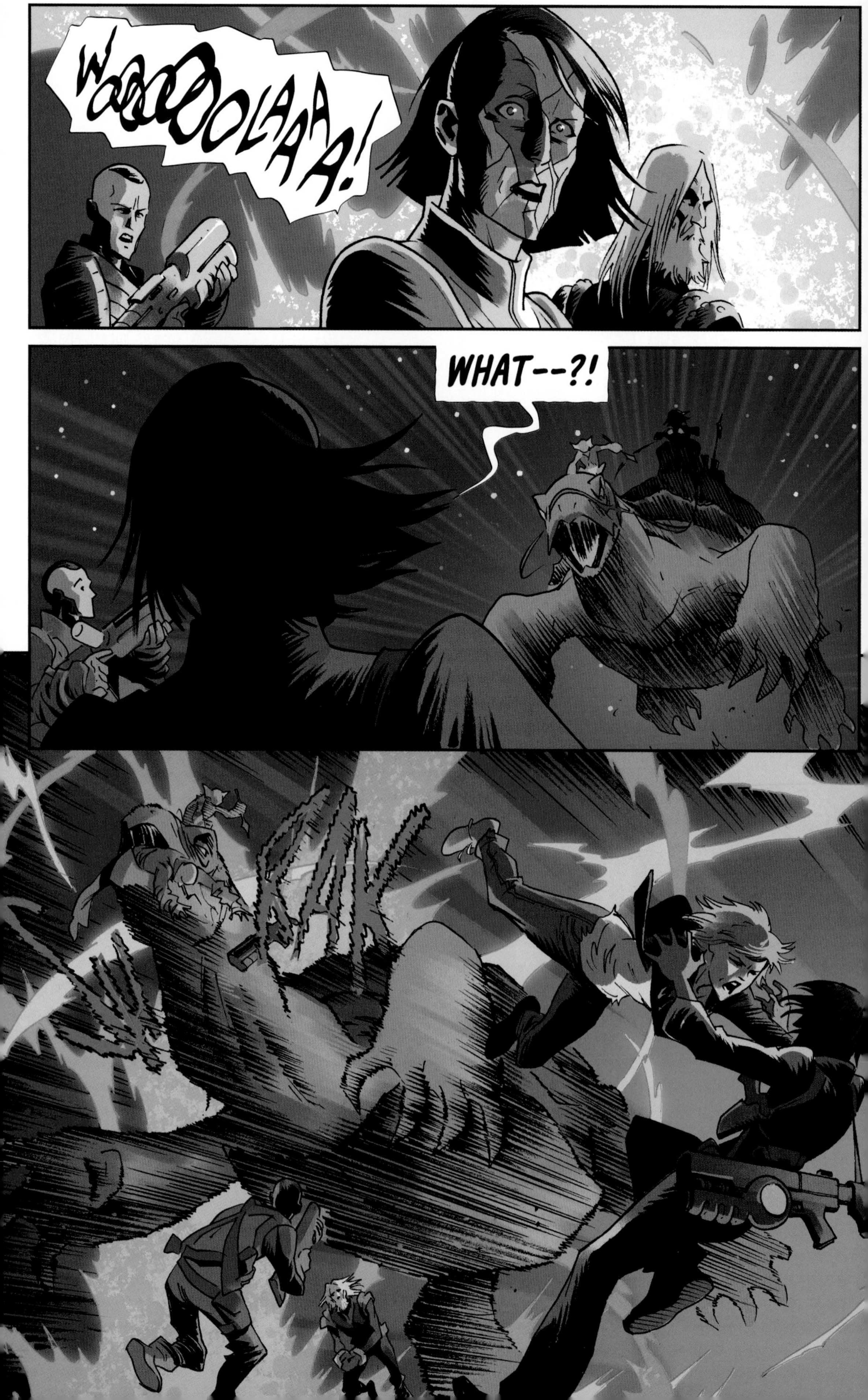
WOOOOOLAAAA!
WHAT--?!

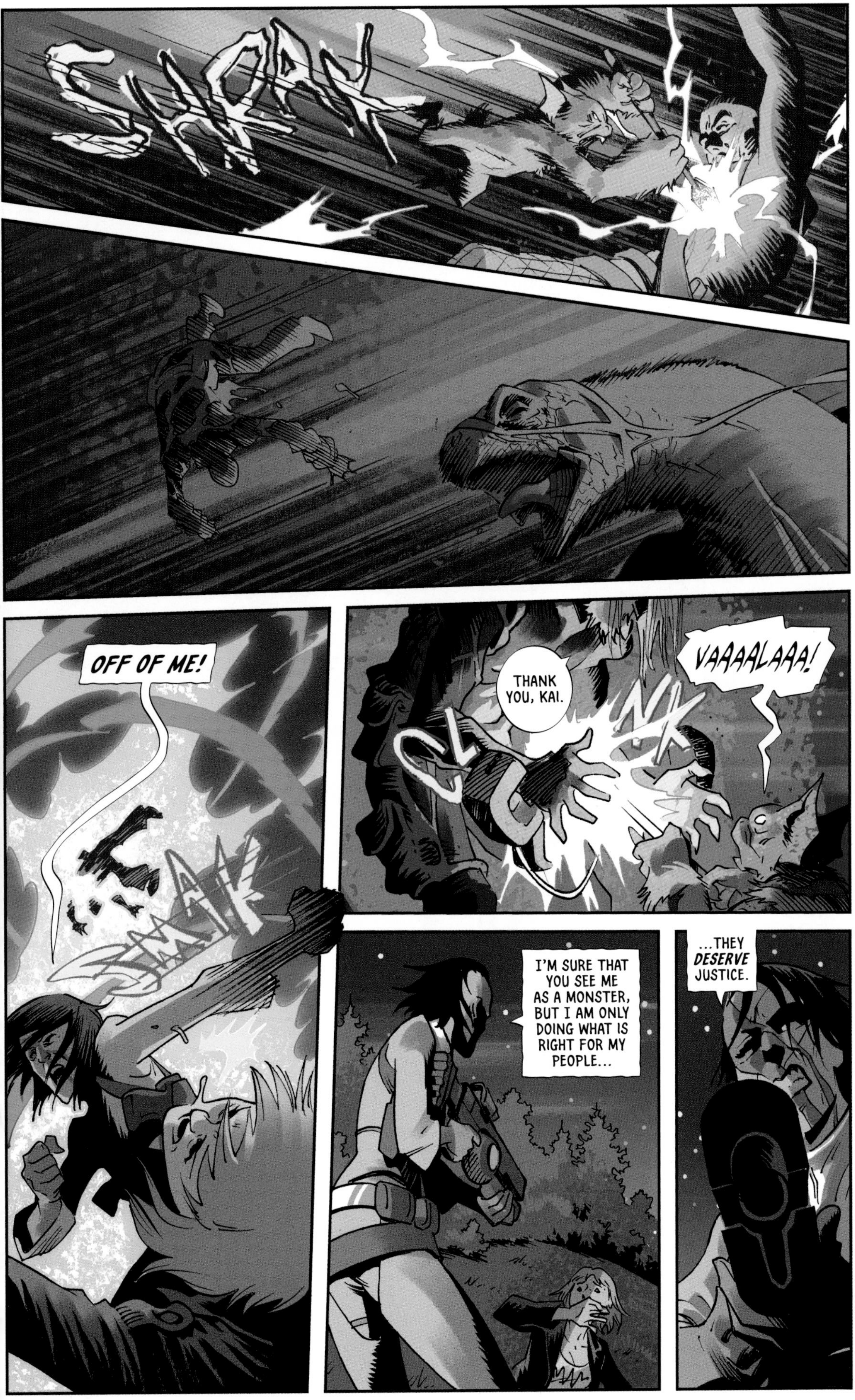
SHRAK
OFF OF ME!
THAT
THANK YOU, KAI.
CLANK
VAAAALAAA!
I'M SURE THAT YOU SEE ME AS A MONSTER, BUT I AM ONLY DOING WHAT IS RIGHT FOR MY PEOPLE...
...THEY *DESERVE* JUSTICE.

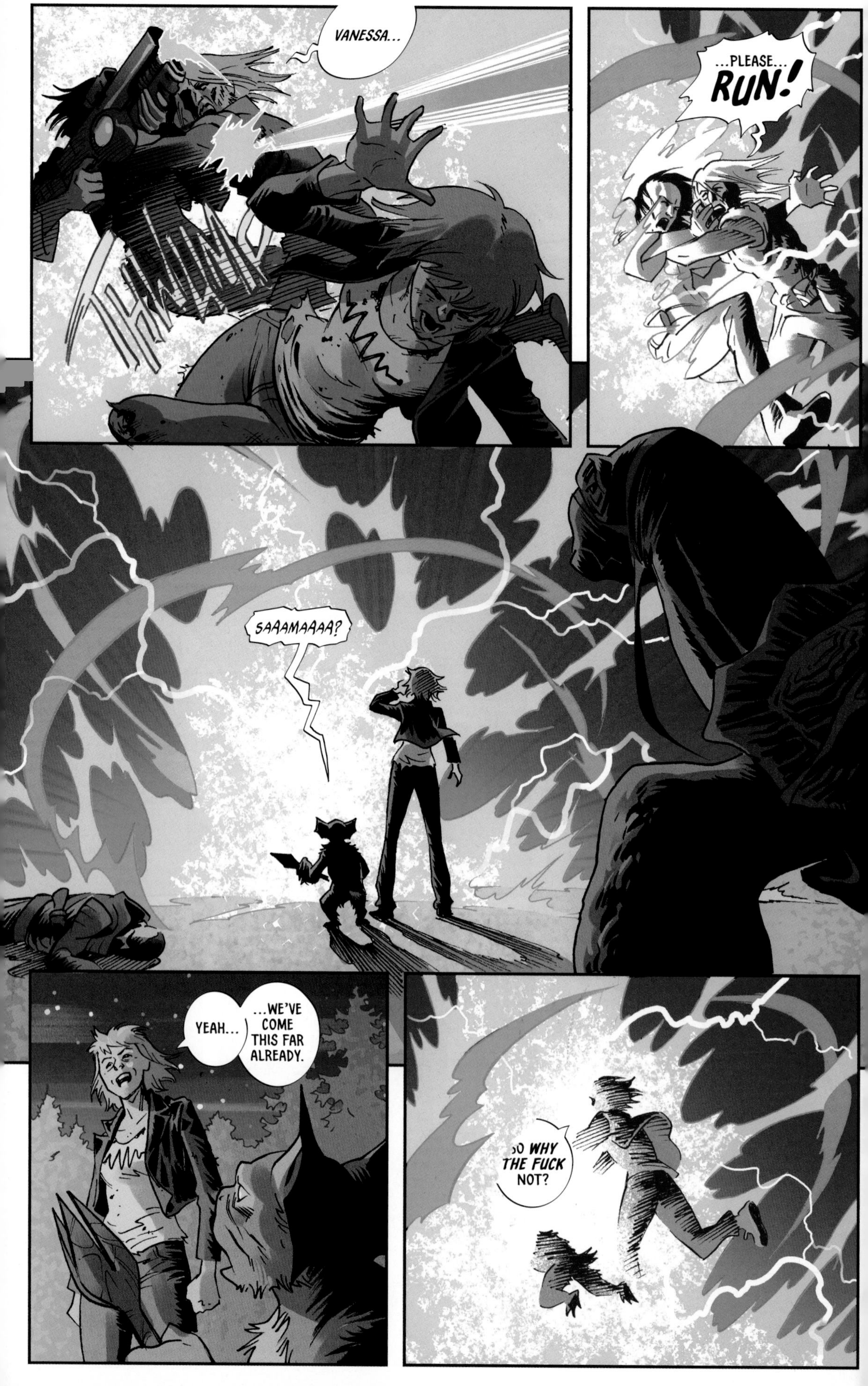
VANESSA...
...PLEASE... RUN!
SAAAMAAAA?
YEAH...
...WE'VE COME THIS FAR ALREADY.
SO WHY THE FUCK NOT?

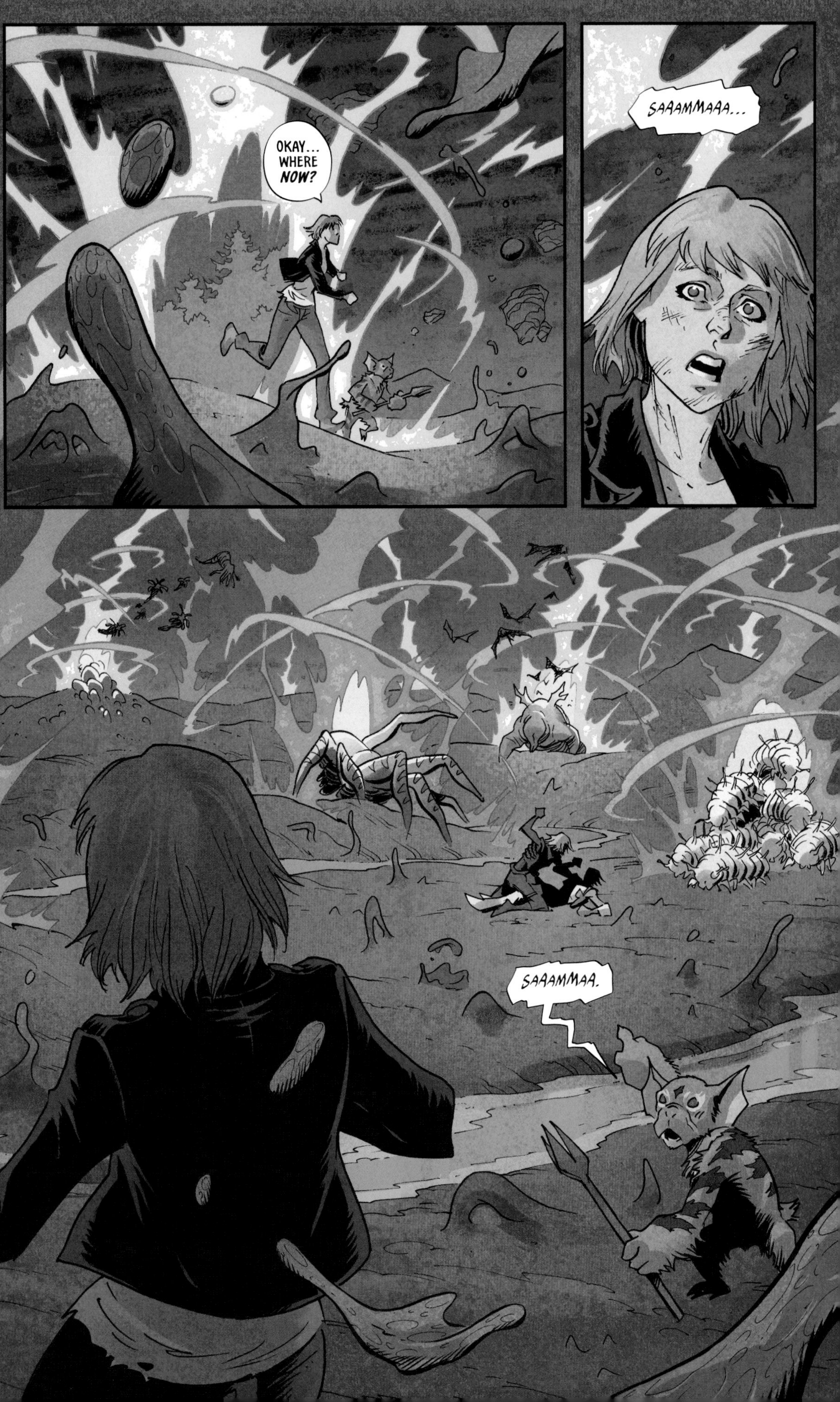
OKAY... WHERE *NOW?*
SAAAMMAAA...
SAAAMMAA.

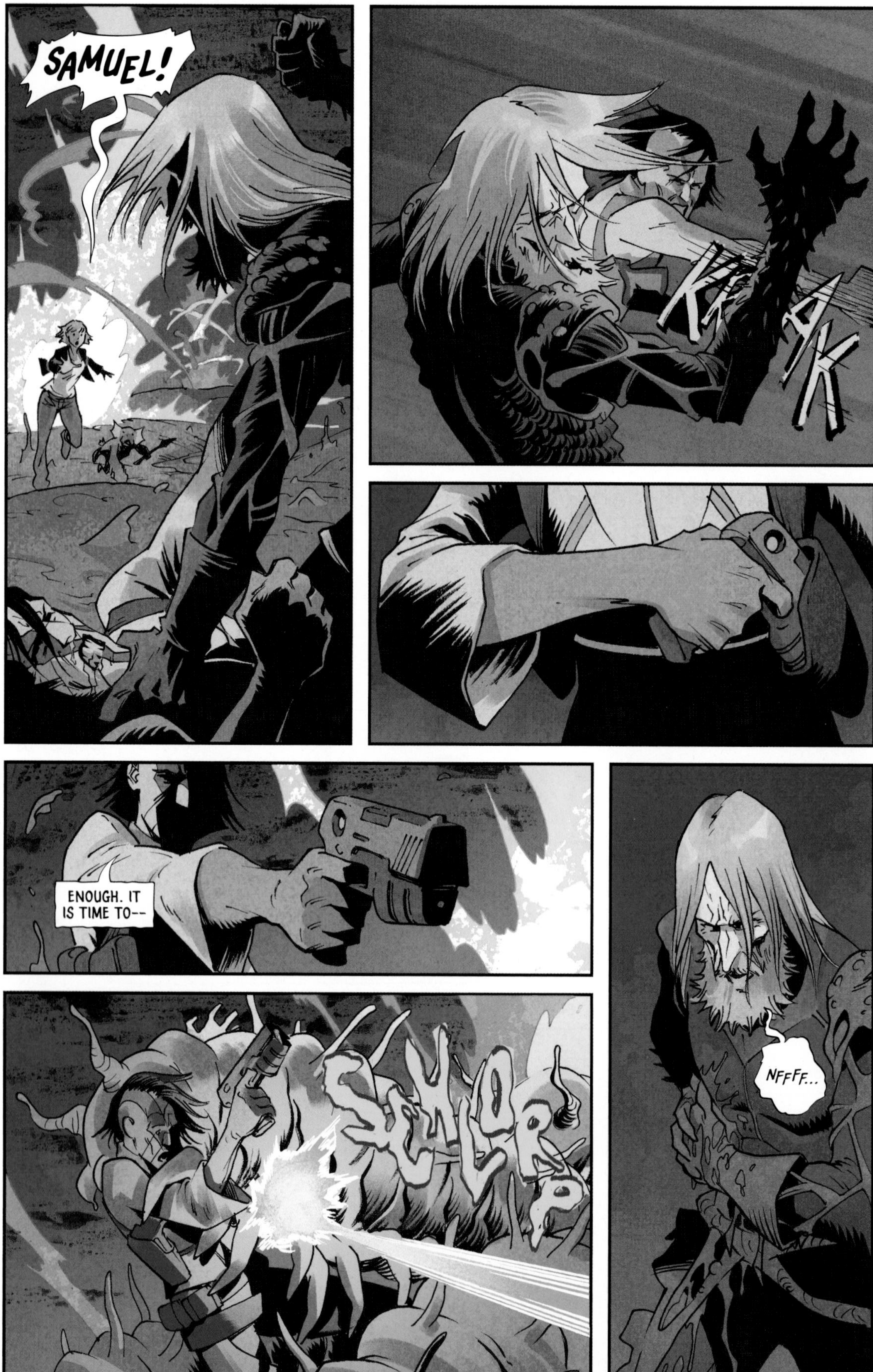

SAMUEL!
KRAAK
ENOUGH. IT IS TIME TO--
NFFFF...
SCHLORP

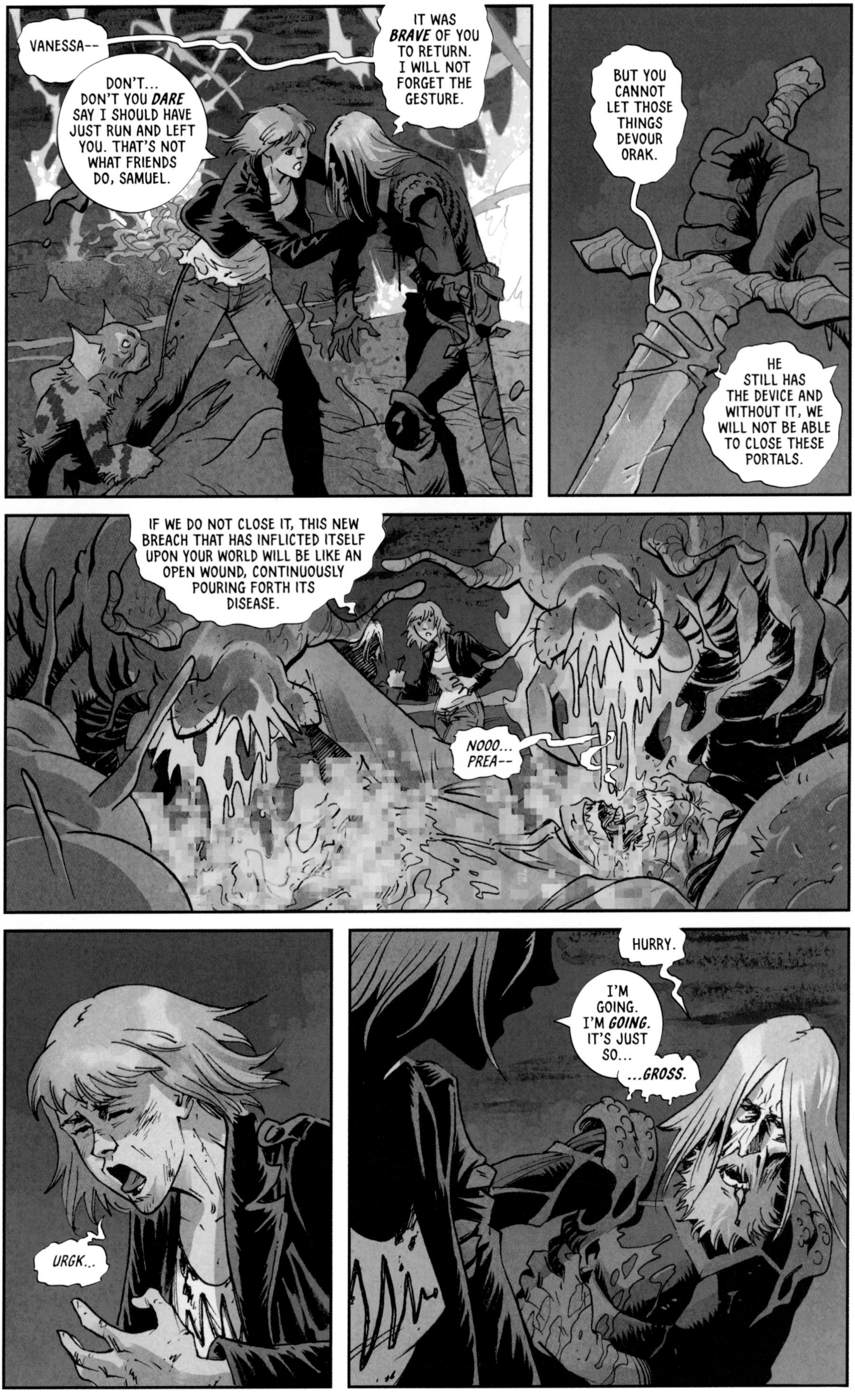
VANESSA--
DON'T... DON'T YOU ***DARE*** SAY I SHOULD HAVE JUST RUN AND LEFT YOU. THAT'S NOT WHAT FRIENDS DO, SAMUEL.
IT WAS ***BRAVE*** OF YOU TO RETURN. I WILL NOT FORGET THE GESTURE.
BUT YOU CANNOT LET THOSE THINGS DEVOUR ORAK.
HE STILL HAS THE DEVICE AND WITHOUT IT, WE WILL NOT BE ABLE TO CLOSE THESE PORTALS.
IF WE DO NOT CLOSE IT, THIS NEW BREACH THAT HAS INFLICTED ITSELF UPON YOUR WORLD WILL BE LIKE AN OPEN WOUND, CONTINUOUSLY POURING FORTH ITS DISEASE.
NOOO... PREA--
URGK...
HURRY.
I'M GOING. I'M ***GOING.*** IT'S JUST SO...
...GROSS.

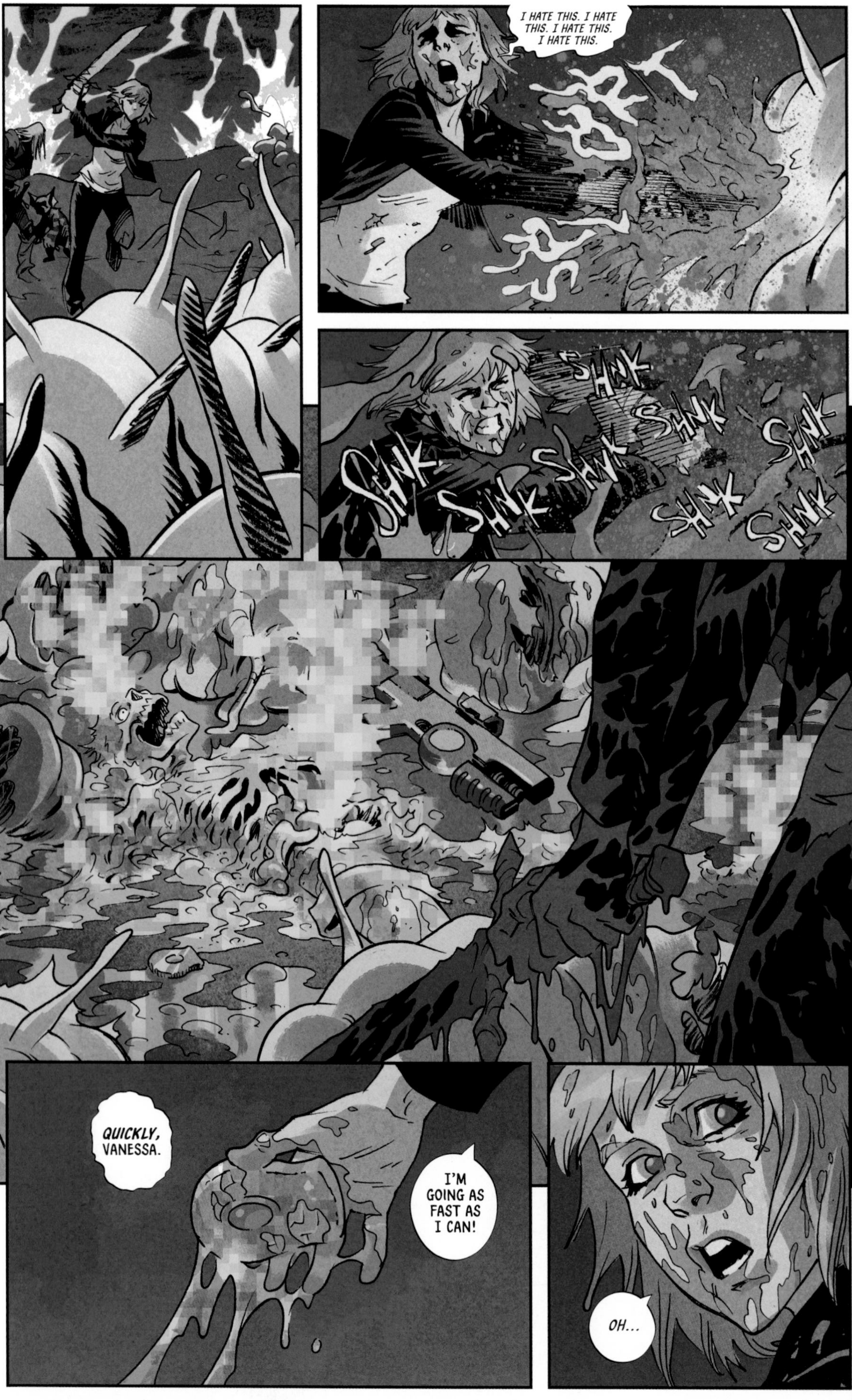
I HATE THIS. I HATE THIS. I HATE THIS. I HATE THIS.
SHNK SHNK SHNK SHNK SHNK SHNK SHNK SHNK
QUICKLY, VANESSA.
I'M GOING AS FAST AS I CAN!
OH...

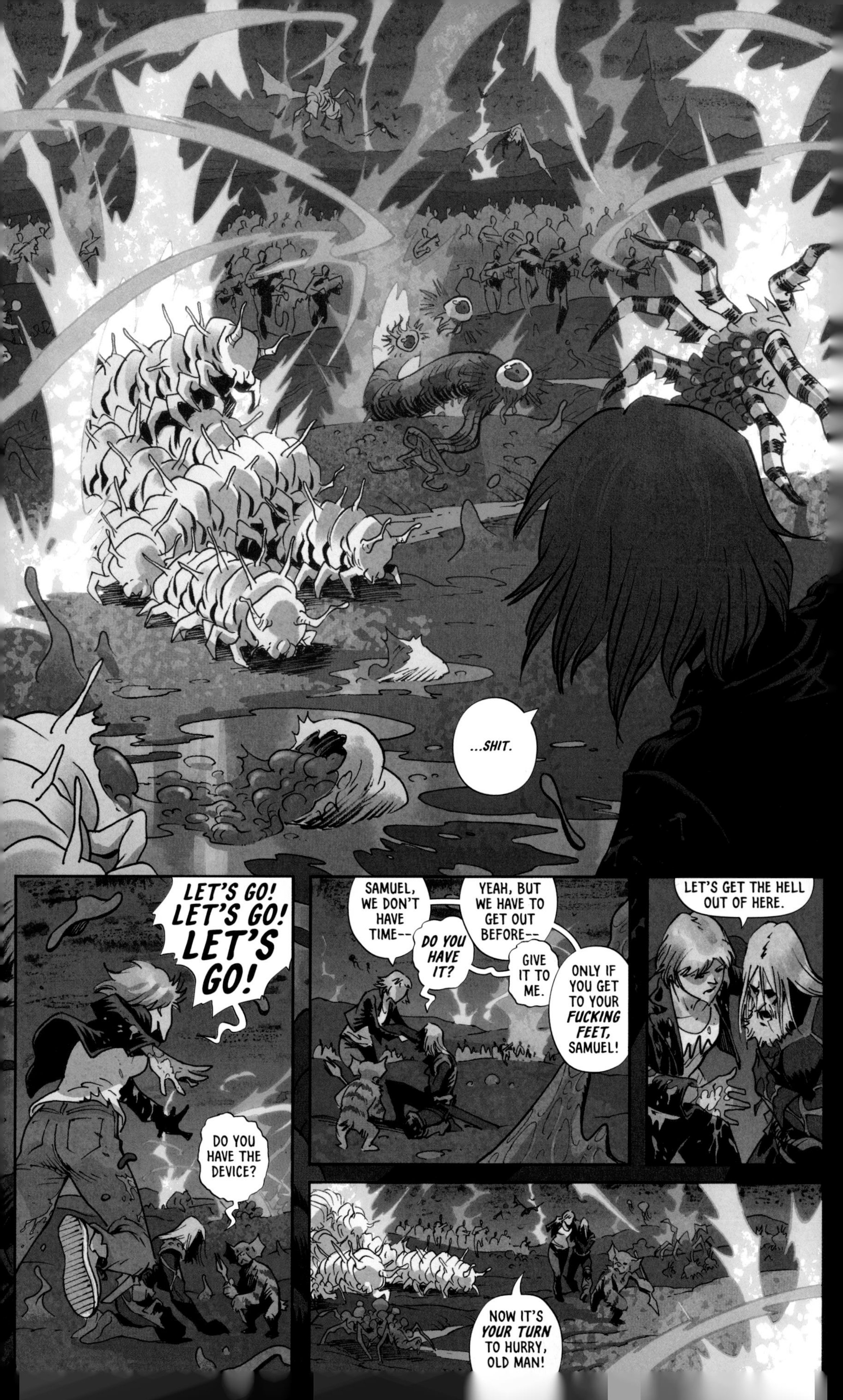
...SHIT.
LET'S GO! LET'S GO! LET'S GO!
DO YOU HAVE THE DEVICE?
SAMUEL, WE DON'T HAVE TIME--
YEAH, BUT WE HAVE TO GET OUT BEFORE--
DO YOU HAVE IT?
GIVE IT TO ME.
ONLY IF YOU GET TO YOUR ***FUCKING FEET,*** SAMUEL!
LET'S GET THE HELL OUT OF HERE.
NOW IT'S ***YOUR TURN*** TO HURRY, OLD MAN!

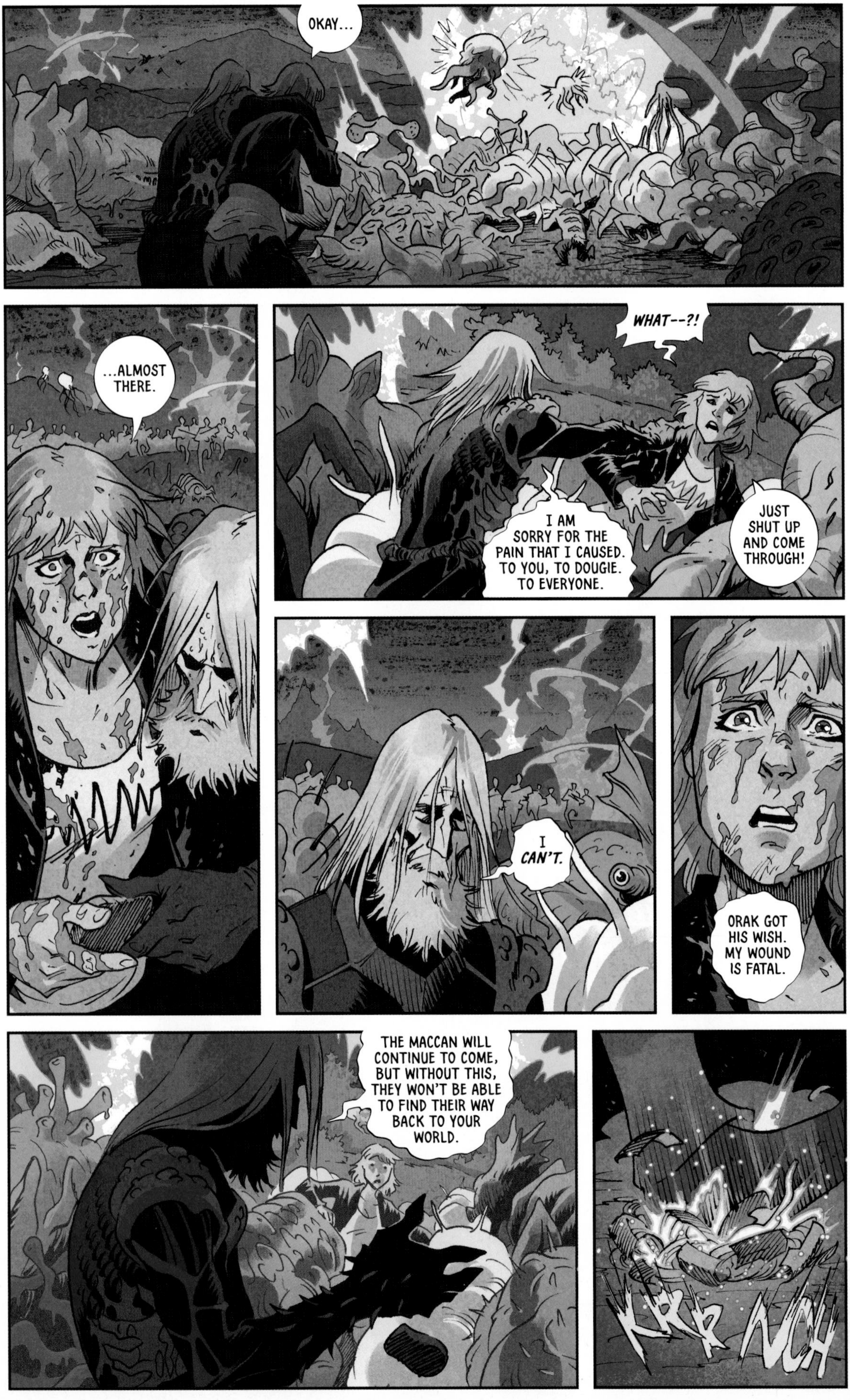
OKAY...
...ALMOST THERE.
WHAT--?!
I AM SORRY FOR THE PAIN THAT I CAUSED. TO YOU, TO DOUGIE. TO EVERYONE.
JUST SHUT UP AND COME THROUGH!
I CAN'T.
ORAK GOT HIS WISH. MY WOUND IS FATAL.
THE MACCAN WILL CONTINUE TO COME, BUT WITHOUT THIS, THEY WON'T BE ABLE TO FIND THEIR WAY BACK TO YOUR WORLD.
KRRR NCH

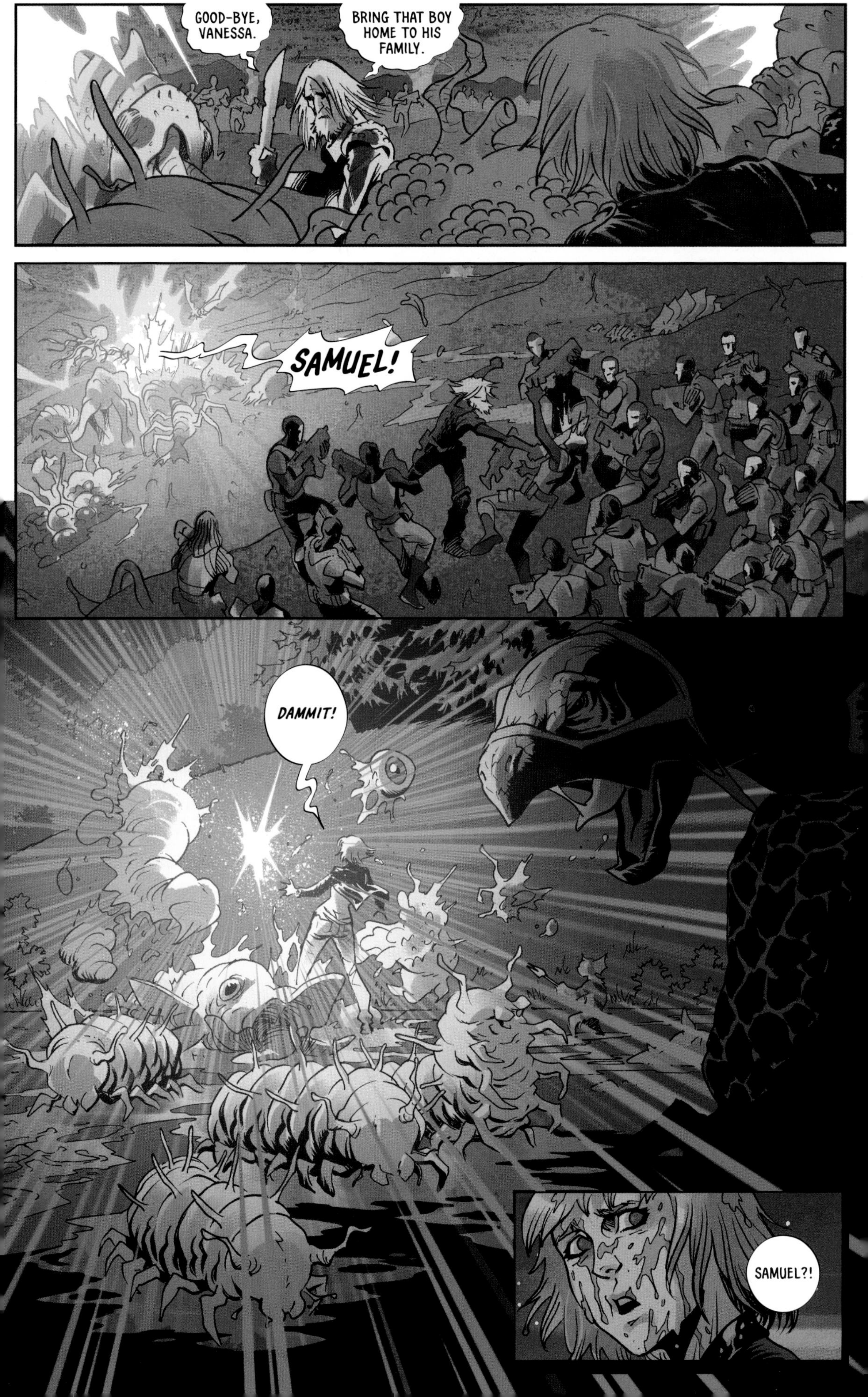
GOOD-BYE, VANESSA.
BRING THAT BOY HOME TO HIS FAMILY.
SAMUEL!
DAMMIT!
SAMUEL?!

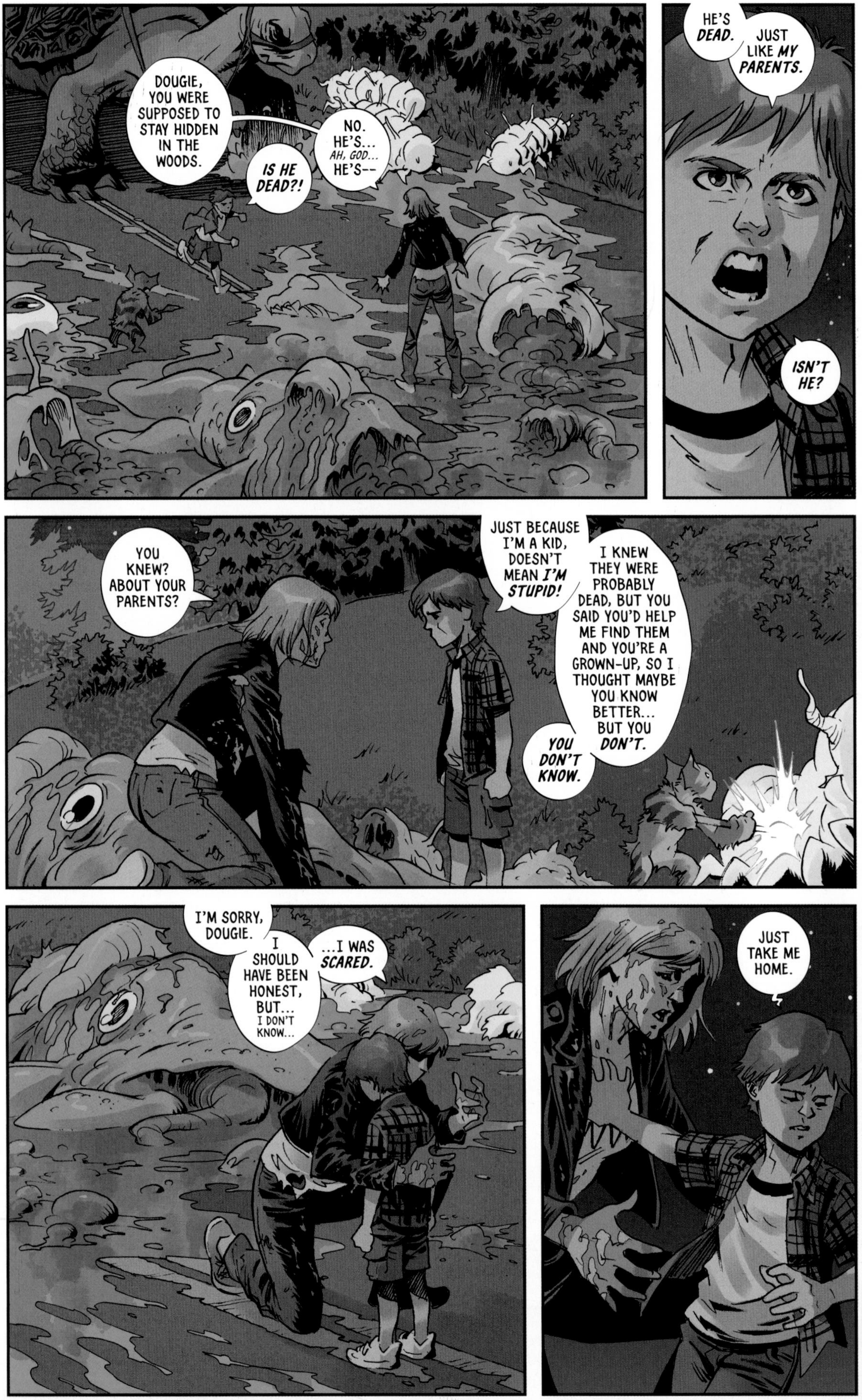
DOUGIE, YOU WERE SUPPOSED TO STAY HIDDEN IN THE WOODS.
IS HE DEAD?!
NO. HE'S... AH, GOD... HE'S--
HE'S DEAD.
JUST LIKE MY PARENTS.
ISN'T HE?
YOU KNEW? ABOUT YOUR PARENTS?
JUST BECAUSE I'M A KID, DOESN'T MEAN I'M STUPID!
I KNEW THEY WERE PROBABLY DEAD, BUT YOU SAID YOU'D HELP ME FIND THEM AND YOU'RE A GROWN-UP, SO I THOUGHT MAYBE YOU KNOW BETTER... BUT YOU DON'T.
YOU DON'T KNOW.
I'M SORRY, DOUGIE.
I SHOULD HAVE BEEN HONEST, BUT... I DON'T KNOW...
...I WAS SCARED.
JUST TAKE ME HOME.

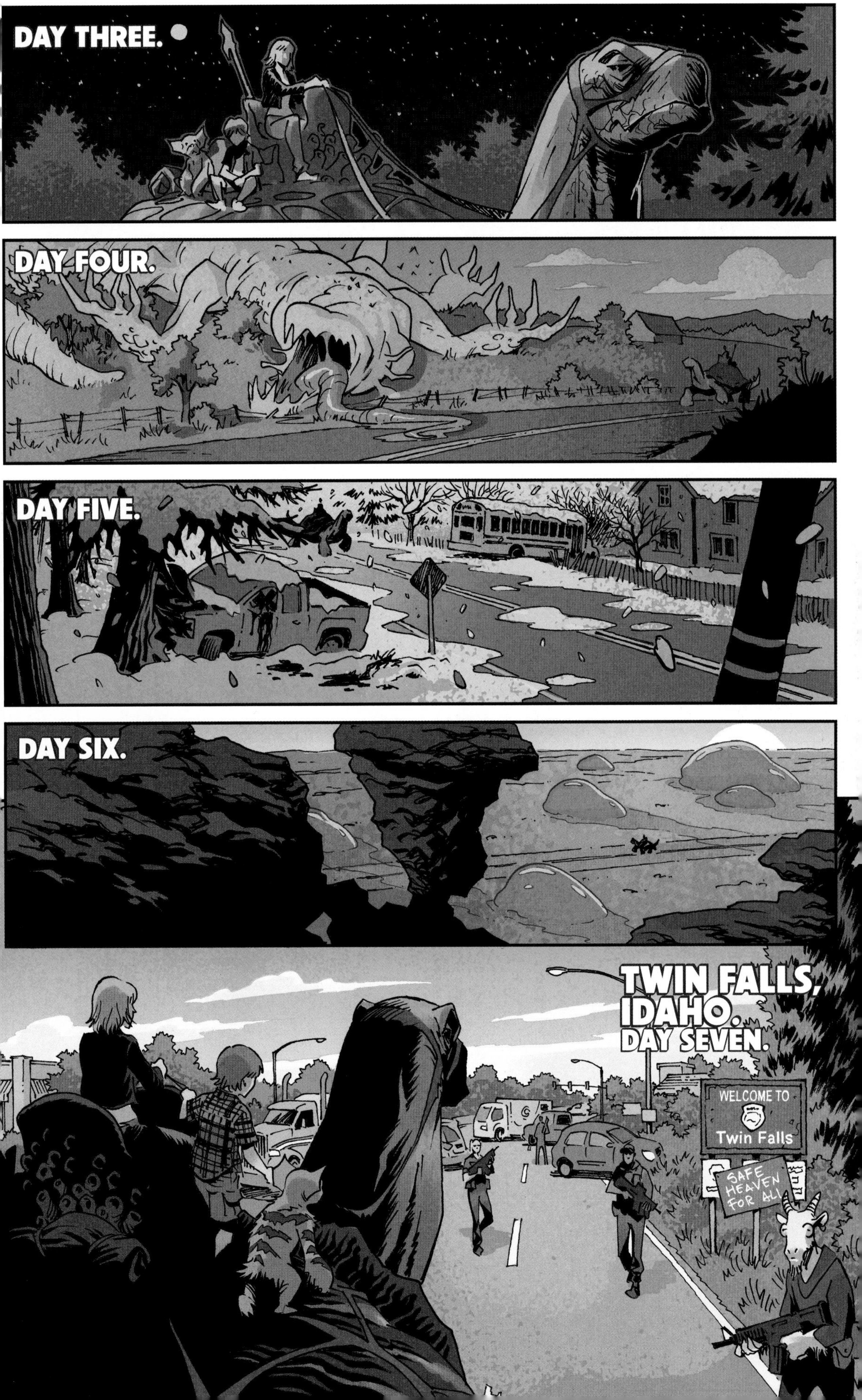
DAY THREE.
DAY FOUR.
DAY FIVE.
DAY SIX.
TWIN FALLS, IDAHO. DAY SEVEN.
WELCOME TO
Twin Falls
SAFE HEAVEN FOR ALL

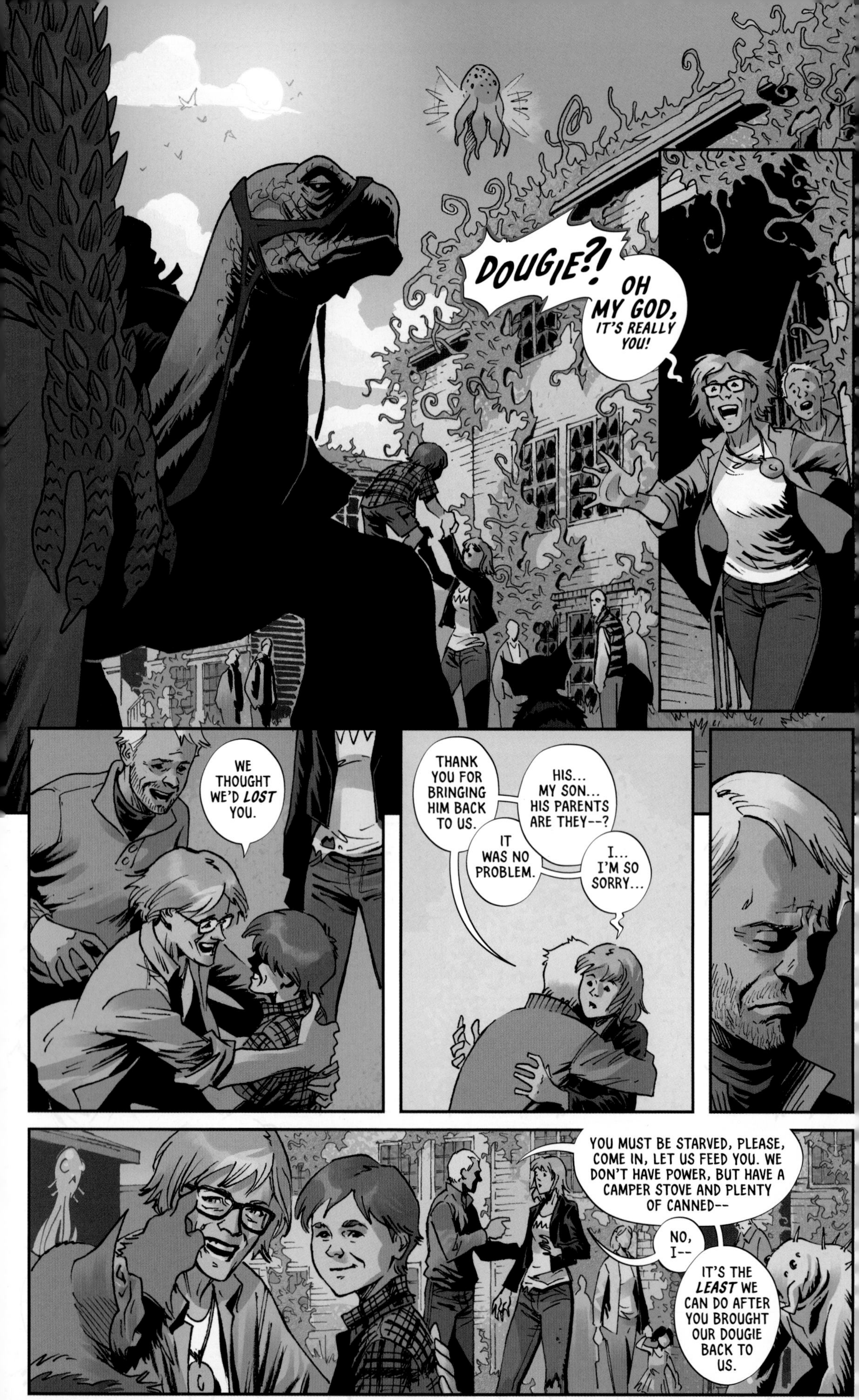
DOUGIE?!
OH MY GOD, IT'S REALLY YOU!
WE THOUGHT WE'D LOST YOU.
THANK YOU FOR BRINGING HIM BACK TO US.
HIS... MY SON... HIS PARENTS ARE THEY--?
IT WAS NO PROBLEM.
I... I'M SO SORRY...
YOU MUST BE STARVED, PLEASE, COME IN, LET US FEED YOU. WE DON'T HAVE POWER, BUT HAVE A CAMPER STOVE AND PLENTY OF CANNED--
NO, I--
IT'S THE LEAST WE CAN DO AFTER YOU BROUGHT OUR DOUGIE BACK TO US.

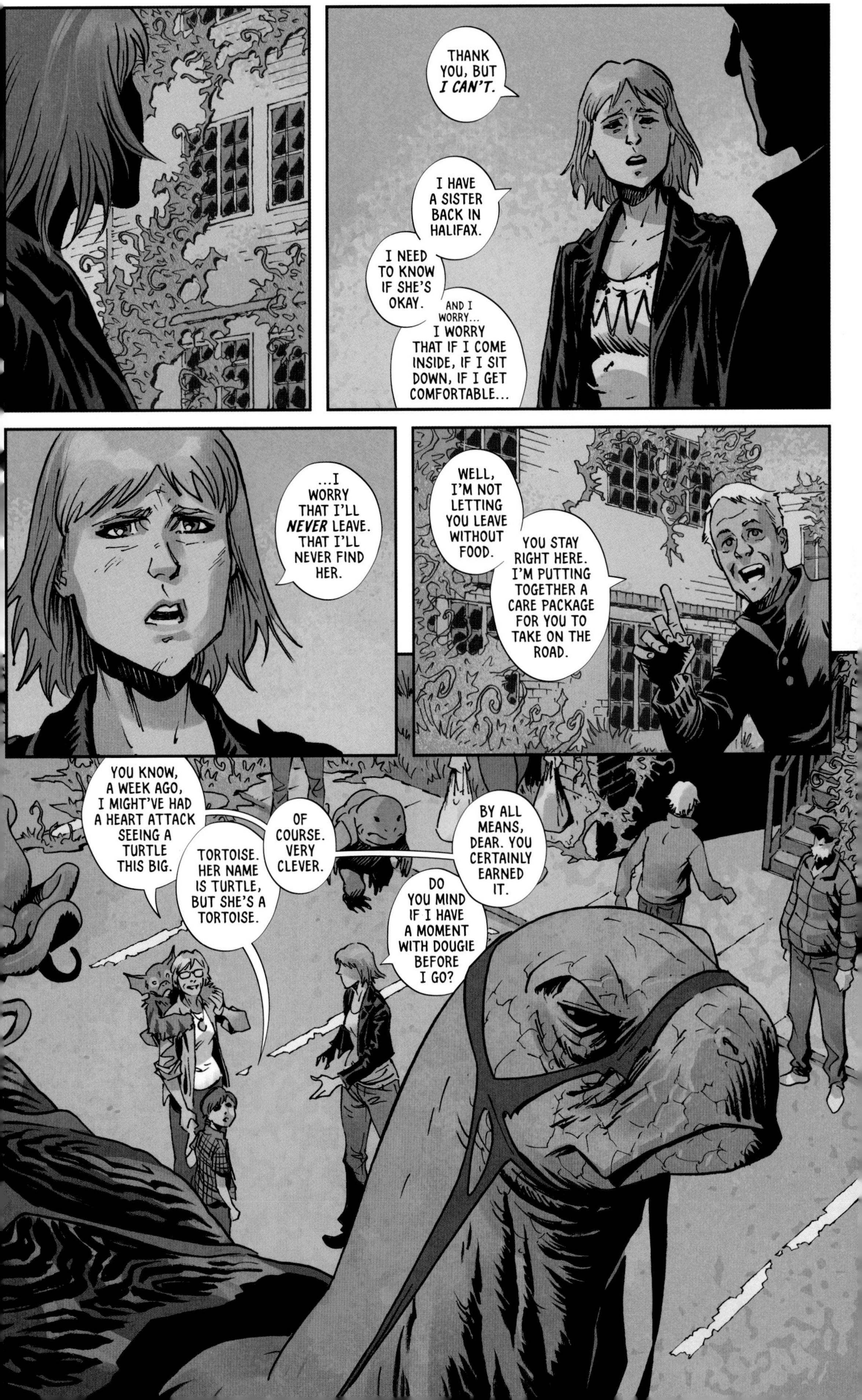
THANK YOU, BUT *I CAN'T.*
I HAVE A SISTER BACK IN HALIFAX.
I NEED TO KNOW IF SHE'S OKAY.
AND I WORRY...
I WORRY THAT IF I COME INSIDE, IF I SIT DOWN, IF I GET COMFORTABLE...
...I WORRY THAT I'LL *NEVER* LEAVE. THAT I'LL NEVER FIND HER.
WELL, I'M NOT LETTING YOU LEAVE WITHOUT FOOD.
YOU STAY RIGHT HERE. I'M PUTTING TOGETHER A CARE PACKAGE FOR YOU TO TAKE ON THE ROAD.
YOU KNOW, A WEEK AGO, I MIGHT'VE HAD A HEART ATTACK SEEING A TURTLE THIS BIG.
TORTOISE. HER NAME IS TURTLE, BUT SHE'S A TORTOISE.
OF COURSE. VERY CLEVER.
DO YOU MIND IF I HAVE A MOMENT WITH DOUGIE BEFORE I GO?
BY ALL MEANS, DEAR. YOU CERTAINLY EARNED IT.

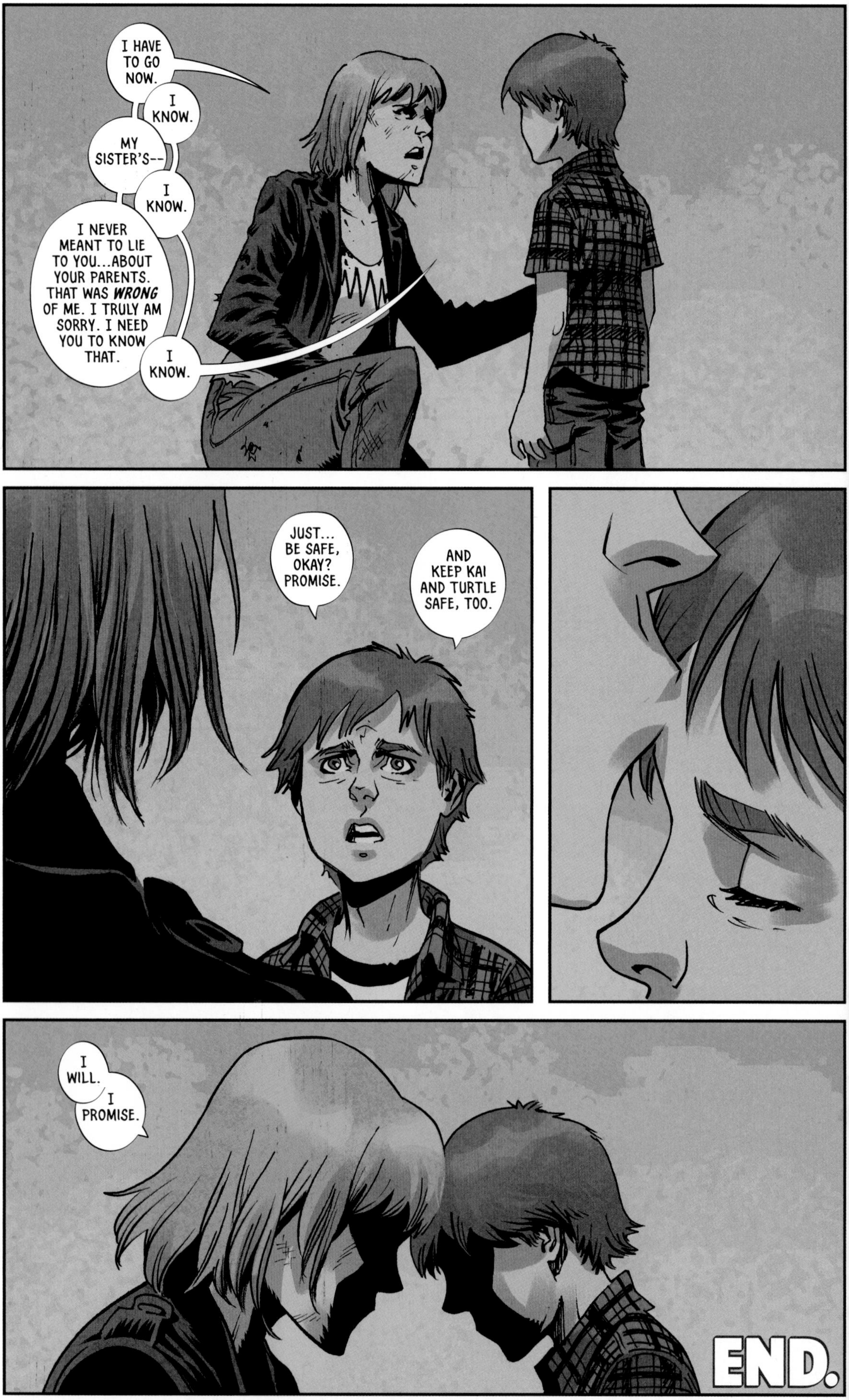
I HAVE TO GO NOW.
I KNOW.
MY SISTER'S--
I KNOW.
I NEVER MEANT TO LIE TO YOU...ABOUT YOUR PARENTS. THAT WAS *WRONG* OF ME. I TRULY AM SORRY. I NEED YOU TO KNOW THAT.
I KNOW.
JUST... BE SAFE, OKAY? PROMISE.
AND KEEP KAI AND TURTLE SAFE, TOO.
I WILL.
I PROMISE.
END.

BEYOND THE THE BREACH™

COVER GALLERY & EXTRAS

Issue 1
DECLAN SHALVEY
Incentive Cover

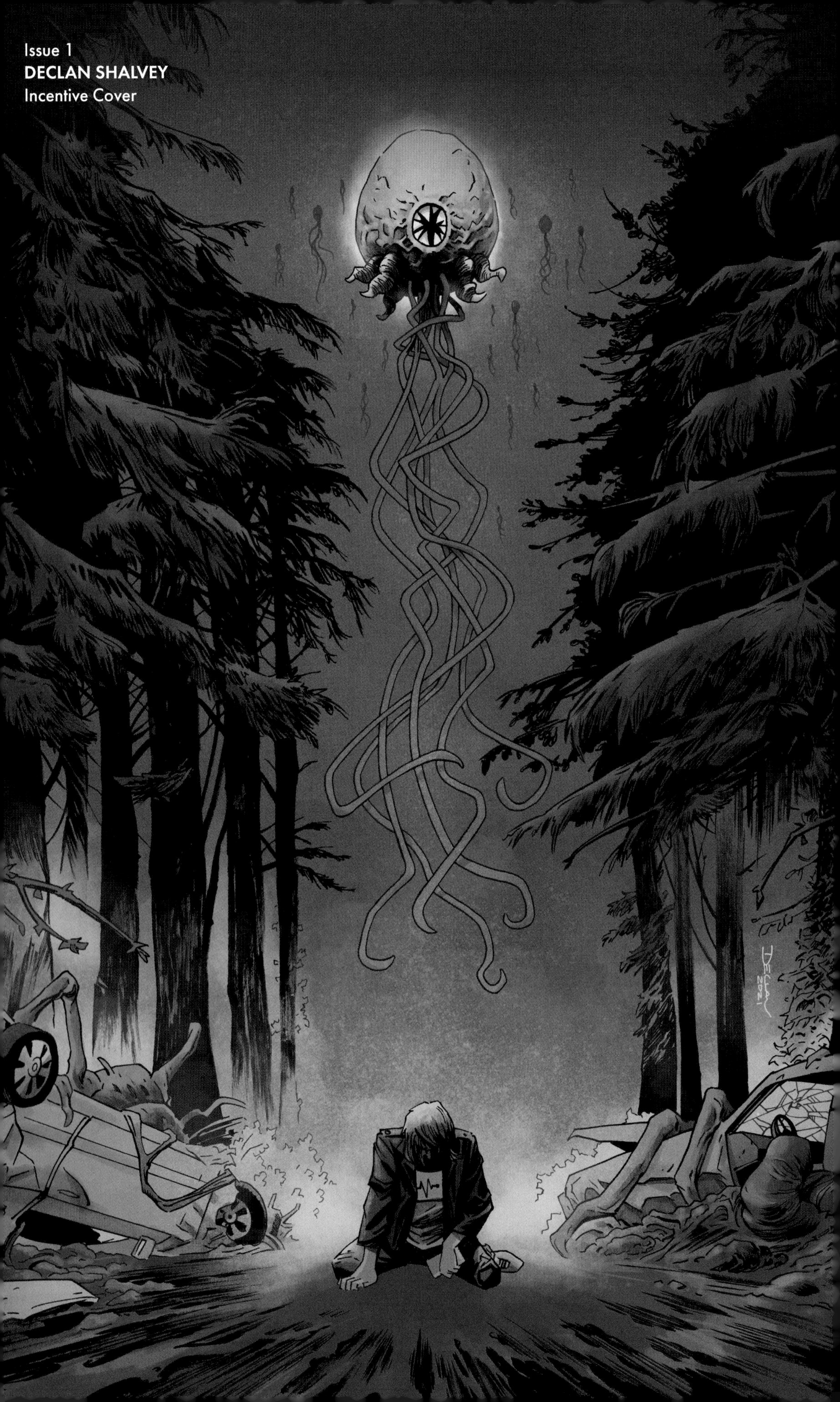

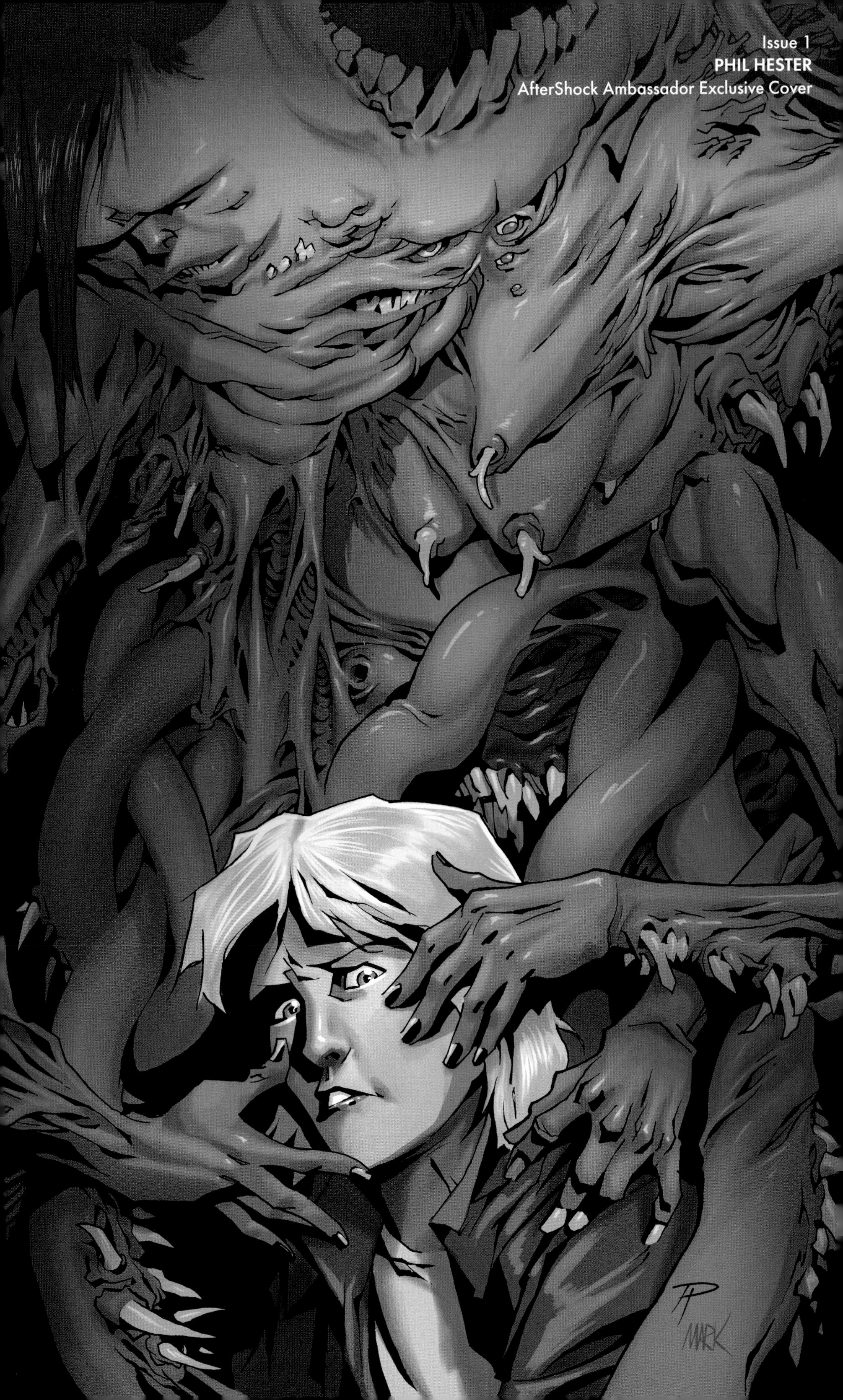

Issue 1
PHIL HESTER
AfterShock Ambassador Exclusive Cover

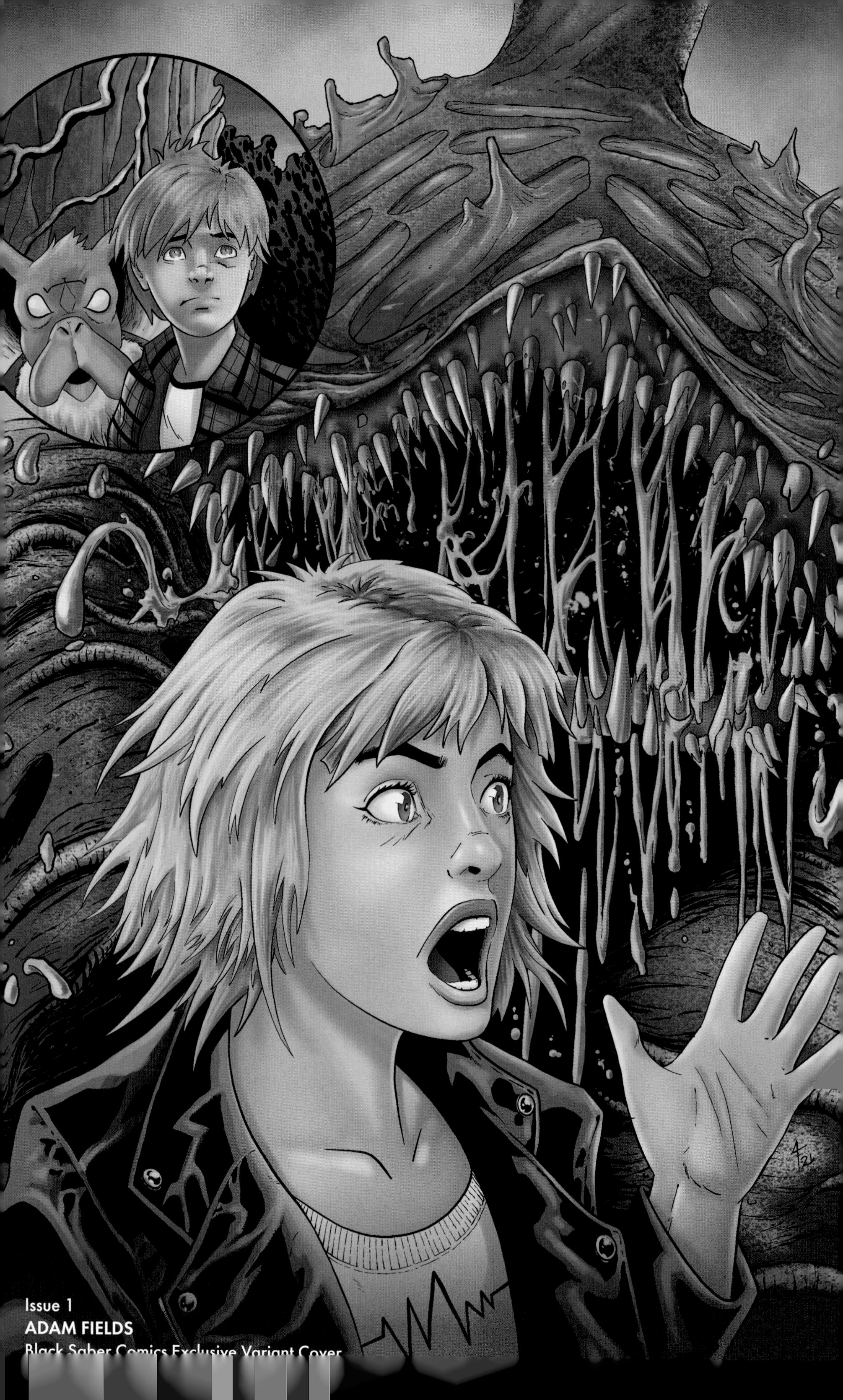

Issue 1
ADAM FIELDS
Black Saber Comics Exclusive Variant Cover

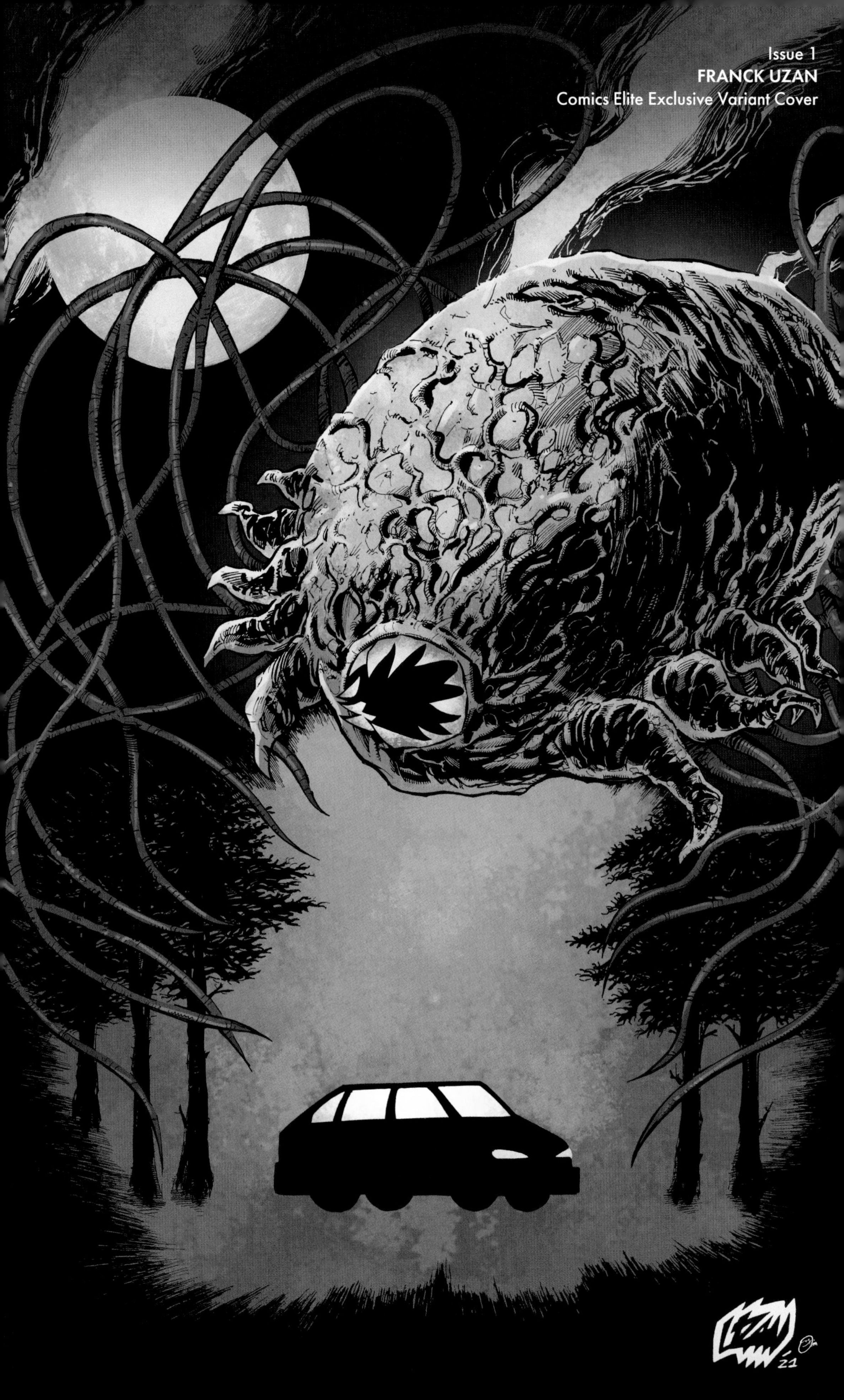
Issue 1
FRANCK UZAN
Comics Elite Exclusive Variant Cover

Issue 1
FRANCK UZAN
Comics Elite Bloody Breach Exclusive Variant Cover

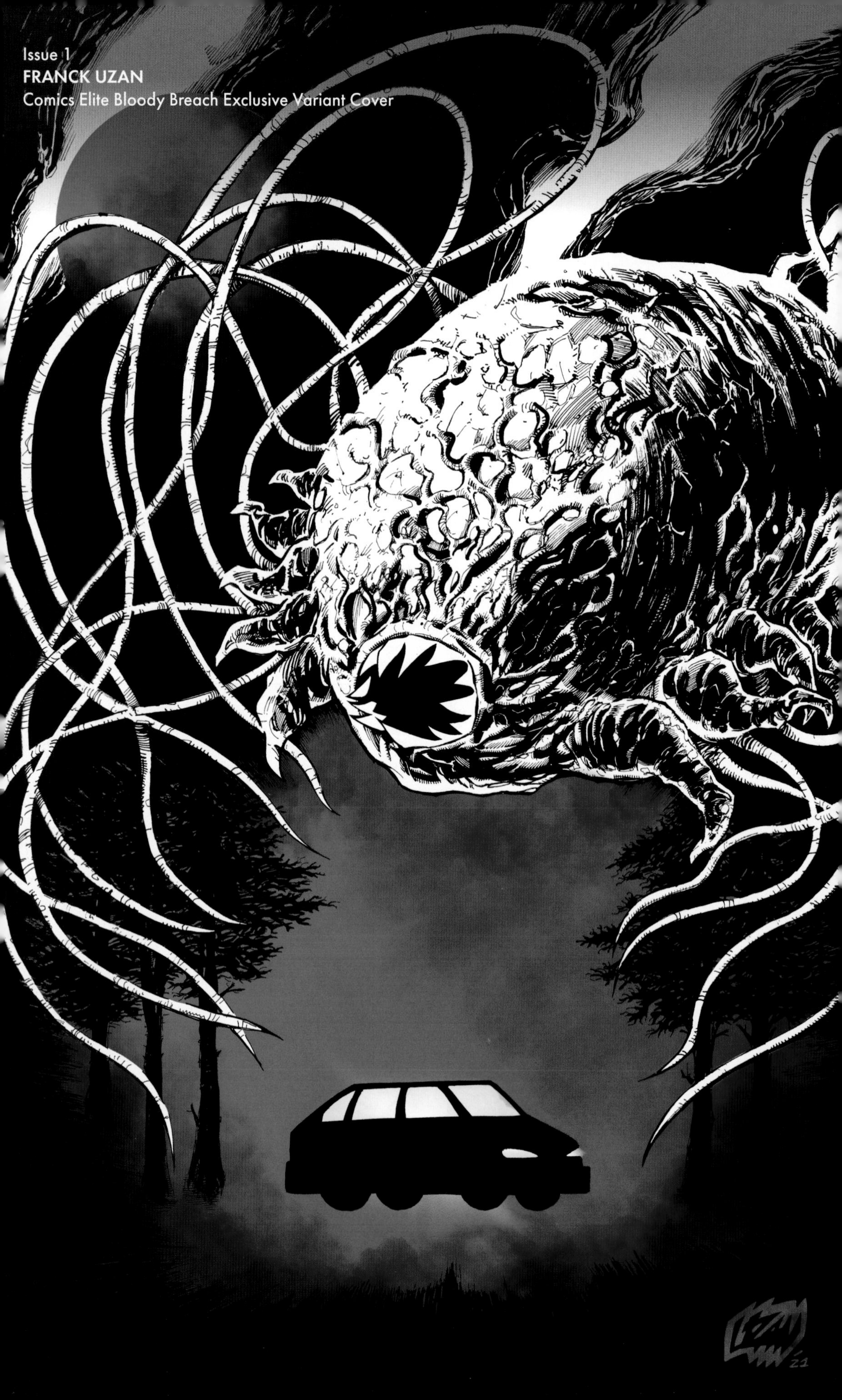

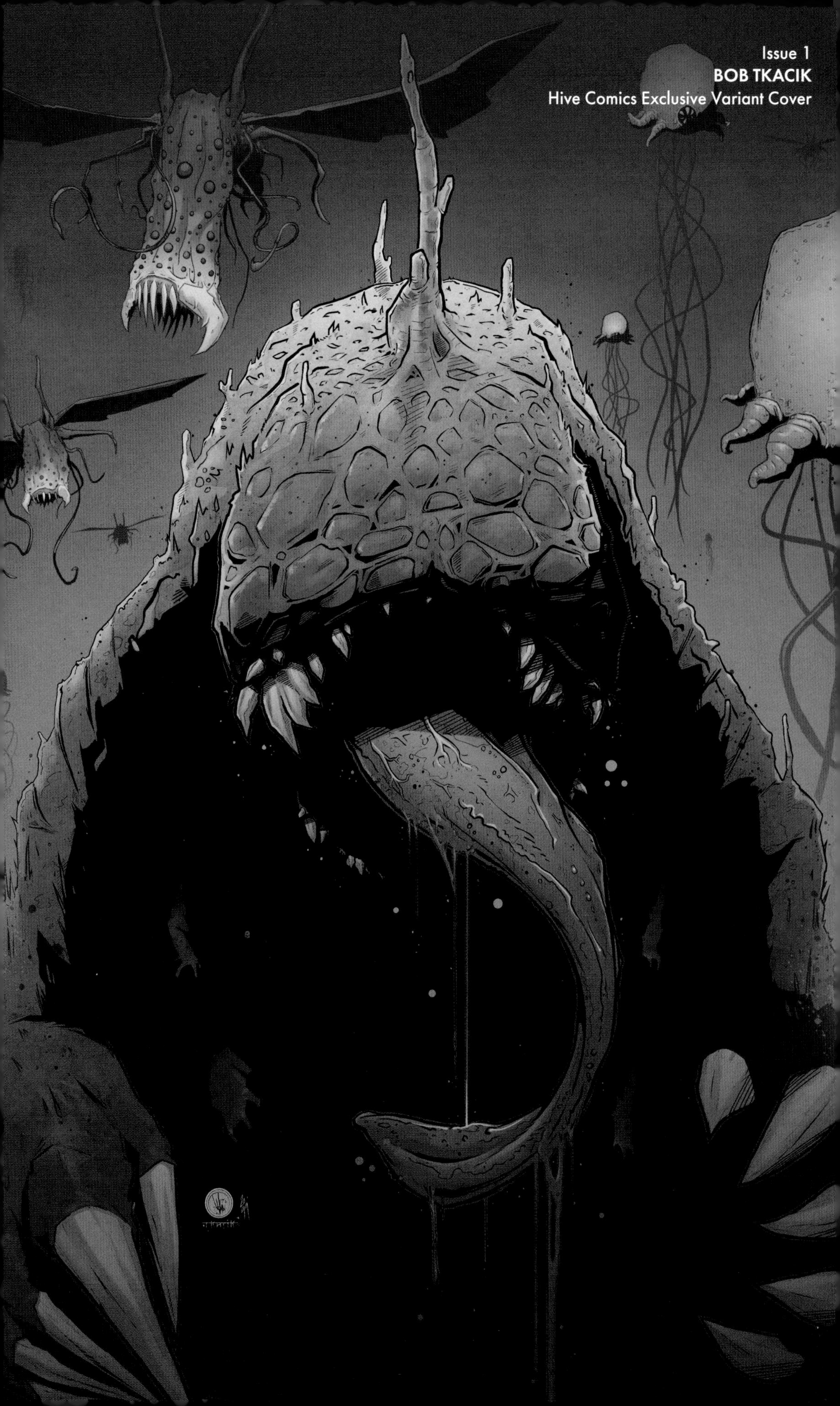

Issue 1
BOB TKACIK
Hive Comics Exclusive Variant Cover

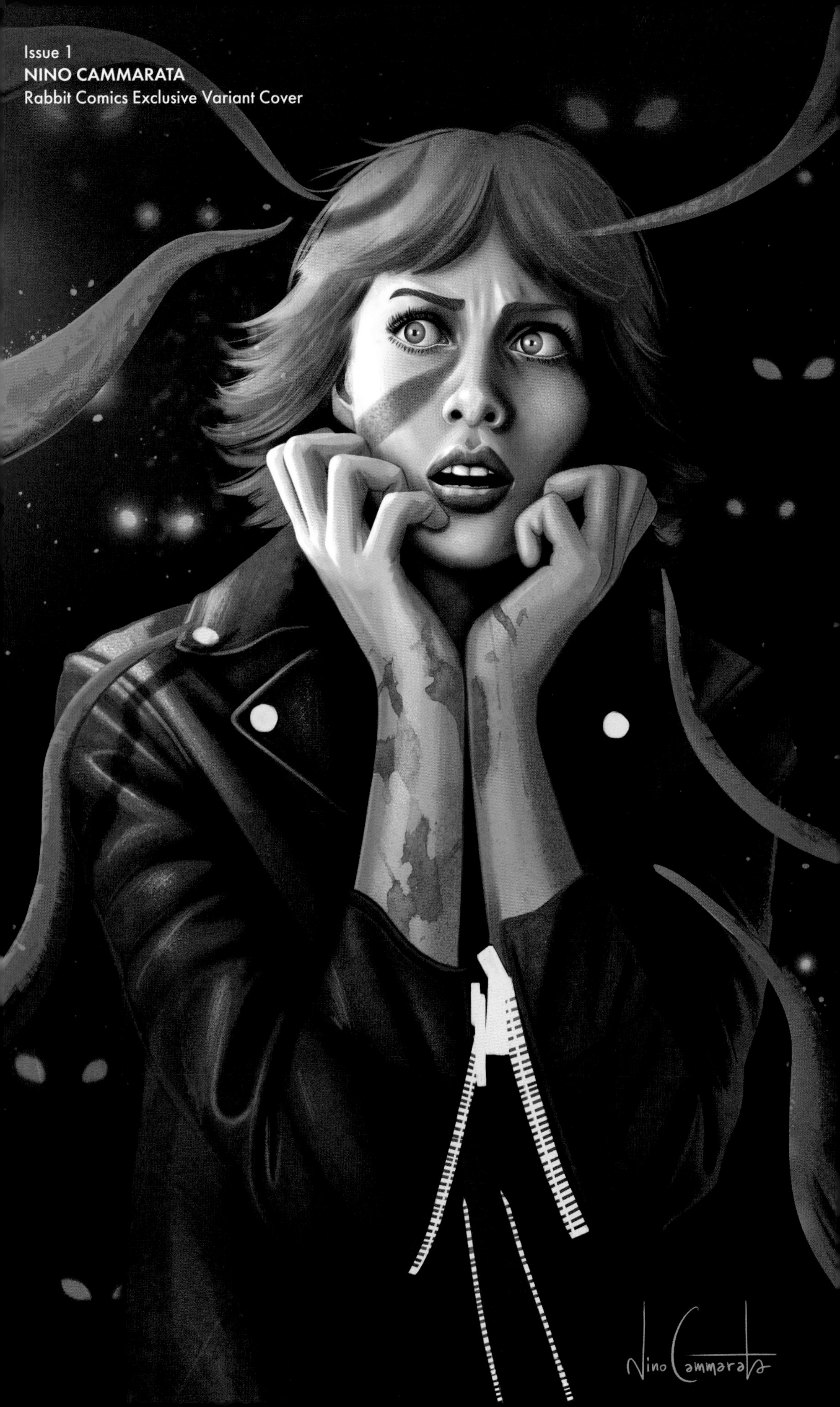
Nino Cammarata

Issue 1
NINO CAMMARATA
Rabbit Comics Exclusive Variant Cover

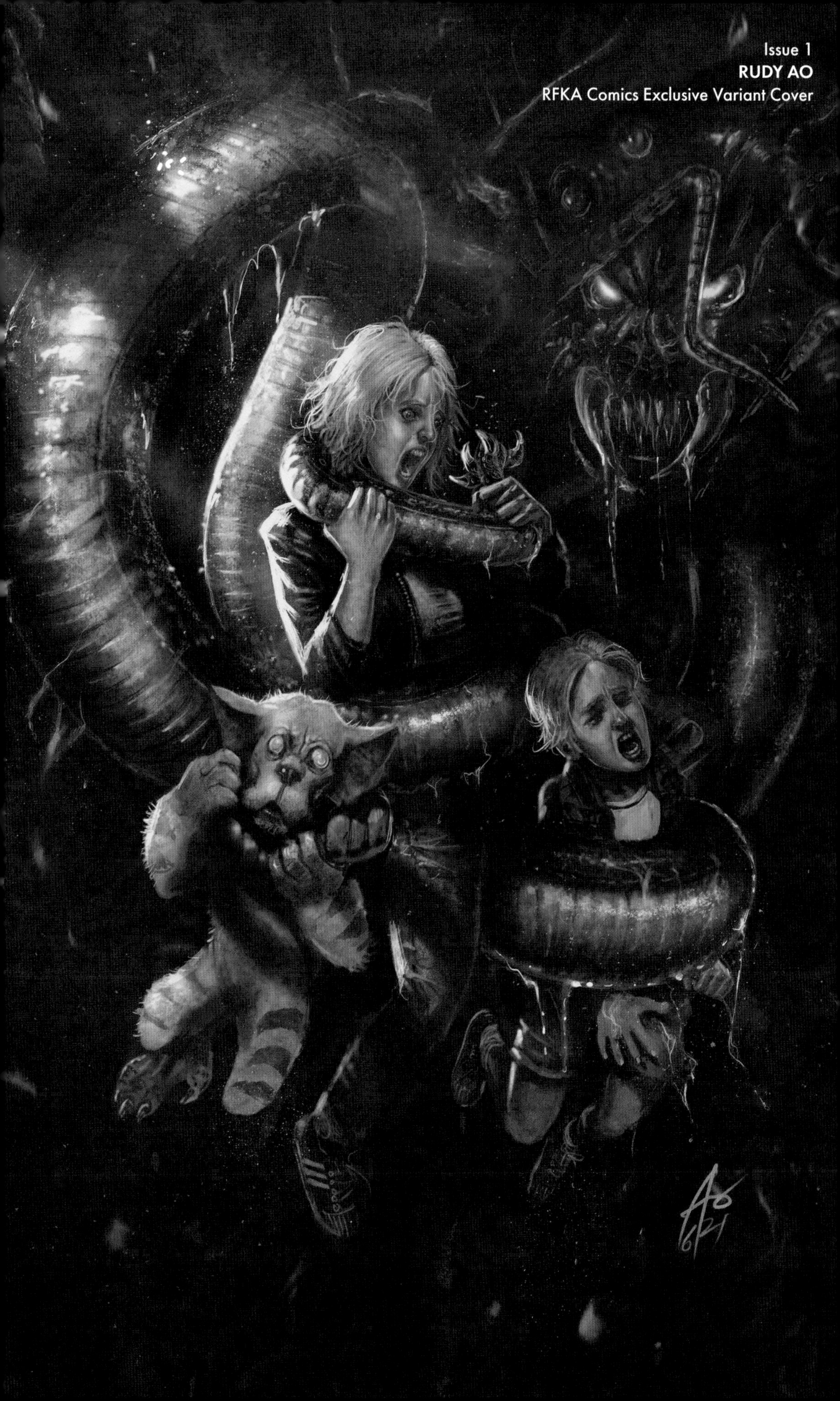

Issue 1
RUDY AO
RFKA Comics Exclusive Variant Cover

Issue 1
GÖRKEM DEMIR
Slabbed Heroes Exclusive Variant Cover

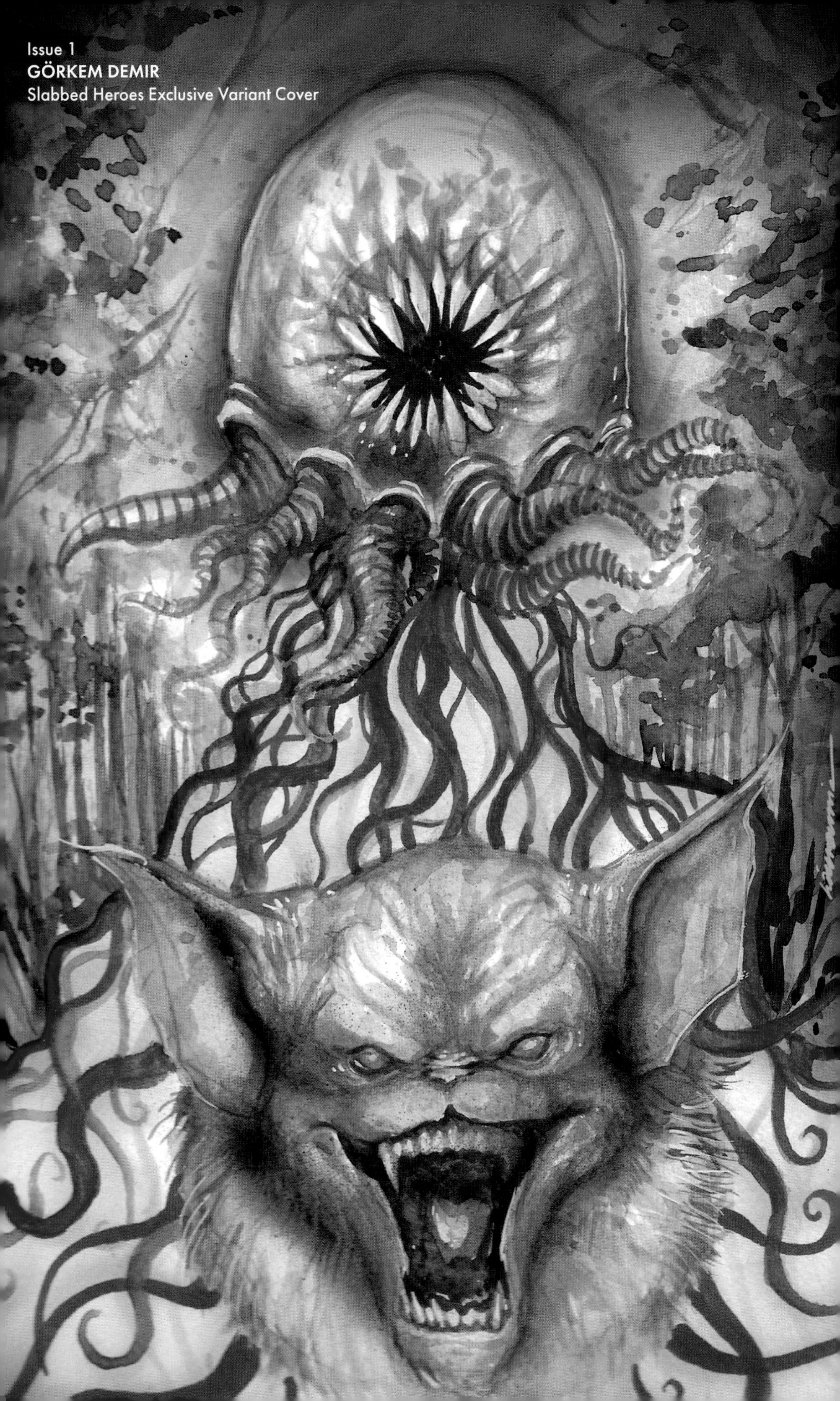

Issue 1
PEEJAY CATACUTAN
Wicked Gator Comics Exclusive Variant Cover

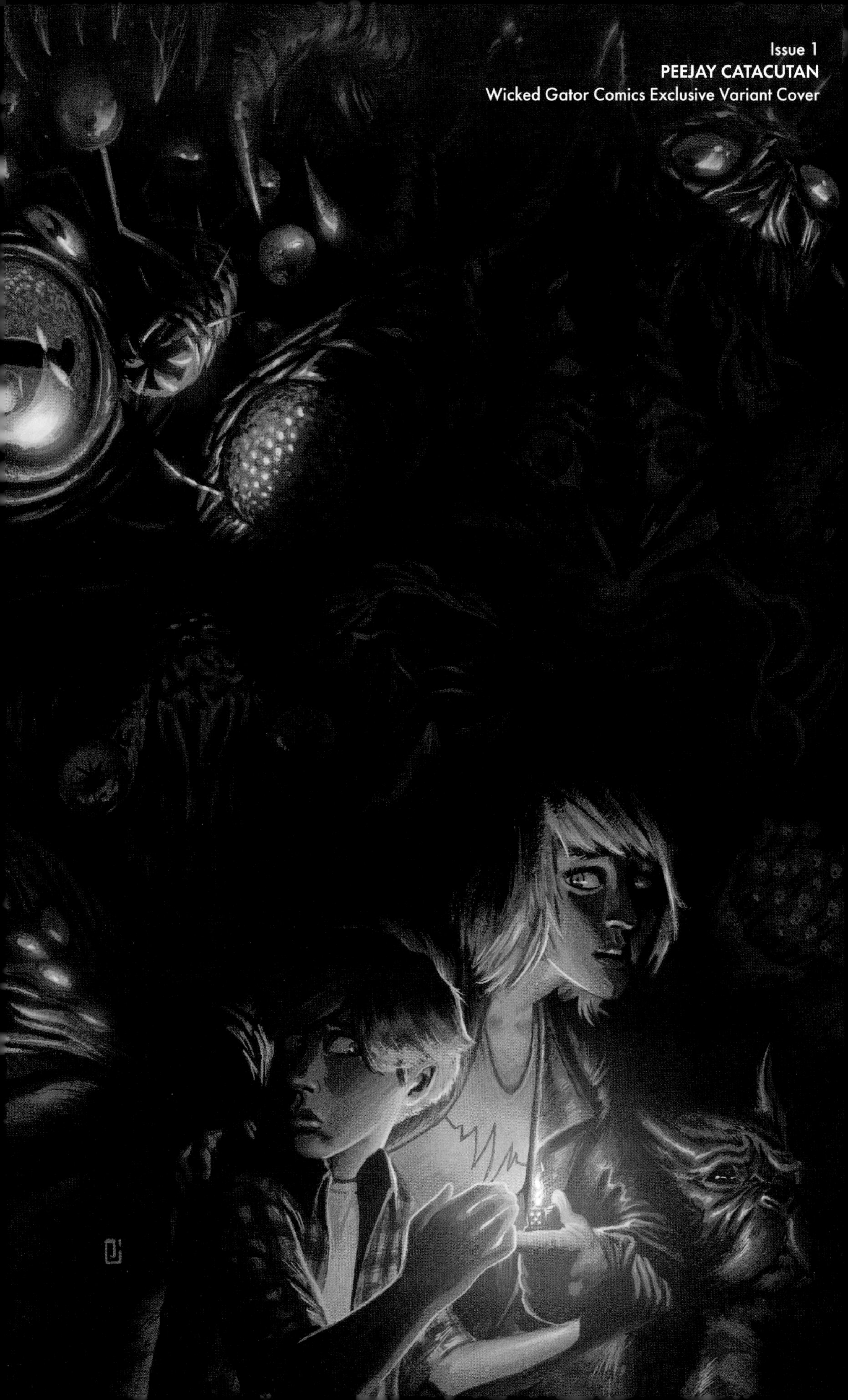

Road to Freedom
One week to get it All in!

Day One (hippies/redwoods)

- Arrive San Francisco at 10:56AM.
- Pick Up Rental from Cheeps
- Breakfast (Lunch?). Haight/Ashbury somewhere maybe?
- Amoeba Music.
- Find donuts for the road.
- Hit 101 to 1 and prepare your eyeballs for Redwoods & the Pacific Ocean!
- ~~Visit Castello Di Amorosa.~~ Not enough time. Too far out of way.
- Take Avenue of Giants for Shrine Drive-Thru tree.

Reservation at Elk Field Cabins.
18 Green Glen Drive
Orick, CA. (Three Nights)

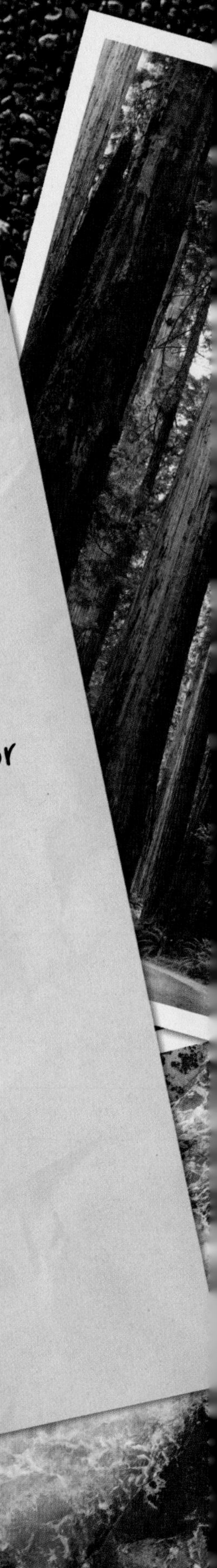

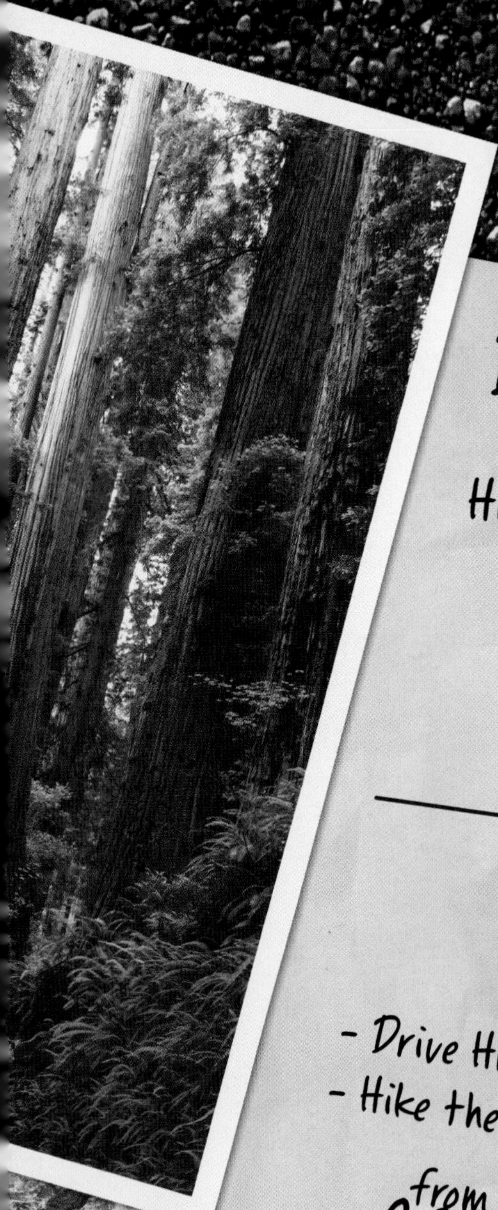

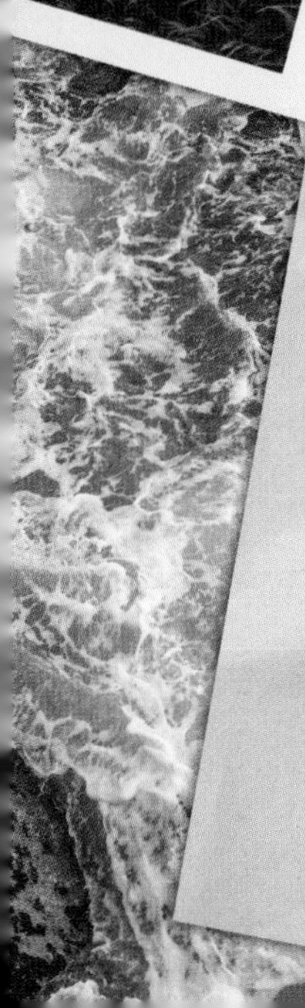

Day two & Day Three

Hike Redwood National Park!

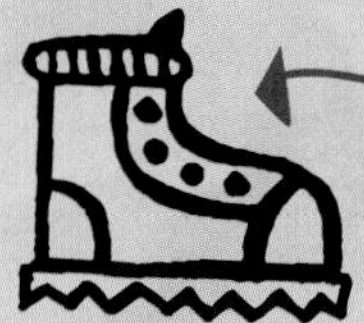

Forgot my shoes! find somewhere to buy good hiking shoes!

Day four

- Drive HWY 101 to Cannon Beach, Oregon.
- Hike the shore, see the Haystack Rock from GOONIES!

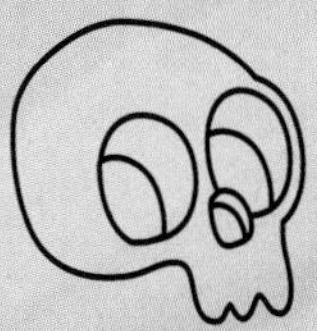

NEVER SAY DIE!

- Rest & recover from drive and hiking. Take it easy!

- Reservation at:
  The Sea Horse Lodge
  15 E Lincoln Street, Cannon Beach

Day Five (Portland!)

- Seaside: Go Karts
  Seaside Carousel Mall, Promenade
- Astoria: Goonies House!

Closed Down ☹ Though, maybe not? Reviews unclear. Get a picture anyway.

Reservation at:
Kennedy School Hotel. 5763 NE 33rd Ave
(two nights)

Day Six

(more Portland!)

- Visit Cart Pods. Gorge on good street food!
- Voodoo Doughnuts.

Explore!

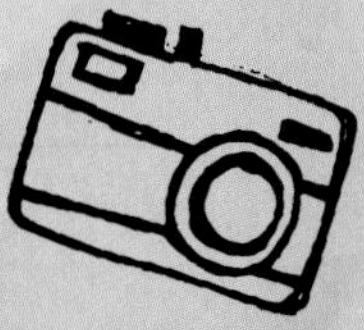

- Powell's Books.

  Careful! Remember you have to bring back everything you buy!
- Book Brewery Bike Tour

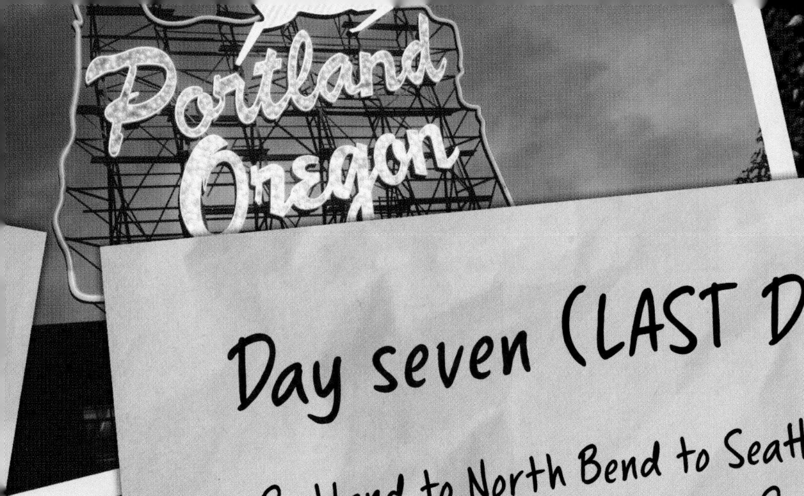
Portland
Oregon

Day seven (LAST DAY!)

- Portland to North Bend to Seattle
- Twede's Cafe for lunch (Twin Peaks!).
  Coffee and pie!!!
- Pike Place Market.
- Fremont Troll.
- Seattle Art Museum.

Get some rest!

Reservation at:
Hotel Franklyn 1531 7th Ave.

Day Eight (home)

SeaTac Flight @ 6:01am
Flight number BA647.

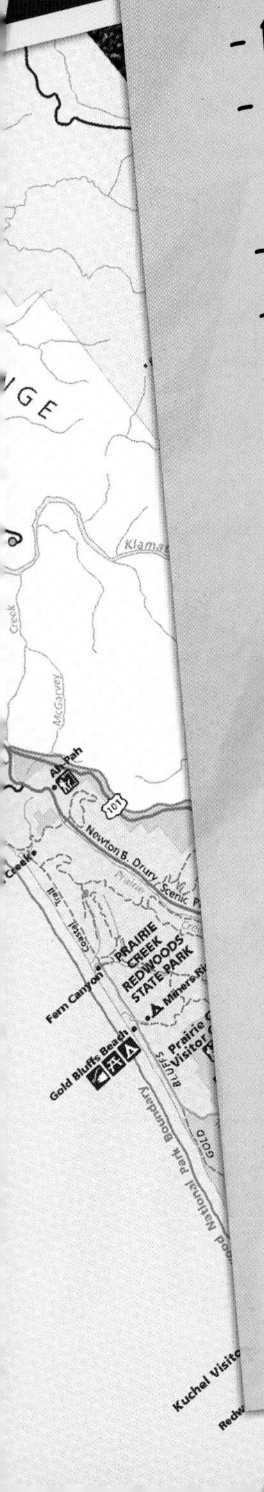

BEYOND THE BREACH

DAMIAN COUCEIRO
artist interview

AFTERSHOCK COMICS: What were your influences behind the overall look of BEYOND THE BREACH?

DAMIAN COUCEIRO: When Ed and I started talking about this project, I visualized it as a straight horror story, so I watched a lot of Junji Ito art, but also a lot of Alex Toth's short stories from *Creepy* and *Eerie*. I even played at first with the idea of adding some grey tones to the line art, like Toth. But I realized soon after that it only worked on black and white, and they were pointless after coloring. As the project moved on and we started to add more elements of sci-fi and fantasy, I started to get more influences from artworks like Moebius'. As for the designs of creatures and monsters, I took a lot of influences from photos of flora and fauna. There is a lot of weird stuff in nature that you can take and give a spin to create something original.

ASC: If you were going on a similar road trip as Vanessa, which character would you bring along?

DC: Kai, for sure. It probably won't be as helpful as another human or an inter-dimensional warrior, but it will definitely bring joy and comfort along the trip. Plus, I used my lovely French bulldog as a reference when creating Kai, so I have a special bond to that character.

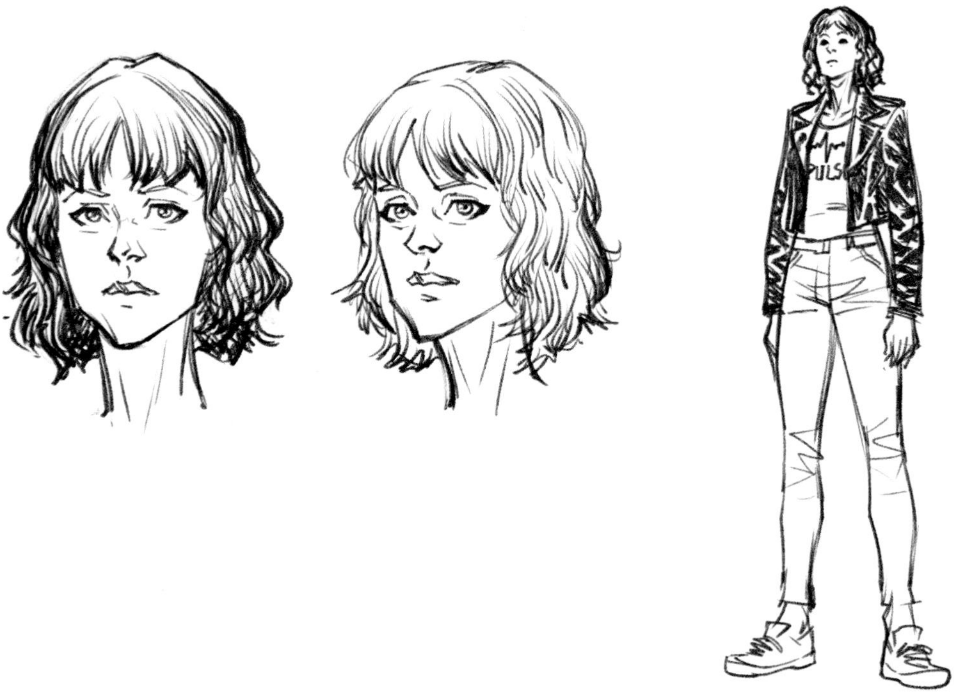

ASC: What is your creative process when illustrating such a character-driven story like this one?

DC: Well, I take a fair amount of time designing those characters for sure. I looked a lot at actors and photos for reference to find their look that I think matches their personality. This process is always made side by side with Ed, who provides his ideas and suggestions. So, together we came up with the characters' looks that are best suited for the story. When it came to working on the comic itself, I took special care on characters acting and body language to reflect their feelings and dialogues. I used photo references of myself when needed. Plus, I wouldn't move on to drawing the backgrounds until I was satisfied with all the characters illustrated in each panel.

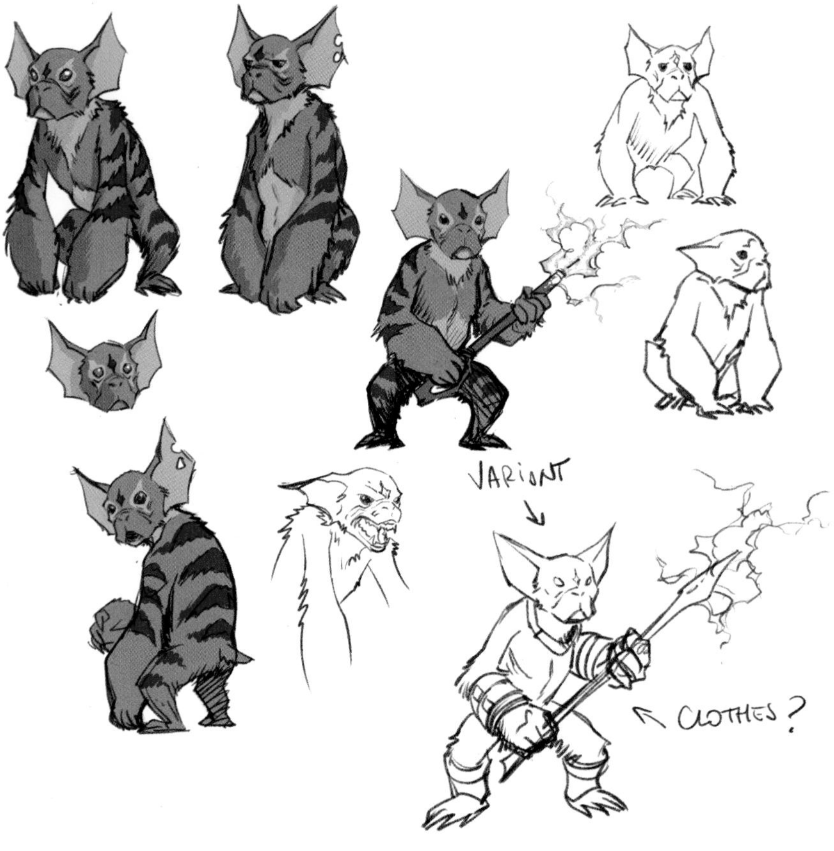
VARIANT
CLOTHES?

ASC: Any advice for artists trying to break into the industry?

DC: This is a tough one because I think every person has a different experience, and the tools to break into comics are probably different now from when I did it ten years ago. But still, I think there are three aspects to consider. The first one is working hard. Try very hard to be the best at what you do. Study, practice, practice and practice and have an open mind to be inspired and learn from every different form of art. Second, show your work. You can be an extraordinary artist, but nobody will find you if you don't show yourself. It can be really hard to expose yourself to rejection and bad feedback, especially when you're starting out, but put yourself in those positions and try to learn from it. And the third one I think is simple — luck. I feel I've been very lucky along the way. But the only way of taking advantage of the stroke of luck when it comes, is if you have done your best on the first two aspects.

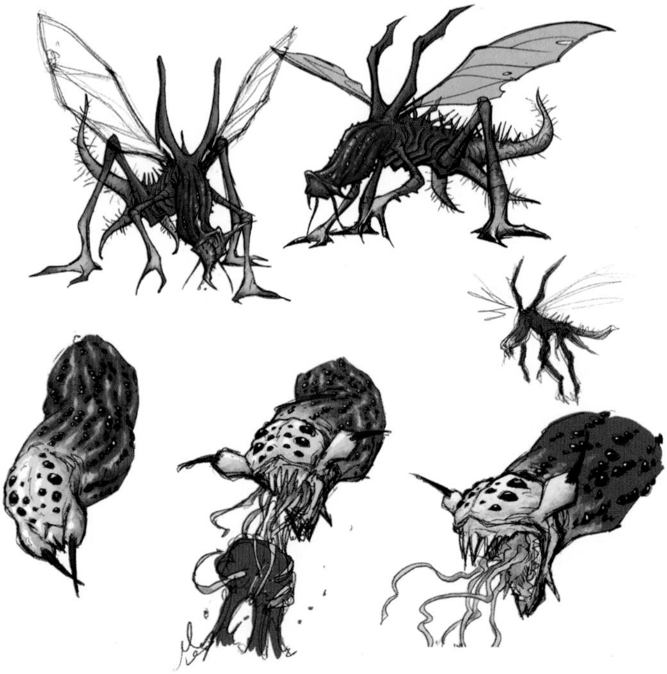

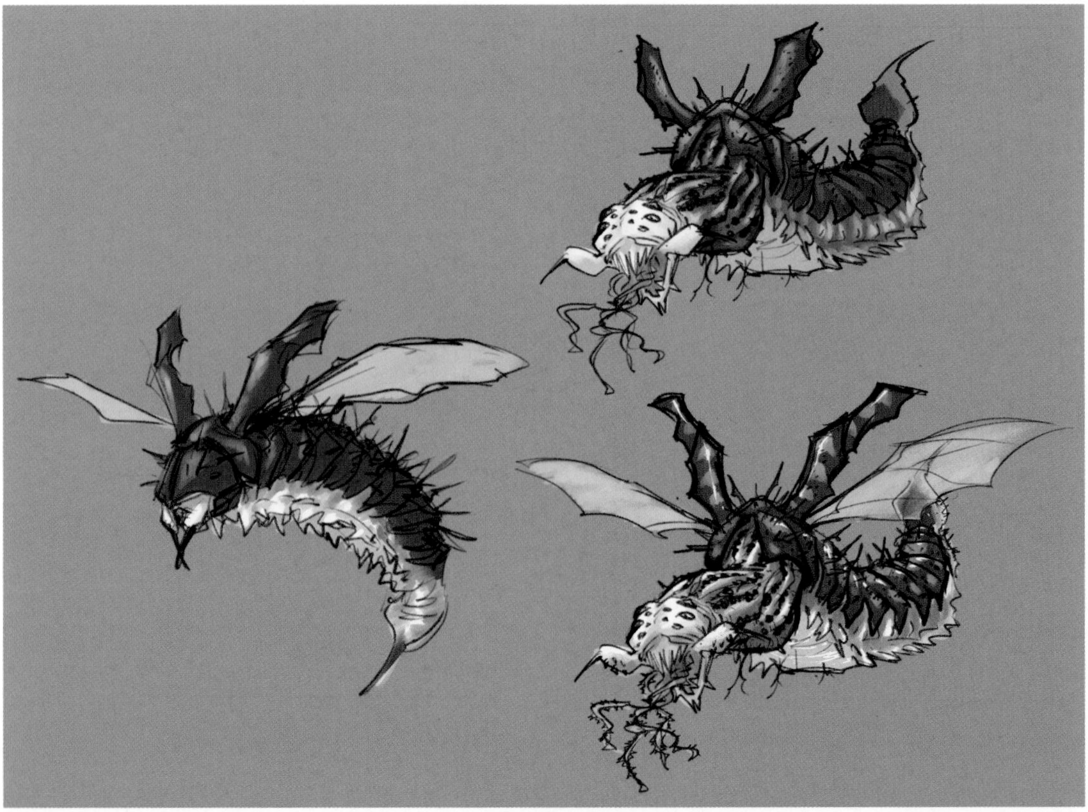

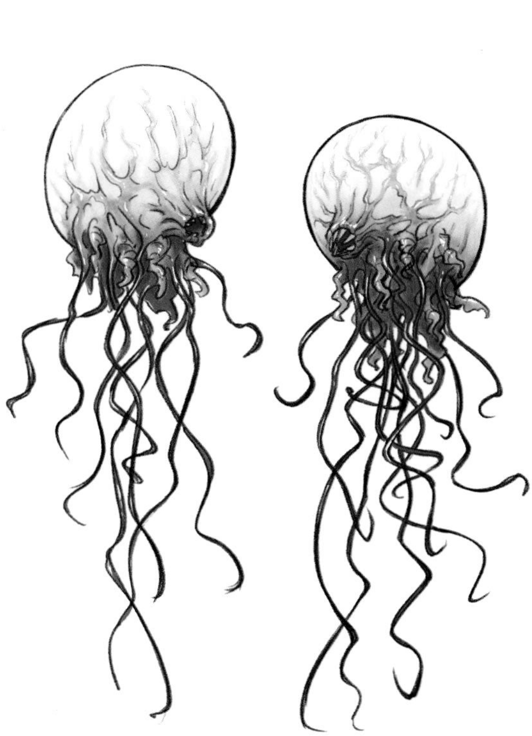

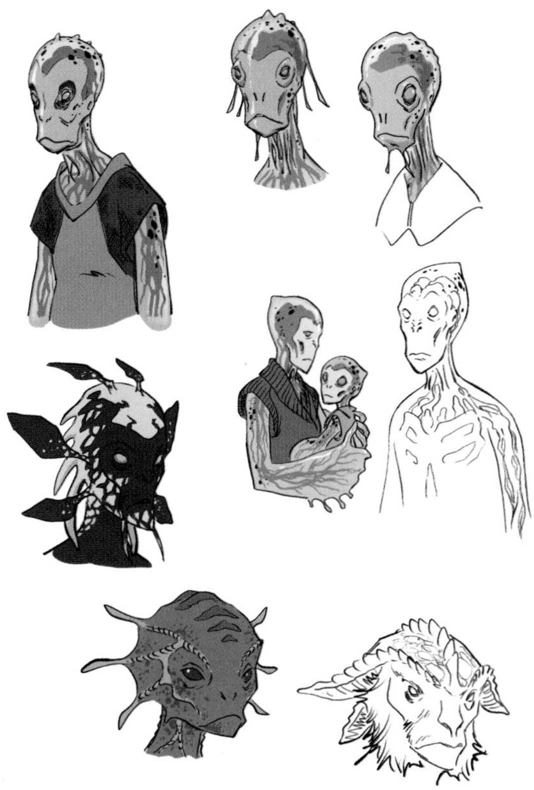

ASC: What was the most challenging aspect for you when illustrating BEYOND THE BREACH?

DC: I think the most challenging aspect was trying to be original. It's always hard to create these worlds and creatures while making sure they are unique and different from anything you've seen. I hope I have succeeded — I do know I had a lot of fun making them. Also, Dougie was tough. I had never illustrated a book with a child character, so that was a bit of a challenge.

ASC: Do you have a favorite road-trip themed film, television show or book?

DC: When I think of road-trip movies, I think of classics like *Thelma and Louise* and Spielberg's *Duel*. More recently, I loved the film *Nebraska* and, I don't know if it counts but, *Mad Max Fury Road*. Isn't that one an extreme road trip movie after all? Haha!

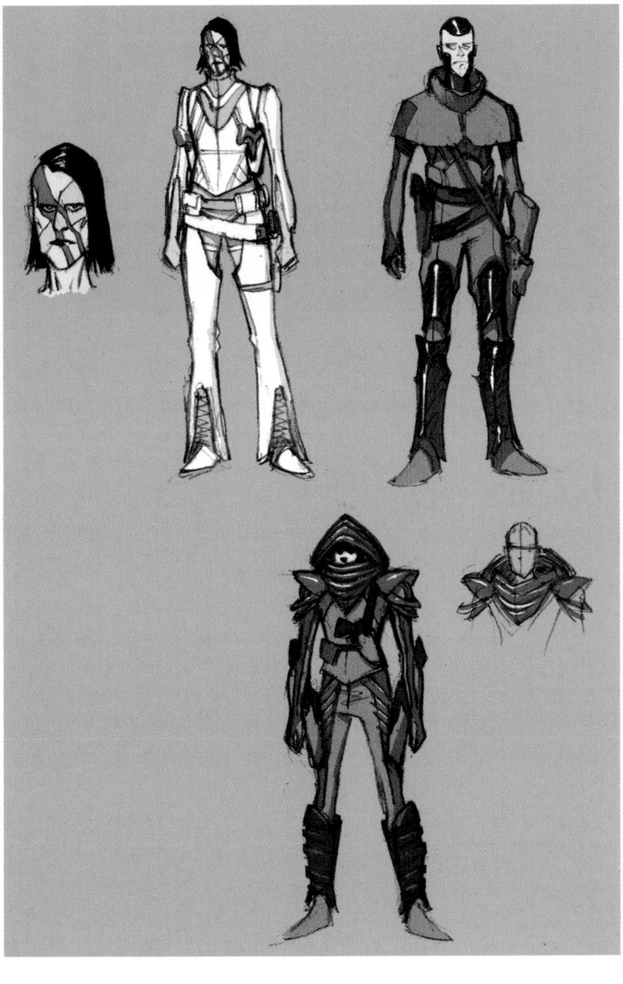

BEYOND THE BREACH

PATRICIO DELPECHE
colorist interview

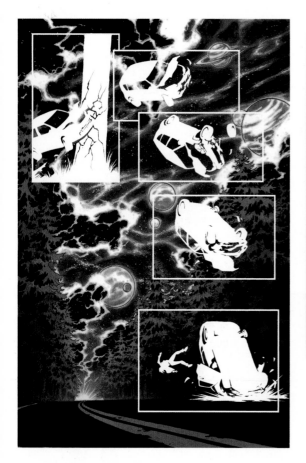

AFTERSHOCK COMICS: What were your influences for bringing those unique characters and moments found in BEYOND THE BREACH to life?

PATRICIO DELPECHE: It is always difficult to define with certainty what influences us but colleagues that I deeply admire, like Matheus Lopes, Brennan Wagner or Jordie Bellaire, are a constant inspiration. The nightscapes and the colorful portals to other dimensions are also greatly influenced by the palettes that Jean Giraud (Moebius) used.

ASC: Do you have a favorite page, moment or panel?

PD: My favorite moment is, without a doubt, the flashback where Samuel shares how the Maccan attacked his planet. The insertion of such a different palette to describe that alien world made it an extremely fun sequence for me.

ASC: What was the most challenging aspect while working on BEYOND THE BREACH?

PD: The greatest difficulty was showing those portals to strange worlds as interesting places that left the reader wanting more and managing to integrate it with our reality, our world.

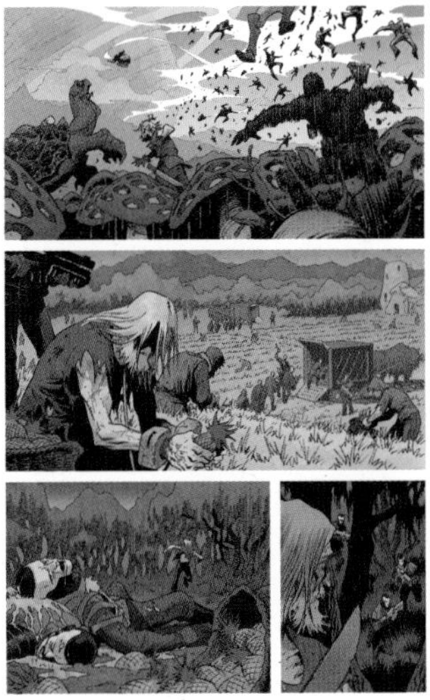

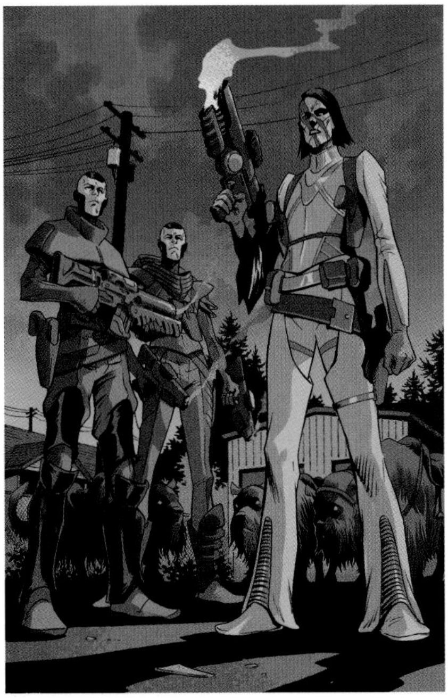

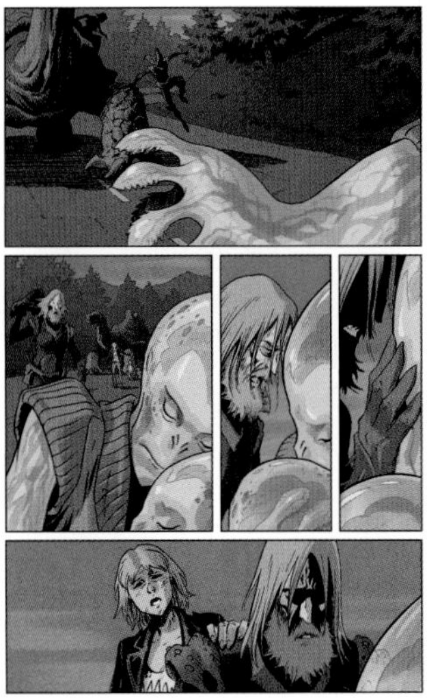

ASC: If you had to choose between Kai or Turtle as your new pet, who would you choose?

PD: Without a doubt, Kai! He's warm in winter and has a fascination for getting into toilets... or do you know a better way to clean them?

ASC: Any advice for creators who are trying to break into coloring?

PD: I have always colored my own drawings. It was by chance that one day a colleague asked me to collaborate with him for a monthly comic. Since then, I have done both; color my own work and color others. I think the best advice is to look for a collaborator and make an effort to offer something that is not there, something that not even the cartoonist considered but elevates the work and allows the reader to have more reading dimensions.

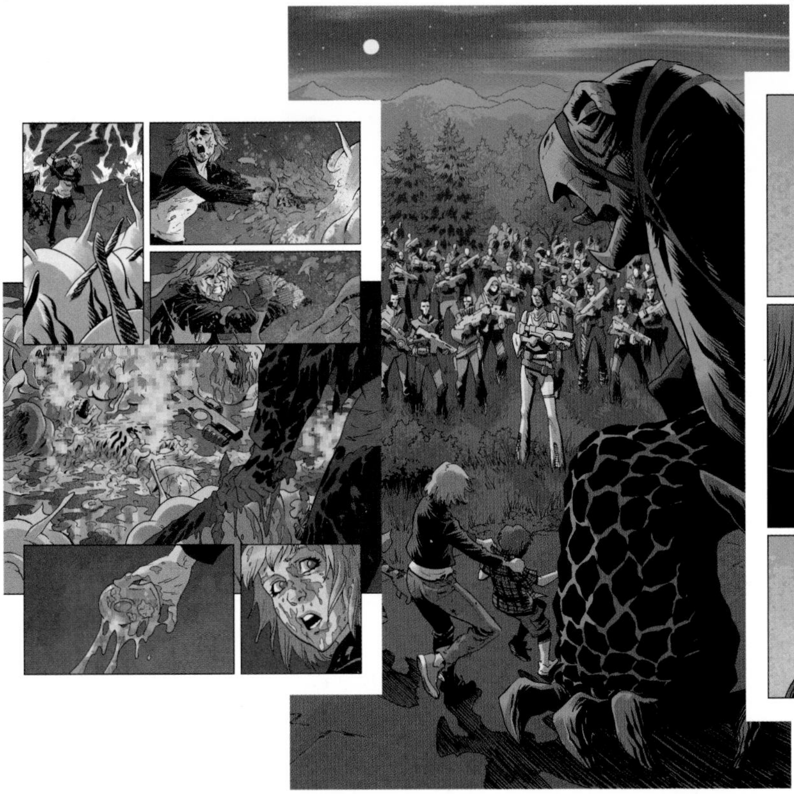

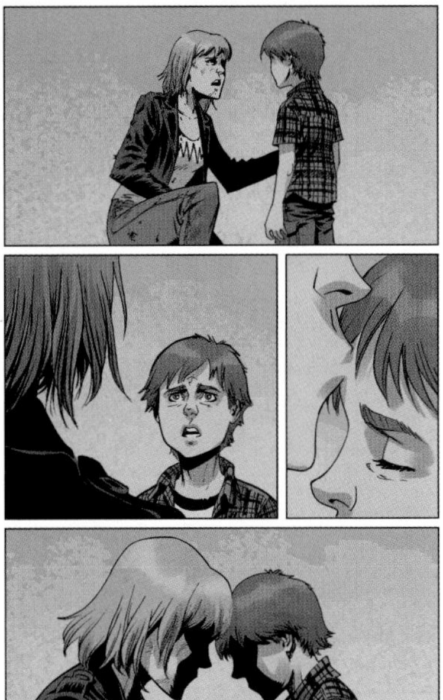

BEYOND THE BREACH

ED BRISSON writer

🐦 @EdBrisson

Ed Brisson is a comic book writer who first started to garner attention with his self-published crime series *Murder Book*. He broke into the public spotlight in 2012 with the crime/time-travel thriller series *Comeback* (Shadowline/Image Comics). In the short time since then, he's written and co-created four other series published by Image: *Sheltered, The Field, The Mantle* and *The Violent*. Ed's credits include: *Uncanny X-Men, Old Man Logan, Iron Fist, Batman & Robin Eternal, Ghost Rider* and more. He lives in Halifax, Nova Scotia, Canada with his wife and daughter.

DAMIAN COUCEIRO artist

🐦 @DamianCouceiro

Damian Couceiro is an Argentinian comic book artist. His professional breakthrough came working at BOOM! Studios on titles like *Sons of Anarchy, Planet of the Apes: Cataclysm, Robert E. Howard's Hawks of Outremer, Dracula: The Company of Monsters* and his contributions to series like Mark Waid's *Irredeemable* and *Incorruptible*. Since then, Damian has illustrated different titles like *TMNT* and *TMNT Universe* (IDW) and *Iron Fist, Old Man Logan, X-Force,* and *Ghost Rider 2099* (Marvel). Along with writer Ed Brisson he co-created the sci-fi series *Cluster* (BOOM! Studios) and the webcomic *The Big Idea* (Stela). The pair reunite for AfterShock's BEYOND THE BREACH.

PATRICIO DELPECHE colorist

Patricio Delpeche is a South American comic book artist and graphic designer born and raised in Buenos Aires, Argentina. He works for Vault, Heavy Metal, IDW, Glénat and currently Boom! Studios. His next projects to be published this year are *Origins*, together with Clay McLeod Chapman and Jakub Rebelka, and *Elles se Rendent pas Compte* with JD Morvan.

HASSAN OTSMANE-ELHAOU letterer

🐦 @HassanOE

Hassan Otsmane-Elhaou is a writer, editor and letterer. He's lettered comics like *Shanghai Red, Peter Cannon, Red Sonja, Lone Ranger* and more. He's also the editor behind the Eisner-winning publication, *PanelxPanel*, and is the host of the *Strip Panel Naked* YouTube series. You can usually find him explaining that comics are totally a real job to his parents.